Recommendations

"Finally! A parenting book that gives mothers (and fathers) permission to listen to their God-given intuition to find the parenting style that works for them and their baby. Chickering and Yoder recognize and celebrate that God creates both parents and babies as unique individuals, and that there is no one-size-fits-all recipe. They blend scientific evidence-based recommendations with Biblical grace to help each family find a good balance."

Dr. Rebecca Saenz, MD, IBCLC, FABM
Mississippi Breastfeeding Medicine Clinic, PLLC
Madison, MS

"This book will be what every new mom needs to read. I love the practical comments on how and why you rock a baby… and the proper use of a baby sling. The whole thing is very practical. It is written very well and is easy to follow. I LOVE how it teaches the Biblical view. That is so needed! I have explained this view to many girls. I really love it and I will recommend it to every pregnant lady I know."

Mrs. Anna Teis
Pastor's Wife, Liberty Baptist Church
Las Vegas, NV

"One of the chief regrets of my earthly life is that I did not know the Lord until many years after my babies were born. Not having His presence, nor a godly heritage, I made so many serious mistakes which have affected their lives even to this day. Since the disintegration of our culture (even in Christian homes) and lack of intergenerational wisdom, *The Gentle Art of Mothering* provides a rich foundation for establishing life patterns that will channel an infant toward God, not away from Him. I heartily and enthusiastically recommend this detailed 'workbook' on mothering of infants to anyone entering that most blessed and sometimes, terrifying, life process. May God use the information and principles found in it to bring many infants (and their parents) into a loving and satisfying relationship with their heavenly Father."

Mrs. Mina Oglesby
Ladies Conference Speaker
Chattanooga, TN

THE Gentle Art OF Mothering

A Christian Guide to Infant Care

Miriam Chickering, BSN, RN, IBCLC

Ronda Yoder, DSN, ARNP

Grace & Truth Publishing, LLC

Copyright © 2012 by Grace & Truth Publishing, LLC
226 Second Street, Manning, IA 51455
www.GentleArtofMothering.com/gtp

All Scripture quotations, unless otherwise noted, are from the Holy Bible, King James Version.

Printed in the United States of America.
Editor: Stephanie McMillian
Cover Designer: Michelle Johnson
Interior Designer: Rebecca Wind
Photo Rendering Illustrator: Rhonda Autrey
Technical Assistant: Rob Yoder
Calligrapher: Stan Shimmin

ISBN-13: 978-0-9887799-4-5 (paperback edition)
ISBN-13: 978-0-9887799-3-8 (ebook edition)

Dedication

To the babes of the world:
May this book help your mothers to delight in you, and
may you take comfort and delight in your mothers.

To my mother: Thank you for the love you have always shown your children and the joy you continually have in us. My children are receiving the benefits of your investment as I delight in them.

Miriam J. Chickering

To my mother, Carol, Jayne, Susan, and Karen: You have had the most profound influence on my understanding of the role of breastfeeding in the mothering relationship. Thank you for sharing your wisdom, persistence, patience, and humor with me. You have each made a difference in my life that will be carried on in those who are influenced by this book.

Ronda E. Yoder

The wisdom
that is from above
is first pure,
then peaceable,
gentle, and easy
to be intreated,
full of mercy
and good fruits.

James 3:17

Table of Contents

Section One · A Framework for Mothering

Section Two · The Early Days

Section Four * Putting It All Together

Appendices

Preface

God's Word provides direction for our lives. Although the Bible doesn't give us specific instructions about how to care for our infants, there are many verses that give us a sense of God's heart toward parenting. We have found the following verses to be very encouraging about God's love for us:

Psalm 139:13-18

¹³ For thou hast possessed my reins: thou hast covered me in my mother's womb.

¹⁴ I will praise thee; for I am fearfully and wonderfully made: marvellous are thy works; and that my soul knoweth right well.

¹⁵ My substance was not hid from thee, when I was made in secret, and curiously wrought in the lowest parts of the earth.

¹⁶ Thine eyes did see my substance, yet being unperfect; and in thy book all my members were written, which in continuance were fashioned, when as yet there was none of them.

¹⁷ How precious also are thy thoughts unto me, O God! how great is the sum of them!

¹⁸ If I should count them, they are more in number than the sand: when I awake, I am still with thee.

Sometimes a section of Scripture can be paraphrased in such a way as to bring special emphasis to what God is saying. A particularly beautiful and telling paraphrase of the previous verses is found in The Message.

viii

Psalm 139:13-18

Oh yes, you shaped me first inside, then out;
you formed me in my mother's womb.
I thank you, High God—you're breathtaking!
Body and soul, I am marvelously made!
I worship in adoration—what a creation!
You know me inside and out,
you know every bone in my body;
You know exactly how I was made, bit by bit,
how I was sculpted from nothing into something.
Like an open book, you watched me grow from conception to birth;
all the stages of my life were spread out before you,
The days of my life all prepared
before I'd even lived one day.
Your thoughts—how rare, how beautiful!
God, I'll never comprehend them!
I couldn't even begin to count them—
any more than I could count the sand of the sea.
Oh, let me rise in the morning and live always with you!
(Peterson 2002)

This is how much God knows your baby! What a comforting thought. You and your baby are precious in God's eyes.

Miriam Chickering   *Ronda Yoder*

Manning, Iowa   *Pensacola, FL*

October 2012

Acknowledgments

There have been many wonderful people that helped with this book project. We would like to thank Jennifer Roy for her contribution about twins. Thanks to Aresia Watson, who helped us with the wording in one section of the book. Thanks to Heidy Hayden, ARNP for infant healthcare advice. Thank you, Rachel Nikolaiev, for helping at the beginning of the project and for your extended discussions throughout the writing. Your friendship has been a true gift! Thanks to Dr. Patricia Posey-Goodwin who helped us obtain research articles when needed. Thank you to all the mothers who shared their stories on Miriam's Facebook and gave encouragement and input on Ronda's Facebook. That interaction really helped us stay focused!

We want to recognize the contribution of graphic design artists, Joe Digangi and Grace Larson, who gave us advice about the appearance of the cover. Rhonda Autrey, Faith Goetz, and Jackie Hoppe were a great help with the photo illustrations. We also appreciate the assistance of Sally Stuart at an early point in the publishing process and Sallie Randolph for valuable advice throughout one difficult part of our journey to being authors. She has been readily available with great advice on many subjects over the past few months. We also want to thank: Pat Lindsey, IBCLC; Mina Oglesby; Anna Teis, and Dr. Rebecca Saenz, MD, IBCLC, FABM for reviewing and sharing their thoughts about the book.

A heartfelt thanks to Stephanie McMillian whose copyediting of the entire book encouraged us to eliminate or clarify a number of passages. Her patience and editing expertise were both greatly needed and appreciated. Thanks to Rebecca Wind who designed the interior layout and made our words look great on the page. We so appreciate our cover designer, Michelle Johnson, who had a beautiful vision for the overall design and appearance of the book, which has carried over to the interior of the book and the website. Ronda's son, Rob, has provided invaluable technical assistance with many facets of the book and website. Thanks to Jewell Lowe and Jessica Edwards for our author photos on the back cover.

Miriam: To my loving husband, Shannon Chickering, none of this would have been possible without you. You are Superman! Thank you to my wonderful children: Beka, Jac, Eli, Lily, and Shannon James. You have added immeasurable joy to my life. Thanks, Dad, for teaching me to be tenacious and attempt hard things for the right reasons. I never would have begun this project without my grandfather's influence. Abiding faith, curiosity, love of science, and truth seeking characterized his life and defines his legacy. The women in my life: my mother, Grandma Whittington, Grandma Judy, Aunt Becky, Aunt Debbie, my mother-in-love Linn Chickering, and my cousin Jewell, your love and support have been so necessary. To my sisters, Ruth and Judy, you have encouraged me, loved my children, and become my dearest friends. A special thanks goes to the Calvary Baptist Church of Manning, Iowa for your prayer support during the writing of this book.

Ronda: Thanks to my wonderful husband, Bob Yoder, your love, faith in me, and support of my projects has made all the difference. You are an amazing husband and father, and I'm glad God gave us to each other! Thanks to my amazing kids: Rob, Sarah, Jenny, and Kathy, the source of much of my understanding of infant parenting. The five of you are my life on this earth. Your love and patience has been so undeserved, yet so needed and cherished. For the countless loads of laundry, mounds of dishes and endless meals that you have waded through over the past two years, you deserve more gratitude than I could ever adequately show. Maybe now we can get back to work on those school projects! To the women who have urged me to make this book a reality: Anna Teis, Karen Shelton, and Patti Reymond, thanks for that needed encouragement. To my dear friends, Joyce, Stephanie, Lorraine, Rachel, and Maybeth, thanks for your encouragement and availability when I needed to talk. To the board members of ECABS who have helped me have a greater influence on breastfeeding in our community, thanks for the work you do. I am especially thankful for my friends at Campus Church and around the country who provided prayer support during the writing of this book.

And finally and most importantly, our love, adoration, and gratitude to our Savior, Jesus Christ who has loaded us with so many benefits and aided us in the conception, writing, and editing of this book. He deserves our utmost praise for our lives and all that we endeavor to do.

> 2 Corinthians 9:8 "And God is able to make all grace abound toward you; that ye, always having all sufficiency in all things, may abound to every good work:"

Introduction

Jude 1:25 "To the only wise God our Saviour, be glory and majesty, dominion and power, both now and ever. Amen."

This book began out of our desire to encourage both new and experienced parents to understand that children are gifts from God to be enjoyed. Parents, new parents especially, are often afraid of doing something wrong. They try to find the "right" way to do every parenting task. The problem is that every baby is different and every parent is different. Each family will also experience its own unique set of circumstances. No rigid formula will work for all of us. We all want the best for our children. We have expectations for our little one and sometimes very clear pictures in our heads about what parenting will be like. Some of these expectations may include ideas about infant sleep, scheduling, and feeding. We can trust God to help us parent in a way that is healthy for our family.

Ronda: I read books before my children were born that influenced my parenting. The main book about breastfeeding that I read before my first child was by the La Leche League. This book emphasized that newborns need to be fed on a flexible schedule and often during the night. I knew I would be away during the day at work, so I understood that I would have to nurse more frequently at night. Since I didn't expect my first or second child to sleep through the night right away, it was more than a year until they did. I did find some helpful advice in one of the more rigid baby books for my third child, and she was able to sleep through the night most nights after eight weeks. Our fourth child didn't sleep through the night until she was four to five months old. I was very blessed to have an abundant milk supply and three babies who could handle it. My last child could not, so she would spit up a great deal after each feeding and need to be fed again in two hours. It was very frustrating, but I followed her feeding cues and we survived. Feeding her every three hours and ignoring her need would not have been a healthy experience for either of us.

I was influenced strongly by what I read. It affected the way I did things with each child. Fortunately, I had not read a very structured advice book until I had my third child. By that time, I was willing to take the good I found in the book and ignore the things with which I didn't agree. Unfortunately, new parents aren't confident enough to do that. If you try to follow some advice too closely, it can lead to physical problems for your baby. This is particularly true of feeding advice. The point of this is that my babies were all different and my expectations and actions played an important role in the way each baby responded to us and our activities.

Today, we are very concerned with living by a schedule. Many of us have decided opinions about how we want our day to go. We want our children to be unspoiled and to know that they are a part of our family, but not, as one parenting author writes, "the center of our universe." There are gentle ways to help a baby move to a predictable routine and we will discuss those in this book.

We need to adjust our expectations in appropriate ways. There are some basic Biblical principles that we can follow in parenting. You will have successful and satisfying times with your baby. What we want for you, after reading this book, is to understand that there is more than one right way to care for your baby. By using God's principles and some helpful suggestions in this book, you will become more comfortable parenting. You will gain your own style and form realistic expectations without worrying if the expectations of others have been met. God gives us grace in every area of our life, and He didn't withhold it from parents. This is something for which we all can be very thankful!

We often use male pronouns to talk about your baby as we discuss various aspects of baby care. We do this because we usually are talking to moms and using female pronouns. Also, we make reference in several places to seeing your primary care or healthcare provider. For mom, this may be an obstetrician, family doctor, nurse midwife, or nurse practitioner. For the baby, it may be a pediatrician, family practice doctor, or nurse practitioner.

Section One

A Framework for Mothering

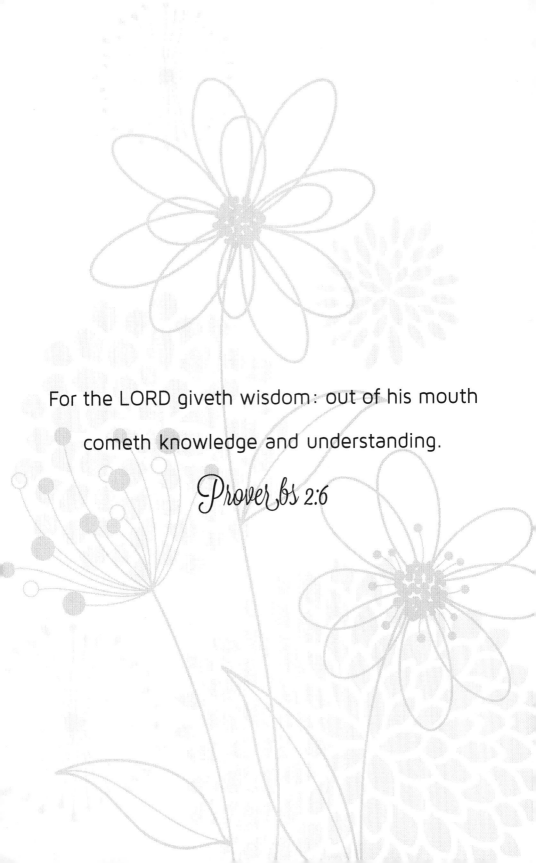

For the LORD giveth wisdom: out of his mouth

cometh knowledge and understanding.

Proverbs 2:6

Chapter One

Wisdom from God to You

This book has been written to enable you to mother well. It is written to those whom God has given either the hope or the blessing of a child. Those who have influence with mothers and young children are welcome to listen in on the conversation. God has given you the opportunity to care for your precious baby, and He gives the grace needed to gain knowledge for this task. He also gives grace to meet your needs and the needs of your baby. It is exciting to know His grace is available and we just have to ask to receive! As you begin this book on the gentle art of mothering your baby, we invite you to pray this prayer.

> *Dear Father, I look to You for comfort and joy just as my baby finds comfort and joy in me. Please help me to delight in Your Word. Give me Your most gracious wisdom to mother this baby in a way that pleases You. I trust Your grace for the strength to love and care for this child. When I am unsure, please help me to seek You first. Thank You for Your goodness towards me and my baby. In Jesus name, Amen.*

God's Grace to Gain New Knowledge through Available Witnesses

We know that you want the very best for your baby. This book will discuss both the knowledge and wisdom needed to care for your baby well. To form a framework from which to mother, you will need to consider information from three main sources: God's wisdom from His Word, the truths that are available to you through observable and discoverable science, and practical knowledge from both experienced mothers and your own developing "Mommy Sense." The Bible often speaks about the need for multiple counselors or witnesses to determine a matter. The above three "witnesses" or ways of knowing will be used to illuminate some very good approaches to motherhood and infant care.

Proverbs 11:14 "Where no counsel is, the people fall: but in the multitude of counsellors there is safety." (See also Proverbs 15:22 and 24:6)

2 Corinthians 13:1b "In the mouth of two or three witnesses shall every word be established."

As you evaluate ideas, think about these three witnesses. Does the idea (insofar as it can apply) line up with Biblical principles and God's expectations regarding motherhood? Does it agree with research? Is the idea you are considering practical? When you find a method that agrees in all or most of these areas, you can feel confident that you have found a good way to care for your baby. And then as you try something, your own conscience and Mommy Sense will confirm if it is the best approach for you and your baby.

Some infant care practices have a clear best answer. Isn't that nice! We all love clear answers. But what about questions like: is a schedule best or should I just follow the baby's cues? This book will be careful to identify those gray areas of mothering, those questions where there may be more than one right answer. We will present research, tell stories from our own experiences and discuss Biblical principles as they apply.

We are all different and each of us tends to rely on one of these witnesses more than the others. Do you know which of these witnesses you rely on the most? You may value learning from stories told by those around you about the way they handled a particular problem. Learn to use other ways of knowing as well. This book will help you to identify ways to care for your sweet baby, to think about motherhood, and to solve problems that arise. This next section will discuss each of the resources you have to discern truth.

Witness One: Biblical Guidance

God's Word provides direction and perspective that is clearly aimed at the maternal relationship. There are general principles of living that can be applied to the relationship between mother and baby.

Much of our Biblical insight can be gathered from situations and principles that are not specifically related to mothers. This gives us a much richer understanding of God's perspective and plan for us.

Biblical Perspective on Motherhood: Here is an example of God's plan regarding the relationship between a mother and her baby. This passage, and others like it, is not necessarily a directive to mothers; but we can safely infer what God expects to be normal for the relationship between mother and baby.

> *Isaiah 66:10-14a* [10] *"Rejoice ye with Jerusalem, and be glad with her, all ye that love her: rejoice for joy with her, all ye that mourn for her:* [11] *That ye may suck, and be satisfied with the breasts of her consolations; that ye may milk out, and be delighted with the abundance of her glory.* [12] *For thus saith the LORD, Behold, I will extend peace to her like a river, and the glory of the Gentiles like a flowing stream: then shall ye suck, ye shall be borne upon her sides, and be dandled upon her knees.* [13] *As one whom his mother comforteth, so will I comfort you; and ye shall be comforted in Jerusalem.* [14a] *And when ye see this, your heart shall rejoice, and your bones shall flourish like an herb:"*

This lovely passage in Isaiah speaks of the end of the ages. It is amazingly beautiful that God chooses to use the imagery of a mother and her young child to illustrate the joy that God's people will experience from Him.

These verses show us what God assumes the relationship between a mother and baby should be. The baby is delighted with his mother's provision of nourishment. He loves to nurse! The mother is depicted as cuddling her baby, playing with him, and carrying him. She is shown as a comforter who brings joy to the infant. The mother and baby take great delight in the relationship. Do you find great joy in your baby?

When you carry, cuddle, comfort, play with, feed, and delight in your infant, you are pleasing God. This relationship is beautiful to the mind of God and is worthy of your time and effort. Just as your baby turns to you to meet his needs, remember to turn to God for your comfort. Oh, that we would seek Him for nourishment, joy, and delight!

Biblical Principles Applied to Motherhood: There are many principles in the Bible that can be applied to a mother's attitude and actions towards her baby. A prime example is the principle of faithfulness.

> *1 Corinthians 4:2 "Moreover it is required in stewards, that a man be found faithful."*

Babies have many needs, and each time you meet your baby's needs you are being faithful. Suppose your baby is lonely and needs your presence. Faithfulness means that you will meet this need by being with your baby rather than find a way to pacify the baby without meeting his need. There is nothing wrong with pacifiers or infant swings. In fact, they can both be good tools. The focus is discerning your baby's needs and meeting them faithfully.

God recognizes and blesses faithfulness. Since God often rewards us in practical ways, the natural, positive reward of your faithfulness is giving your baby the best chance to develop properly.

Witness Two: Knowledge through Science

God is the Creator of all. The laws that govern our universe are His. Science is the study of God's designs and His laws. He designed our physical bodies with our greatest good in mind. David, composing long after the Fall, wrote under the inspiration of the Holy Spirit, *"I am fearfully and wonderfully made." (Psalm 139:14)* We have much research from which we can learn. All truth is God's truth, regardless of the particular worldview of the scientist or researcher.

Before discussing how science is relevant to mothering, we have to come to an understanding of how we view science and particularly the discipline of biology. The Bible is clear that God created man in His image (Genesis 1:27). So, how might the discussion of animals and their behavior relate to the study of man? The study of human beings is separate from zoology. Because humans were created in the image of God, man is distinguished from animals in four basic ways: we have been given a living soul; we have been given stewardship and control of the earth (Genesis 1:28); we have the capacity for moral choices; and we have power for reasoning, speech, and relationships. Man has been given a free will to choose to serve and glorify God with our abilities and speech. He created us for fellowship with Him.

Since God is the Designer of all these things, He used many similar processes in our creation. There are similarities between humans and other living creation because we have the same Creator and share the same environment. Scripture provides us with examples of what we can learn from creation: consider the ants (Proverbs 6:6), lilies (Luke 12:27), spiders (Proverbs 30:28), horses (Psalm 32:9), and ostriches (Lamentations 4:3 and Job 39:13-17) to name a few. When we consider other parts of God's creation, both positive and negative comparisons to motherhood emerge.

The disciplines of chemistry and biology also shed light on God's plan for infant care. One way is through the milk composition of different animals. Milk composition affects how long the mother animal can leave her baby. Nils

Bergman, a medical missionary to South Africa, first noted the differences in milk composition as he was searching for ways to save babies who were born prematurely. Animals that produce milk with a high fat and protein content need to nurse less frequently than those animals whose milk has a low fat and protein content. This means that milk with a low fat and protein content is metabolized more quickly, and these baby animals must be fed more often in order to grow (Kirsten, Bergman, and Hann 2001).

Baby rabbits are left in a safe place alone for most of the day. The mother returns and feeds the babies once every twelve hours. Their milk is high in fat and protein and low in carbohydrates. Bunnies' brains are fairly mature at birth. Rabbits are considered cache mammals because they cache their young; they hide them away and return to them periodically.

Cows' milk is lower in fat and protein and higher in carbohydrates than cache mammals. Cows need to feed their calves more often than rabbits feed their young. Calves are mature at birth and can follow their mothers within a few hours. Elephants, camels, and horses are all examples of follow mammals. They have a higher level of carbohydrates and less fat and protein than cache animals. Follow mammals stay with the mother after birth.

At the other end of the spectrum are baby kangaroos, other marsupials, and primates, which are carried and fed very often. Carry mammals, like the kangaroo, give birth to immature young that will not remain biologically stable without the physical presence of the mother. Their milk has an even lower protein and fat content and a higher carbohydrate content than follow mammals. Milks with a low protein and fat content are metabolized more quickly and these baby animals must be fed more often in order to grow.

The composition of human milk gives us clues as to how often babies need to be fed. Human milk has a lower concentration of fat and protein and a higher carbohydrate content than any of the mammals (Kirsten, Bergman, and Hann 2001). Protein content determines the number of feeds a baby will need. Human milk contains 0.8-0.9% protein (Riordan and Wambach 2009). Out of all of God's creation, He designed human milk to be digested the most quickly. He intended for human mothers to feed their babies very often (Mohrbacher and Kendall-Tackett 2010).

Witness Three: Practical Wisdom

Other Mommies' Sense: Practical wisdom comes from the experiences of people—the stories we all have. Ronda taught Nursing Research for many years, which enables her to understand research studies and apply her knowledge to motherhood. She also has four children of her own and has worked with thousands of nursing students over her career. She treated patients as a nurse practitioner and has earned a doctorate in nursing. Mothers can take advantage of Ronda's experiences to help them make good choices for their babies.

Miriam is a lactation consultant and a labor and delivery nurse who cares for moms and babies. She is an adjunct clinical instructor who works with nursing students at a community college. She also counsels in her role as a pastor's wife and cares for her five children. Her experiences have gained her practical wisdom that she can share with other moms.

There may be people in your life with practical wisdom that can help you. Even if they are not healthcare professionals, they may have a good deal of wisdom and knowledge to help you in your journey of godly motherhood. Practical wisdom is also developed from your own set of experiences when it comes to mothering your baby. God has given you a conscience and a body that is uniquely designed to mother. As you grow as a mother, you will develop your own practical wisdom that can be shared with others in your sphere of influence.

Your Mommy Sense: God made you in a special way. Your sensitive emotions make you perfect to mother your baby. It is natural after delivery for your emotions to run away with you a time or two, but it is important to listen to your Mommy Sense when deciding how to care for and respond to your baby.

God made you both emotionally and physically sensitive to your baby. All during your pregnancy and after delivery your brain changes in measurable ways. Those lost car keys; the misplaced purse – all those brain cells were busy doing other things, preparing for a newborn!

When you sense that your baby has a need, your whole body responds. God made you this way so it would be easier for you to meet your baby's needs. We can respond to our baby by rationally thinking about how to meet his needs, but our emotions, mind, and body also play a part in helping us know if we have made a good choice.

Along with our Mommy Sense, God gave us a conscience to help us make choices that please Him. We also have the Holy Spirit working through God's Word and in our hearts to direct our decisions. God has not left us alone to figure out how to do this job of mothering. You do have many different ways of knowing and confirming to yourself what is right for your baby.

Understanding the Challenges of Motherhood

We need God's help as we parent. There is so much to learn. Taking care of a newborn is one of the most challenging and rewarding experiences of your life. These first few months can be times of incredibly sweet memories but also times of extreme stress. Mothers and fathers can both experience emotions at each end of the spectrum.

As a new parent, you will have to cope with a baby's unpredictable needs, learning everything for the first time, and making choices that may permanently affect your parenting style. Most moms want to be told exactly what to do. Unfortunately, in many areas of parenting, it's hard to know what will work best for you until you try. Knowing that you will have to decide this for yourself doesn't give you a sense of security. The good news is that God will give you grace as you learn to care for your baby.

It is imperative that you learn how to deal with your initial lack of knowledge and the stress that it causes. All new parents struggle at times as they learn how to accept the unpredictable needs of their newborn. You will need God's grace and wisdom as you come to understand your expectations for your family and prayerfully decide how those expectations will be adjusted to meet with reality.

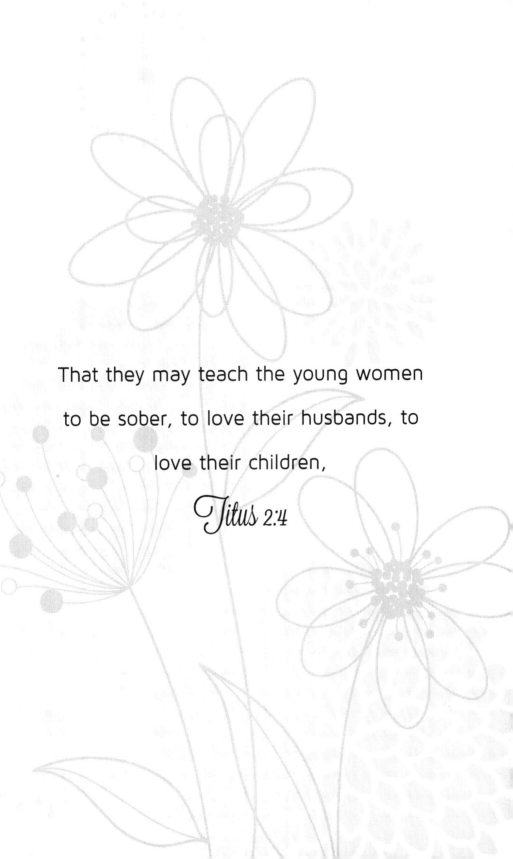

That they may teach the young women

to be sober, to love their husbands, to

love their children,

Titus 2:4

Chapter Two

Growing into Motherhood

Become the Mother God wants You to be

On the Fast Track to Womanhood

*B*ecoming a mother encourages a woman to mature faster than anything else. Maturity has little to do with age and everything to do with character. There are some key characteristics found in a woman who is prepared to please God through her mothering. It is important to understand those aspects of growth and heart preparation needed for motherhood.

We may not approach the birth of our first baby thinking that it is the start of a whole new life. It might be said, but we don't understand what that really means. As we have grown and hopefully matured, we now understand that some aspects of maturing had to be learned on our journey, but for other attributes, having a road map would have been very helpful. This chapter will discuss several points of interest on the motherhood road map.

Accurate Perception of Control

Releasing Control

As a growing mother you learn you have control of your personal actions and practically nothing else. We may think we have control over life's circumstances, but this is an illusion. Our actions can influence outcomes, but there are many events we have little control over. For example, a woman cannot control the events of labor and delivery. Although she can do things such as exercise or gain the appropriate weight to give her a better chance, she cannot guarantee an easy labor. If she has chosen to deliver with little medical intervention, she does not control the beginning of labor. *The key is to distinguish between the events we can exert control and influence over and the events we have little or no control over.*

As a mother, you will have control over much of what your baby does, and you can make wise decisions about his care. But if father or a grandparent watches the baby for several hours or you put the baby in daycare, you yield control. You have to trust that the Lord will protect your child, even if you aren't the one caring for your baby. It is natural to worry, but we are told to release our anxieties to the Lord.

> *Philippians 4:6-7* [6] *"Be careful for nothing; but in every thing by prayer and supplication with thanksgiving let your requests be made known unto God.* [7] *And the peace of God, which passeth all understanding, shall keep your hearts and minds through Christ Jesus."*

A strong trust in God can protect you from needless concern. Two Bible verses really complement each other and can be an important part of our response to stressors in our lives.

> *Psalm 56:3 "What time I am afraid, I will trust in thee."*

> *Isaiah 26:3 "Thou wilt keep him in perfect peace, whose mind is stayed on thee: because he trusteth in thee."*

You can rest in knowing that God is working in your life desiring to make you like Christ. The uncontrollable factors in life become more bearable when you remind yourself that God has your best interest at heart.

> *Romans 8:28-29* [28] *"And we know that all things work together for good to them that love God, to them who are the called according to his purpose.* [29] *For whom he did foreknow, he also did predestinate to be conformed to the image of his Son, that he might be the firstborn among many brethren."*

Reclaiming Control

While we cannot control everything, we can determine our own actions. God expects us to do this, and He promises to give us the strength and wisdom to respond appropriately (James 1:2-5). In fact, God's Word promises that He will not give us anything that His grace cannot help us handle (1 Corinthians 10:13). So when the toilet backs up, the baby eats a plant leaf, and the dog escapes from the house, we can call on God to give us the grace to handle the emergencies with a clear head, without losing our temper, or sitting down and bawling.

It is normal that our emotions greatly influence our actions. The problem arises when our emotions are out of proportion to the circumstances of life. Unfortunately, new mothers are especially vulnerable. For the first week or so, our hormones are in a state of profound flux. Even moving into the second week postpartum and beyond, we are usually sleep deprived and challenged to learn and perform mothering behaviors that are completely new to us. The good news is that we do not have to act on our feelings. We don't have to throw the phone down, scream at our three-year-old, or even post an angry status update on Facebook. We can choose appropriate responses that please God; responses like stopping to pray for grace, answering the door with a pleasant face, and quietly giving the three year old a bath while deciding how to clean up a mess. When we respond appropriately during difficult times, God rewards us. We feel better about ourselves knowing that we responded correctly.

> Miriam: I remember an instance when Beka woke up for the second or third time during the night. My husband and I were both working at that point and very tired. I went into her room to nurse, but she wouldn't stop crying. I didn't want to be up with her in the first place, but when she wouldn't stop crying I found myself furious! The instant anger was overwhelming, so I put her back in bed and walked away. After I calmed down I felt frightened and guilty. How could I have such feelings toward my baby? I told Shannon the next day. He said, "Yep, I've felt that way before." He was so matter of fact about it. I am so glad that even at that moment of anger, I knew I was still responsible for my actions.

The best thing to do in a moment like that is to cry out to God for help (Psalm 18:6; 34:6). He will give you the strength and patience to respond in a way that pleases Him.

> Jonah 2:2 "And said, I cried by reason of mine affliction unto the LORD, and he heard me; out of the belly of hell cried I, and thou heardest my voice."

Flexibility and Adaptability

Mothering demands flexibility and adaptability. Being able to adapt, problem solve, and become flexible may not be familiar, but they are skills you will develop. You are in your journey towards godly motherhood, and God has promised to give you the grace and strength to meet the challenge.

We do not get to pick the type of baby that God gives us. You may find yourself with a very sensitive, high-needs baby. This can be a very exhausting and challenging experience, but God can teach us to grow through experiences like this.

God often encourages us in Scripture to be willing to change. He asked Abraham to leave his family and homeland and move to a new, unknown place (Genesis 12:1). I'm sure Sarah loved that idea, wouldn't you?

Ronda: I can imagine the conversation my husband, Bob, and I would have had in a situation similar to Abraham and Sarah's:

"Honey, we are going to move away from Florida."

"Where are we going?"

"I don't know."

"What will we do there?"

"I don't know."

"Can we come back to visit?"

"Probably not. I think it's over near Washington or Montana. It will be too far to travel back here." Yes, I'd be very excited about that!

Scripture also reminds us that we shouldn't set our hearts on doing things our way by having inflexible expectations. Instead of being focused on our own plan, we are to focus on Christ and His plans.

> *Colossians 3:1-2* [1] *"If ye then be risen with Christ, seek those things which are above, where Christ sitteth on the right hand of God.* [2] *Set your affection on things above, not on things on the earth."*

> *Psalm 62:5, "My soul, wait thou only upon God; for my expectation is from him."*

We are to accept changes in our plans and even expect them. God's plan for our lives usually differs from our own. We can seek and ask Him to give us our expectations. In other words, let the Lord show us what we can expect or plan. Sometimes we are following Scripture and trying to listen to God's voice, but we still may be surprised by life's challenges. Changes to our plans can be especially hard to accept since most women love security and stability. Once again, we can call on God for strength and grace.

Ronda: At the doctors' office where I've worked, things change constantly: policies, employees, and schedules. The common response of the women in the office is, "I hate change!" Then we go ahead and learn a little more about flexibility every day.

Miriam: I have a friend with six children. Two of her babies were very sensitive. Her first baby cried so much that the mom often received unwanted advice. "Feed her more." "Feed her solids (at six weeks)." Her baby was not hungry and was growing well; she just cried frequently. That child today is happy, well-adjusted, and has earned a doctoral degree.

My friend's fourth baby was also a screamer. On her second day of life, the hospital nurses refused to keep her in the nursery because she kept waking up the other babies! My friend said that she could hear her baby crying in the nursery from her own room. The hospital staff was eager to see her leave the next day. The medical doctor couldn't find anything wrong with the baby, and today that baby is a successful college student.

My friend had to adapt and learn to cope with those particular stressors of motherhood. Facing challenges as a young mom prepared her for the many challenges that arose as the mother of a large family while helping run two businesses and a farm. She learned to ignore the poor advice she was given by others and to persevere in love for her children even when it was difficult.

Courage

It is easy to pout and give up when we are faced with difficulties, but maturity demands that we face challenges with courage. This courage can only come from God. Because we trust Him to provide the strength to meet the challenges, we can face them with courage (John 14:1). Mother, you cannot rely on yourself, or your spouse, or your mom, or your best friend to fix all the difficulties of life. You and your support network are not enough.

God has set up life in such a way that we cannot do it without Him. We are weak, and we make mistakes. Sometimes life is overwhelming, but God is sufficient. We must rely on His strength and grace. We must meet with Him in daily, personal worship to experience His presence. Call out to Him when you have a need, when you are angry, sad, lonely, worried, or fearful, and you will find that He can bring you the comfort and strength you need to meet the day's challenges.

As your child grows into an adult, you will no longer be able to provide for all of his needs, but if you have learned to rely on God, it will be easier for your child to do the same. God is the ultimate parent who meets your needs and the needs of your child.

> Joshua 1:9 *"Have not I commanded thee? Be strong and of a good courage; be not afraid, neither be thou dismayed: for the LORD thy God is with thee whithersoever thou goest."*

Ronda: Courage is not an easy task for many of us as we very humanly want to rely on anything or anyone but God. I've often struggled with an over-reliance on myself and others. There have been several specific times that God has used circumstances to help me see I had nowhere else to turn. I could no longer rely on my abilities or even the friends around me to meet my needs. God removed relationships that were hindering my fellowship with Him. He showed me that I needed Him for every area in my life. Even better than that, He convinced me that He loved me enough to meet all my needs. I have always known that God had the power to meet my needs, but there have been times I have doubted that He wanted to meet them. I now rely on the fact that God will meet my need, and that He will use the circumstances in my life to shape me into Christ-likeness. This knowledge gives me the courage to face the challenges of each new day.

Creative Problem-Solving

As a mom, you are a problem solver and proactive planner anticipating the needs of your family. You will need to search for solutions to your problems and work to gain knowledge to better care for your family. We have talked already about accepting difficult circumstances beyond our control. However, accepting difficult circumstances does not mean we stop looking for solutions. For instance, if you have a child that is diagnosed with an illness, you may accept the diagnosis, but you also look for a cure.

Acceptance does not render us helpless. When a difficulty arises, try to immediately identify potential solutions. For example, if you have problems with low milk supply, you can find ways to increase your supply by offering more feedings, taking herbal supplements or medications recommended to you by your provider or lactation consultant, and increasing pumping frequency. Being resourceful in looking for a solution allows us to serve the family God has given to us.

2 Kings 4:8-37 gives the story of the great Shunammite woman who, with her husband, built an apartment for Elisha when he traveled. Elisha asked her what he could do for her but she would request nothing. Then Elisha's servant mentioned that she did not have any children, so Elisha told her God would give her a son within the year. Several years passed, the child grew, and then one morning he became sick and died.

> [20] *"And when he had taken him, and brought him to his mother, he sat on her knees till noon, and then died.* [21] *And she went up, and laid him on the bed of the man of God, and shut the door upon him, and went out.* [22] *And she called unto her husband, and said, Send me, I pray thee, one of the young men, and one of the asses, that I may run to the man of God, and come again.* [23] *And he said, Wherefore wilt thou go to him to day? it is neither new moon, nor sabbath. And she said, It shall be well."*

She did not weep and wail, knowing that God had given her this child and that the prophet was the only one who could resolve this problem. She chose a plan, executed it speedily and did not take time to explain or cause her husband added grief.

> ²⁴ *"Then she saddled an ass, and said to her servant, Drive, and go forward; slack not thy riding for me, except I bid thee.* ²⁵ *So she went and came unto the man of God to mount Carmel. And it came to pass, when the man of God saw her afar off, that he said to Gehazi his servant, Behold, yonder is that Shunammite:* ²⁶ *Run now, I pray thee, to meet her, and say unto her, Is it well with thee? is it well with thy husband? is it well with the child? And she answered, It is well."*

She didn't bother with the servant; she wanted to talk to the man of God. So she kept travelling and once she got to Elisha, he could tell something was wrong.

> ²⁷ *"And when she came to the man of God to the hill, she caught him by the feet: but Gehazi came near to thrust her away. And the man of God said, Let her alone; for her soul is vexed within her: and the LORD hath hid it from me, and hath not told me.* ²⁸ *Then she said, Did I desire a son of my lord? did I not say, Do not deceive me?* ²⁹ *Then he said to Gehazi, Gird up thy loins, and take my staff in thine hand, and go thy way: if thou meet any man, salute him not; and if any salute thee, answer him not again: and lay my staff upon the face of the child."*

Isn't it interesting how she didn't even say the child was dead? Elisha knew based on her actions and words, and he proposed a solution, but this mother wasn't having it!

> ³⁰ *"And the mother of the child said, As the LORD liveth, and as thy soul liveth, I will not leave thee.* ³¹ *And he arose, and followed her. And Gehazi passed on before them, and laid the staff upon the face of the child; but there was neither voice, nor hearing. Wherefore he went again to meet him, and told him, saying, The child is not awaked."*

Looks like the child's mother was right not to trust the servant to do the prophet's work!

> ³² *"And when Elisha was come into the house, behold, the child was dead, and laid upon his bed.* ³³ *He went in therefore, and shut the door upon them twain, and prayed unto the LORD.* ³⁴ *And he went up, and lay upon the*

child, and put his mouth upon his mouth, and his eyes upon his eyes, and his hands upon his hands: and stretched himself upon the child; and the flesh of the child waxed warm. [35] *Then he returned, and walked in the house to and fro; and went up, and stretched himself upon him: and the child sneezed seven times, and the child opened his eyes.* [36] *And he called Gehazi, and said, Call this Shunammite. So he called her. And when she was come in unto him, he said, Take up thy son.* [37] *Then she went in, and fell at his feet, and bowed herself to the ground, and took up her son, and went out."*

What an example of a resourceful, active, and creative mother. She knew there was a solution and she didn't stop until she had found it.

Many of us may read a story out of the Bible and think, "Well, that's nice, but God doesn't care about me in the same way." You may read about God's love and feel that it is meant for someone else. It is true that we do not hear stories today of prophets raising people from the dead. This is because God works differently today. Instead of working through prophets, He has chosen to work through the Holy Spirit in the heart of the Christian and the church. However, there are still times when God performs miracles that are beyond the explanation of medical science. As you continue to walk with God, ask Him to make His love for you obvious in your daily life. He delights to do this for His children (2 Chronicles 16:9).

Miriam: When I was 16 we moved from Texas, where I had lived all my life, to upstate New York. We moved in the middle of winter and I had to attend public school for the first time. What a change from my previous experiences at a small, private, Christian school and with home school! We lived in the basement of the church until the snow melted because it really is not a good idea to buy a house when everything is covered in snow!

In the spring, my parents bought a beautiful home on a small acreage adjacent to a state park and a buffalo ranch. It was the perfect size for a horse. I looked and looked for a horse, but I couldn't find one. At one point, I remember sobbing in my room. My mom came in, "What's wrong?" she said. I said, "If God loved me, He would give me a horse." She looked a little shocked by that statement.

As I reflect on the multiple ways God was working in my life at that time, I can now see how He used circumstances for my good and was actively showing His love for me. But as a 16 year old, I did not recognize any of that. I needed tangible proof of His love and I needed it desperately.

Graciously, very soon after that, God did provide a horse. I look back now and am a little shocked by my audacity, but God wasn't. He understood my immaturity and need at that time. He answered me in mercy.

> There have been other times in my life that I have earnestly prayed for something that God did not give me. He chose to meet my needs in other ways, but in that critical moment He met my need in a way that my 16-year-old brain could understand, and my faith was increased.

God loves you. He proves His love every day when the sun rises and the birds sing. He shows us His love in the beauty of nature. He gives the common joys of life freely to all men: things like a baby's smile, a puppy, a kitten, food, water, fire, and laughter. He further shows us His love by writing His law in our hearts, so that every man knows the difference between good and evil. God has ultimately shown His love by sending Jesus Christ to reconcile us to Himself for eternity. Beyond all of this, God delights to show us His love in our daily lives.

Growing mothers are not committed to just one way of doing things; they are committed to finding the best solution for the problem. Sometimes this means asking an experienced friend, calling a healthcare provider, reading a book, or trying several different solutions until they find something that works.

Teachable Spirit

A growing mother needs to be teachable. You will always be learning. Seek to learn from God's Word and others who are farther along in life's journey. Mothering, and the events surrounding early motherhood, are some of the most intimate and profound moments of our lives. We want to do it all right, and there is much to learn. Nothing is as important to most women as being a successful mother. Because these things are so important, it is difficult at times for us to accept the teaching and help we need.

As new moms, we know that we don't know everything and must sometimes seek help or advice, even when we would rather not. We must show discernment in who we ask or the advice we follow. Both refusing to ask for help and seeking or following wrong advice can leave women without accurate knowledge, so it is critical to know who to ask for advice.

> *Titus 2:3-4* ³ *"The aged women likewise, that they be in behaviour as becometh holiness, not false accusers, not given to much wine, teachers of good things;* ⁴ *That they may teach the young women to be sober, to love their husbands, to love their children,"*

An older, godly lady can give you great advice on learning the character traits that we talk about in this chapter. Notice what the older ladies are to teach, "to be sober, to love their husbands, to love their children." Look for someone who routinely exhibits the character traits of a godly mother and work to befriend her. Older ladies are to teach younger women how to be "grownups" and how to love their families.

Notice that the text does not say that older women should be used as a Google tool for infant feeding and medical advice. For practical advice about feeding and medical care, seek out a healthcare professional. Many churches have at least one nurse in the congregation that can direct you to good resources or recommend other good advisors. It is also important to ask advice from someone who shares your core values. Ultimately, we go to the Word of God to help us weigh advice that is given about parenting. We must be very careful to use Scripture in context, to pray over our decisions, and to seek the help of the Holy Spirit.

Dealing with Advice

We should be ready to listen and learn from those around us who have something helpful to say. Don't be ready to discount or ignore everything being said, just because the speaker has a different situation than you do. It is important to ask the right people for advice. Healthcare providers can be good resources for healthcare and feeding advice.

There may be a tendency for family and friends to give outdated feeding or medical advice that they received and used. Unfortunately, they sometimes experienced negative outcomes, which we now know how to avoid. For example, if they didn't have success with breastfeeding, they may be less encouraging for you to stick with it. They may say something like, "Well, it will be okay if the baby has to take a bottle. Why don't we supplement now, then you can try again later?" This type of advice may not help you reach your breastfeeding goals. Try to surround yourself with people who will encourage your efforts and help you continue with a comfortable parenting style. If you have doubts about the advice you receive, consider doing your own research from a reliable source

If you do encounter negative feedback from your family regarding your infant care decisions, it may help to take your mother, sister, aunt, or even father to the doctor at the infant's check-up. Encourage your family to ask questions. Don't feel embarrassed if they challenge your healthcare provider. The healthcare professional is accustomed to answering questions. You might even take a family member with you to visit the lactation consultant. Ask your lactation consultant or other healthcare professional what books or information on infant care they recommend. Get a copy for your family members to refer to when they have concerns.

Miriam: My mother and grandmother attended much of my labor and the newborn follow-ups. My dad was in the room when the doctor came with the discharge instructions. My husband attended prenatal classes and read parts of several books on infant care. All of this was helpful as we were able to agree.

Sharing Stories, Giving Advice

Beyond any other accomplishments, the births of our children are at the top of the list. We will talk about our child's birth for the rest of our lives. If there were problems with the birth, or the first weeks, or breastfeeding, we remember every detail and love to share it with others, especially new or expecting mothers.

Some people will share their story, even if it was traumatic, with a pregnant mother whether she wants to hear it or not. You need to be aware that many people just want to share and have someone listen to their story. Sometimes it is difficult to sit back and take it all in.

The important thing to do when someone is telling you a sad or traumatic story about a birth or breastfeeding experience is to remember to listen with grace. You might say, "Wow, that must have been difficult for you. I'm sorry that happened." Sometimes a woman will share a story that is reassuring; make sure you let her know how much you appreciate that and encourage her to share her story with others. The stories that are shared are just another person's experience.

Miriam: One day recently, while I was working hidden in an alcove at the library, a group of older ladies who were knitting began discussing their childbirth experiences. Not one in the group was under seventy. I was surprised to hear them discussing this without a younger woman in the group. They talked about the events as if they had happened months ago, not decades. One lady mentioned that she had given birth to a baby five weeks early. The routine practice at the time was to give formula, but the baby was failing to thrive and unable to tolerate it. The doctor told the young mother that her milk was probably the best for this particular baby and that there really wasn't any more that they could do.

This young mom was sent home with her preterm baby, and she breastfed her. She said, "She took my milk better than the formula; it kept her alive." I could hear the pride in her voice. "I held her." She explained, "The nurses told me I was the best thing for her." This older woman was almost in tears remembering those first weeks with her baby. "When she got bigger and was doing well, I started giving her formula. I wish I had kept breastfeeding her."

It was amazing to hear the pride, joy, and then a little bit of regret in her voice as she shared one of the most significant events of her life. Each of the ladies shared her birth story and I was taken aback at this entire conversation and thought, "Will I be talking about my birth experiences in my seventies and eighties? Probably!"

Your experiences will be just as important, and you, too, will want to share them. You will want others to do things that you found successful, exactly as you did them. Remember this when it comes to giving your advice to others later.

Sacrificial Love and Trust

Mothers all desire a sense of connection and intimacy with their babies. As much as you desire that, God desires connection and intimacy with you more! God desires you. He longs for you to walk in fellowship with Him daily, to cry out to Him in all your troubles and to seek Him as your first choice of counselor in difficulties.

Growing mothers show sacrificial love by putting the needs of others above their desires. Sacrificial love is the ultimate mark of maturity. It is the driving force that motivates us to master the other characteristics we so desperately need in order to mother our children properly. This is the type of love that God showed for us. God's love and provision is the ultimate example of the way we should love and care for our babies. Now that you have the responsibility for another person, knowing these principles and implementing them requires a new compassion, patience, and resilience. The exciting part is that with God's grace, you are up for the challenge.

Ronda: I remember many times that we had to stop what we were planning to do to feed a baby. It was important for Bob and I to have appropriate expectations about the needs of each baby even when those needs interfered with our plans. I'm sure we are all prone to try to get "one more thing" done before we feed the baby, or even while we feed the baby.

Sarah, Jenny, and Kathy were all very jealous of my attention while nursing. As they got a little older, maybe four to six months, they became very aware if I was paying attention to something else besides them. They would look at my eyes and see that I was not looking at them. I would try to read a book while one was nursing. Invariably, a little arm would pop up, reach back, and cover up the page of the book or move the book. Then I would look down at her. Sometimes she would pop off the breast and give me a wide, toothless grin. "See, I have your attention now! Let's keep it that way!" I valued those opportunities to sit and rest. Sometimes it was a sacrifice to give up whatever I was doing, but the blessing of getting to hold my precious baby while she nursed was invaluable.

Overcoming Fear and Guilt

Trust can sometimes be a difficult character trait to achieve for new mothers. We want to keep our baby safe and make right decisions. Mothers, especially new mothers, often experience fear when they make decisions for their new babies. Common questions arise like, "Am I doing it right? Why isn't my baby doing this or that?"

> Miriam: My third baby, Elijah, did not smile regularly until he was seven weeks old. I was so concerned. He was supposed to do this at four weeks! What was wrong with my child? He was my third, and I still worried over minor details. By five weeks, I was intentionally spending many minutes throughout the day smiling at him.
>
> I would hand the baby to his daddy, "Shannon, sit there and smile at that child." I laugh about it now, but at the time it felt like a personal failure on my part. Of course, Elijah must not be smiling because I wasn't smiling enough. I didn't feel depressed, but maybe I was, because after all, the baby was perfect. If he wasn't smiling at four weeks it was obviously my fault. Now that baby is four years old and smiles constantly. He has a great sense of humor.

Then there is the guilt. "My baby has jaundice, what did I do wrong?" Someone asks, "Why doesn't your baby have socks on?" You think, "Do babies always require socks?" but still feel the guilt. Then the absolute worst: you take your baby to church before the recommended six week mark, and he gets a cold—major guilt ensues.

How should moms cope with these emotions? Guilt is not necessarily a bad emotion. When guilt is doing its job, it causes us to change destructive behaviors. Fear is not always a bad emotion either. Fear keeps us from doing dangerous things. The problems occur when we feel fear over situations that are not dangerous or we feel guilt over choices that are not sinful.

Many mothers experience irrational fears like thinking (while driving over a bridge), "What if I were to walk onto the bridge with my baby and accidentally drop him?" Some of this is a defense mechanism we have for problem-solving. We can use the thought to reassure ourselves that we have a plan that would prevent such a situation, like keeping the baby in a stroller or infant wrap when walking near a bridge.

Ronda: I've talked to mothers who have no fear of heights, but can't bear to be on a scenic overlook with their children. I remember experiencing that feeling at the Grand Canyon.

Our family took a once-in-a-lifetime vacation a few years ago. We had planned to spend a day at the Grand Canyon, but time got away from us, and we didn't actually have more than a couple hours once we finally arrived. That was really more than enough for me.

I took in the awe and splendor for a time, but I really couldn't enjoy any of the views, because I had four children wandering around taking pictures and looking over edges! I felt physically panicked every time we let Kathy, 22 months, out of her stroller. There were guard rails and four adults, plus her siblings watching out for her, but it didn't matter. I couldn't enjoy being there. Rationally, I knew that we would all protect her, but I did not enjoy the experience.

God wants us to live in freedom from fear and guilt. Legitimate fear or guilt often occurs over a specific event. The solution may not be immediately obvious, but you know the reason for your emotions. A Christian who is walking closely with Jesus should only experience brief guilt, because any sin causing guilt should be immediately confessed and forsaken. The fear a Christian feels should be momentary. It should cause us to evaluate our choices and turn to a better path; it should drive us to seek God.

If you do not know why you are afraid or feeling guilty, these feelings are probably illegitimate. A blanket sense of fear or guilt about your entire life is not healthy. You must pray and ask God to direct you in dealing with these emotions.

It is important to be discerning when we feel these emotions. Sometimes we feel them because we just don't know the answers. We are uncertain of our parenting skills. You can manage these emotions by following these steps:

1. Ask yourself, "Why am I upset?" Determine the specific reason, if possible.

2. "Do I have enough knowledge to determine if I am feeling legitimate fear or guilt?" If not, do what you need to do to gain the knowledge you need: look it up, call a trusted friend, confer with people who are experienced parents, or ask your health care provider.

3. If you determine that your guilt or fear is legitimate, change your behavior appropriately. Seek the help needed to avoid a dangerous situation or remedy it.

4. If your guilt or fear is illegitimate, let it go. Ask God for help combating this emotion. You can trust God to meet your needs and the needs of your baby.

If you cannot resolve feelings of overwhelming guilt or fear, you should consider seeking the help of a trained and experienced counselor. You can mother from a place of love and trust, by trusting that God can meet the needs of your family. As you ask Him for help, He can direct you to the knowledge you need. When we respond appropriately to fear and guilt, they become emotions that are welcome warnings rather than feelings that define our lives. Fear and guilt should never define the life of the Christian, as it is not God's plan for you.

Some women have had long exposure to the principles of freedom, love and trust in God's goodness, but have never been challenged by life's circumstances to doubt the truthfulness of these principles. If your relationship with God hasn't often been tested, parenting may be the first time you feel really stretched in these areas, since motherhood requires more sacrifices than you have ever been called to make. This doesn't mean you are at a disadvantage to other new mothers, but your experiences may be different.

We know God always works in the best interests of those who love Him and can rest assured that we can trust Him even in difficult times (Psalm 56:3). This takes away our reason for living in fear. You are God's child! He loves you and your baby. You can be at peace in Him (Isaiah 26:3) and can respond with confidence to the challenges of motherhood.

> Psalm 56:3 *"What time I am afraid, I will trust in thee."*
>
> Isaiah 26:3 *"Thou wilt keep him in perfect peace, whose mind is stayed on thee: because he trusteth in thee."*

Overcoming Past Loss or Trauma

Many mothers have experienced some level of personal, physical, or emotional loss or trauma. Some may question God's goodness because of circumstances in their lives, but we need to understand that God does feel our pain. Although He doesn't cause our loss, He doesn't always prevent events that occur due to the fallen nature of man but allows them to help us grow. By allowing God to teach us through these difficult times, we learn to rely on Him. The result is a growth in our love of Him and in our ability to love those around us. How past challenging situations have been handled will influence your response to situations you will face as a parent.

If you see yourself as damaged, it will influence your current relationships, your parenting, and your perspective on situations now and in the future. It takes work to get past the loss and allow God to work. If you recognize past situations or losses are wrongly influencing your emotions and behaviors, you can find resources to work through these experiences.

Reaching out to a Christian counselor in your local area may be particularly helpful. Working with a counselor who has a Christian foundation for practice will help you learn to deal with wrong emotions and behaviors that have come from past experiences. There is actually a secular form of counseling that is consistent with Biblical teaching. The Biblical principle of replacement, putting off the old man and putting on the new (Ephesians 4:22-24), is in line with Cognitive Behavioral Therapy (CBT).

> *Ephesians 4:22-24* [22] *"That ye put off concerning the former conversation the old man, which is corrupt according to the deceitful lusts;* [23] *And be renewed in the spirit of your mind;* [24] *And that ye put on the new man, which after God is created in righteousness and true holiness."*

CBT can help you succeed in this process of replacement as it addresses how our thoughts impact our mental and physical health. *Proverbs 23:7a* says *"For as he thinketh in his heart, so is he:"* Although the founders of CBT are secular, all truth comes from God, and He will bless the use of Biblical principles.

Overcoming Unforgiveness

One aspect of dealing with loss and trauma is to deal with the residual unforgiveness that can result from how we respond to our past. Some of our readers may be dealing with their response to terrible physical or sexual abuse. Others may be concerned with something much less horrifying, but for that mother, something that has influenced her life dramatically. As we will all come to understand as mothers, parents make mistakes and do wrong. Most parents do not willfully want to harm, but they make wrong choices and fail to correctly deal with challenging life experiences. Even parents that abuse their own children are caught up and enslaved to sins and selfish responses that are a response to their own sinful nature.

> *Romans 6:19-23* [19] *"I speak after the manner of men because of the infirmity of your flesh: for as ye have yielded your members servants to uncleanness and to iniquity unto iniquity; even so now yield your members servants to righteousness unto holiness.* [20] *For when ye were the servants of sin, ye were free from righteousness.* [21] *What fruit had ye then in those things whereof ye are now ashamed? for the end of those things is death.* [22] *But now being made*

free from sin, and become servants to God, ye have your fruit unto holiness,
and the end everlasting life. 23 For the wages of sin is death; but the gift of God
is eternal life through Jesus Christ our Lord."

Christ's sacrifice frees us from the slavery of sin. Because of Him we can each overcome our past and serve Him, our spouse, and children the way we were intended to. This requires sacrificial love. Unfortunately, some parents aren't prepared to make any kind of sacrifice for their offspring. That is very sad, but it is a fact in this world.

The adult who has been abused or treated poorly as a child needs to realize that her response to past situations will harm her more than the actual events. We probably all know people who have been abused by parents or family friends, yet the victim now as an adult is full of joy and is a shining example of how to deal with trouble. Others remain victims and are controlled by their previous experiences. The difference is the victim's response to the situation.

Hebrews 12:14-15 14 "Follow peace with all men, and holiness, without
which no man shall see the Lord: 15 Looking diligently lest any man fail of the
grace of God; lest any root of bitterness springing up trouble you, and thereby
many be defiled;"

Being wronged is painful at the time, and grows much worse as you continue to remember and dwell on those memories. The bitterness and resentment that grows from being abused can control your life within just a few years. Forgiveness is the Biblical solution to bitterness, and the heart of forgiveness is focused on pleasing God rather than man.

God promises joy and freedom from the pain of loss when we follow His will. We are commanded to forgive, and when we hold on to unforgiveness, we are in opposition to God's desires for us. We then put up blocks to God's blessings and fellowship in our lives. But when we forgive obediently God says:

Romans 4:7-8 7 "Saying, Blessed are they whose iniquities are forgiven, and
whose sins are covered. 8 Blessed is the man to whom the Lord will not
impute sin."

Forgiveness is not a nebulous action; it is a choice made with the will. We cannot always control how we feel, but we can control our actions and with practice we can also control our thoughts about that person. When angry or negative thoughts come, replacing them with something else, such as Scripture, is a great technique.

Philippians 4:8 "Finally, brethren, whatsoever things are true, whatsoever things are honest, whatsoever things are just, whatsoever things are pure, whatsoever things are lovely, whatsoever things are of good report; if there be any virtue, and if there be any praise, think on these things."

Other techniques that can help include listening to uplifting music, reading a book, or participating in an activity or exercise that absorbs your mind. You may want to take concrete actions such as doing something kind for the person or writing a letter of forgiveness.

Many women have not experienced true mental, physical, or sexual abuse, yet have dealt with mistakes made by parents in child-rearing that have continued to haunt them even into adulthood. The expecting or new mother is working hard to become a good mommy and deciding how she will approach this new responsibility. Often young women identify areas where their own parents failed or made mistakes. It is a very common experience for women to evaluate their upbringing during pregnancy and the early days of motherhood. It is important to avoid the danger of becoming angry or bitter at your parents.

2 Corinthians 2:10-11 [10] "To whom ye forgive any thing, I forgive also: for if I forgave any thing, to whom I forgave it, for your sakes forgave I it in the person of Christ; [11]Lest Satan should get an advantage of us: for we are not ignorant of his devices."

Some of us are very sensitive to injustices and are very aware of the inequalities parents demonstrate among their children. Maybe you had a difficult relationship with your mother or father growing up and promised yourself, "I will never do 'that' to my child." Now you are on the brink of motherhood, and you worry that you won't be able to keep your promise. As you continue to grow as a mother, you will realize you won't always make the best decisions for your children. Sometimes you have a bias toward what you think has occurred; sometimes you have only part of the facts about an argument between your children. It won't take long to realize you will not always be the perfect parent, and will need your children's forgiveness at some point.

Ronda: In my older children, I sometimes see signs of resentment over a decision I make or the way I chose to correct them. I have begun making a real effort to have heart to heart conversations with my children, particularly my daughters, when I see that root of bitterness. I do not want them to experience the consequences of unforgiveness. I work to break down those walls that can be built. I will still make many parenting mistakes, but I try to be aware of how those mistakes affect my children and guard against those problems when possible.

Some teaching on forgiveness instructs people that they do not need to forgive unless the offender repents. It is illuminating to look at the type of forgiveness that Christ demonstrated to us.

> Romans 5:8 *"But God commendeth his love toward us, in that, while we were yet sinners, Christ died for us."*

Creator God sent Jesus to take the punishment for the sins of the world when we were still enemies with Him.

> Romans 5:10 *"For if, when we were enemies, we were reconciled to God by the death of his Son, much more, being reconciled, we shall be saved by his life."*

Some of Christ's last words dealt with forgiveness.

> Luke 23:34 *"Then said Jesus, Father, forgive them; for they know not what they do. And they parted his raiment, and cast lots."*

This forgiveness is available to all who will receive it and is what we need to offer those who have wronged us.

> Mark 11:24-26 [24] *"Therefore I say unto you, What things soever ye desire, when ye pray, believe that ye receive them, and ye shall have them.* [25] *And when ye stand praying, forgive, if ye have ought against any: that your Father also which is in heaven may forgive you your trespasses.* [26] *But if ye do not forgive, neither will your Father which is in heaven forgive your trespasses".*

> Ephesians 4:31-32 [31] *"Let all bitterness, and wrath, and anger, and clamour, and evil speaking, be put away from you, with all malice:* [32] *And be ye kind one to another, tenderhearted, forgiving one another, even as God for Christ's sake hath forgiven you."*

Those we forgive may not request it, acknowledge it, or accept it, but it is there, made available to them when we choose to forgive.

One aspect to forgiveness is choosing to forget the offense. After the offense has been dealt with, it is time to move on. Dealing with the hurt may mean talking with a counselor, praying, or seeking reconciliation. We have all heard the saying "I can forgive, but I'll never forget." This is not true forgiveness. Rehearsing the wrong only multiplies the hurt done to your soul. An intentional releasing of hurts is not denial. We acknowledge the hurt and anger and then we ask God for help in resolving those feelings.

> *Micah 7:18-19* [18] *"Who is a God like unto thee, that pardoneth iniquity, and passeth by the transgression of the remnant of his heritage? he retaineth not his anger for ever, because he delighteth in mercy.* [19] *He will turn again, he will have compassion upon us; he will subdue our iniquities; and thou wilt cast all their sins into the depths of the sea."*

We encourage you to carefully evaluate those areas of resentment or unforgiveness that you have harbored toward your parent(s) or others and seek the Lord's guidance about how to yield your anger and disappointment to Him. Forgiving fully will allow you to experience the freedom to move forward into parenting with much more joy and acceptance of those around you. It will be worth it; we can promise you that.

Summary

As you are growing to become the mother God wants you to be, it can be helpful to realize that mothering that newborn becomes one of your primary roles; a God-given role. God has called you to do this. We should be encouraged, *because mothering your infant as God intended is the way that you serve God, family, and others. It is your ministry.* Mothering will be your most challenging and critical career goal. This is legacy work. It is also short-term work. There is never a more concentrated effort at mothering than in the first year of life. Just as various projects or responsibilities in life take a concentrated focus, mothering the newborn is a discrete period of time that requires a great deal of your focus while other responsibilities are deferred to some extent.

Motherhood is a time of great change and maturing as both a woman and a member of the body of Christ. As we find ourselves taking on this mothering role, there are many traits that we need to demonstrate in our lives. We may not have acquired these attributes prior to this point, and we can't just put them on our baby gift registry and hope to receive them nicely packaged. The traits will take time and effort on our part to develop.

God will help us to become more controlled in our actions and more flexible in our responses to circumstances. We can know that He will help us solve the problems we find in our families, and act in more loving and sacrificial ways. God will accomplish this work in our lives as we rely on Him to meet our needs, worship Him, study His Word, seek to learn from those around us, and trust the Lord for what He will bring our way.

Section Two

The Early Days

So God created man in his own image, in the image of God created he him; male and female created he them.

Genesis 1:27

Chapter Three

The Scoop on Newborns

There is a passage in the Psalms about how God created us and knows everything about us. It is commonly quoted that we are "fearfully and wonderfully made." We are truly amazing works of His hands. Just consider again the miracle of our individual creation by God. He does know all about each of us. How wonderful!

> *Psalm 139: 13b-17* ^{13b} *"thou hast covered me in my mother's womb.* ¹⁴ *I will praise thee; for I am fearfully and wonderfully made: marvellous are thy works; and that my soul knoweth right well.* ¹⁵ *My substance was not hid from thee, when I was made in secret, and curiously wrought in the lowest parts of the earth.* ¹⁶ *Thine eyes did see my substance, yet being unperfect; and in thy book all my members were written, which in continuance were fashioned, when as yet there was none of them.* ¹⁷ *How precious also are thy thoughts unto me, O God! how great is the sum of them!"*

God made us and fashioned us in the womb, and this process of development continues after birth. The newborn undergoes significant transitions during and after delivery; this means in part that a newborn baby looks quite different than a six-month-old baby. There are many unique changes that occur in the weeks following birth. Let's discuss all the ways a newborn can look, shall we say, "different."

Miriam: When I was expecting my first baby, I remember talking on the phone with my mom. "What if she's ugly? I mean, not that many people are truly ugly. You can fix most kinds of ugly. She'll probably be pretty, right?"

Yeah, I was a really mature first time mom! Of course, I was concerned over other important things like, "Will I look like this pregnant unrecognizable self forever?" My mother only laughed at me, and I earned the pleasure of hearing that story repeatedly. Oh, well.

What do you think my daughter looked like when she was born? She enthralled my husband and me. It was amazing to hold her in my arms, and she was beautiful to me, but there were a lot of surprises! She had the following: stork bite, newborn rash, milia, subconjunctival hemorrhages, caput, Epstein pearls, and dimpling on the end of her spine. When we got home, she developed more newborn acne and turned a yellow color from jaundice. Her poor little head had been so squished that I wouldn't let anyone take her hat off!

Let's Examine the Newborn

The Head

Molding: This is the process that allows the baby's head to fit through the pelvis and vagina. The skull bones move and shift causing the baby to appear to have a cone head. Most molding will disappear within the first few days. Molding can also occur after birth from the baby lying in the same position for long periods of time.

When the baby is held, the head isn't resting firmly on one continual surface as when he is lying down, so holding is a good preventive strategy against additional molding. When a baby is laid down for naps, it is important to change the position of his head.

As the baby gets older and gains more head control, he should be positioned in the crib or playpen in such a way that he will be encouraged to turn his head, instead of always looking to his left or right. Babies can be laid on their tummies during playtime. This will prevent constant pressure on the back of the baby's head. This will also encourage the baby to strengthen his head, neck, arms, and chest as he learns to push himself up and interact with his environment.

Fontanels: These are the soft spots or openings between the bones that make up the skull. The fontanel may move up and down with the baby's heartbeat. A sunken fontanel is a sign of dehydration. It may swell slightly if the baby is having a bowel movement or crying. A bulging fontanel is a sign of increased pressure in the brain, and should be reported to your healthcare provider.

The anterior fontanel is diamond shaped. It closes around the eighteenth month. The posterior fontanel is much smaller and will close between 8 and 12 weeks. These openings in the skull are the part of God's design that allows for rapid brain growth. The brain can grow quickly without causing too much pressure within the skull. What an amazing design!

Caput Succedaneum/Cephalohematoma: This is bruising and swelling on the baby's head. It can be caused by the normal forces of a vaginal delivery, as well as the use of forceps or vacuum during delivery.

Cephalohematomas are composed of mostly blood. They are seen on the first or second day of life and will go away within the first few weeks. Each bone in the skull has one of these membranes. Suture lines are the ridges on your baby's skull, the outlines of the skull bones. A cephalohematoma does not cross suture lines, because the bleeding takes place between the bone and the special periosteal membrane that covers the bone.

Caput can be caused by part of the baby's head being squished against his mother's cervix. The part of the baby that is against the cervix before birth is called the presenting part. We want the head to be the presenting part, but when it is squished against the cervix the blood vessels are squeezed. This can cause extra fluids to move out of the blood vessels and into the skin and flesh of the skull. A caput is composed mostly of fluids and possibly some blood and will be gone by the end of the first day. When the swelling is caused by vacuum extraction it may last a few days. A caput occurs in the tissues above the bones and may cross suture lines.

Some babies have both caput and cephalohematoma:, but both usually resolve without difficulty. If your baby has a bruised head or the doctor used a vacuum, the nurse should measure the baby's head periodically to monitor for abnormal swelling. If your baby's head seems to be getting bigger, let your nurse know. The vast majority of babies come through labor just fine.

If you are reading this book before delivery, you should discuss the use of instrument-assisted deliveries with your doctor. Determining his comfort level with the use of a vacuum or forceps will give you information that can help prepare you for delivery.

The Eyes

Edema: The eyelids may be swollen at first, because of the pressure on the face during birth. This will resolve within the first few days.

Subconjunctival hemorrhages: These are bright red spots on the sclera (white part of the eye). They are caused by pressures exerted on the baby during labor. They will resolve in the first few weeks. Only 10% of babies have these.

The Nose

Newborns can smell! The baby will turn his head towards his mother's scent and the scent of her milk:. The baby can smell both you and your milk within 50 feet, which may explain why you can walk around your hungry baby without being in his line of sight, yet he knows you are there! Amazing! Your baby will breathe through his nose for the first few months. Newborns can breathe through their mouths, but they prefer to nose breathe. Of course, nose breathing makes it much easier to suckle.

Ask your nurse to show you how to use the bulb syringe to gently suction out your baby's nose. Always squeeze the air out of the bulb syringe before placing it in your baby's nose or mouth. Using a little salt water (available over the counter) and a nasal syringe is the best way to get your baby over congestion for the first few months. You will learn to do this well. Babies tend to dislike this procedure, but they do like to breathe!

The Mouth

Epstein pearls: These are small cysts found inside the mouth that look like tiny pearls. These will go away within the first few weeks.

Teeth: Occasionally, babies are born with little teeth:. Often the healthcare provider will remove these, because if they are loose, they can choke the baby when they fall out on their own. These are not the baby's true teeth, which usually start coming in around six months.

Your baby's taste buds work! He can taste already! Human milk is the sweetest of all known milks. He's very familiar with the taste and smell of amniotic fluid, which tastes much like colostrum. This familiarity helps the baby find your breast and drives his interest in locating that source. There is wonderful information available about how a baby checks the smell of amniotic fluid on his unwashed hands and uses that as a comparison when he is looking for his first meal (Browne 2008; Klaus and Kennel 2001).

He may make sucking movements when you touch his lips. If your baby is healthy and active, his lips and the inside of his mouth should be pink. When a baby's lips or inside of the mouth is blue, that indicates the baby is not getting enough oxygen. You need to seek medical care if you find this appearance.

The Ears

If your baby is born in the United States, a hearing test will be performed in the hospital during the first few days. The baby's outer ear cartilage may be folded over due to pressure on the ear inside the womb or birth canal. Taping the ear in a desired position is controversial; this can cause skin irritation. Just give the ear a few weeks and it should return to a normal position. If there is a major discordance in the shape of the ears, consult your baby's healthcare provider.

The Chin

Full-term babies have chins that are only 40% developed. Babies' chins are receded and will grow as they age.

The Neck

The neck is short and your baby's chin will usually rest on his chest. His neck muscles are not strong enough to support his head. Support his head with your hand when holding him. Cesarean delivery may allow the neck to maintain stronger muscles, because there is less strain on the muscles during birth.

Some babies have a difficult time turning their heads. This is called torticollis, and it is a common finding in newborns. Torticollis can occur in the mother's womb from the position of the baby in the uterus, but it may not appear until sometime after delivery. It is easily treated with simple exercises and gentle stretches that your healthcare provider can show you.

The Chest

Supernumerary nipples: These small spots can look like moles; they are usually pink or brown in coloration. They are completely harmless and are rarely attached to glandular tissue. They may darken at puberty, and you may choose to have them removed for cosmetic reasons.

Xiphoid cartilage: This is a normal variation (more noticeable in some babies) that can be seen as a knot at the end of the sternum. This will become less noticeable the fatter the baby becomes.

Respirations: A newborn breathes 30 to 60 times per minute, which is about three times the rate adults breathe! The breathing may be irregular. If you have concerns or your baby seems to be struggling to breathe, notify your healthcare provider immediately. Signs of abnormal breathing include flaring nostrils or indentations around or under the ribs or above or below the clavicles.

Miriam: My first night with Rebekah in the hospital I remember feeling embarrassed about asking the nurse, "Is she going to stop breathing?" It didn't matter that I had worked with newborn babies before as a student nurse. This was <u>my</u> first baby. I needed reassurance that I could sleep. Did I need to stay awake and watch her chest rise and fall? If I went to sleep could I trust that she would still be there when I woke? I wasn't objective enough to assess her physical status. I needed help, and you will too!

Please, ask whatever you need. If you feel something isn't quite right, ask your nurse to assess your baby and to explain the findings.

Cry: Newborns should have a strong cry. Some babies are much louder than others! The cry should not be high-pitched. Always report a high-pitched cry. If you don't think you know what a high-pitched cry is, ask your nurse. If your baby ever does it, you will learn and never forget the difference!

Heart rate: The normal rate is between 120 to 160 beats per minute, about twice that of healthy adults. Heart murmurs are common and most will go away on their own. However, your healthcare provider may monitor one closely. Ninety percent of murmurs are normal (Olds, London, and Ladewig 2000).

The Abdomen

Shape of abdomen: The newborn's tummy should be soft and rounded. It should not scoop inwards towards the spine. The tummy should not look or feel tight, rigid, or distended.

Umbilical cord: It will be a creamy yellow color at first. You may even be able to see the three blood vessel openings in the end of the cord. The cord will turn black and shrivel up by the third day. No blood should come out of the cord. It should be tightly clamped. The clamp will be removed before baby leaves the hospital. By then the cord will be very dry at the end. The dried cord should slowly disconnect right above the skin-colored part of the umbilicus and fall off within two weeks.

Routinely rubbing the cord stump with alcohol is no longer recommended. Just leave it alone, but keep it dry. Fold the diaper down beneath the cord stump. If the cord gets wet or soiled from diaper contents, you can clean it with some rubbing alcohol. If you notice foul smelling drainage from the cord stump, or continued drainage after the cord falls off, report these findings to your healthcare provider.

Once the cord falls off, the umbilicus will remain sticking out (an outie) for several months. Over time, it will begin to recede into the abdomen and for most babies become an innie. Taping a silver dollar over the area does not produce an innie more quickly, and the tape can be irritating to the baby.

The Genitals

Girls: There may be vaginal discharge that is white and tinged with blood. This discharge is present because of the mother's hormones. Blood tinged discharge is called pseudo menstruation. This will stop on its own. A thick, white substance called smegma may be seen between the labia. It will go away. If you try to remove it, you may cause abrasions.

Boys: Both testes should be descended into the scrotum at birth. Fluid around the testes is common. This is called a hydrocele and normally resolves on its own.

The foreskin may not be retractable until the end of the second year or sometimes even later. No special care is needed. Just wash the penis as you would any other body part. There is no need to clean under the foreskin.

If you choose to have your baby circumcised, you will need to apply gauze and petroleum jelly to the circumcision site until it heals. This is important, so the circumcision site does not become stuck to the diaper. If it does become stuck, simply pour some warm water over it and wait a few minutes. Do not just pull it away, or more bleeding will occur. Beware, warm water will have another effect on the little guy, be prepared!

At the time of the circumcision, your healthcare provider should use some kind of anesthetic agent. Local or topical anesthetic with a penile block (a numbing medicine injected near the nerve) and a pacifier dipped in sugar water are ways of providing pain control during this procedure. Some facilities use all of these techniques while others do not use any pain control. Check with the baby's healthcare provider and ask for appropriate pain control. Some hospitals routinely order acetaminophen (Tylenol®) for the day after a circumcision.

Be sure to get adequate information about your facility's procedures, and let your doctor or nurse know if you have any special requests. Be aware that circumcision can affect a baby's desire to nurse for up to 24 hours after the procedure. Keeping the baby skin-to-skin as much as possible after the circumcision can help with the pain response. Be sure to feed the baby before the procedure, or even have the procedure done outpatient in the doctor's office a few days after discharge when breastfeeding is better established. Outpatient circumcision can be less expensive with your insurance.

Insider tip: If the procedure being used requires a clamp, ask your provider to wait the full amount of time as specified in your hospital's policies and procedures before removing the clamp from the foreskin. This greatly reduces bleeding. You may request to be present for the procedure to ensure that appropriate pain control measures are performed and the clamp is left on long enough.

Arms and Legs, Hands and Feet

The newborn's arms and legs will be flexed. The hands are often balled up into tiny fists. This is normal and makes the baby feel safe. If your baby's arms and legs are floppy while they are awake, you should seek medical care.

Wrapping the baby in a flexed position will make him feel more secure, especially if he is lying in his bassinet. There is no reason to swaddle your baby while you are breastfeeding him; it prevents holding him skin-to-skin as well as the positioning he needs to do for breastfeeding when you are using a reclined or laid back feeding position.

The Back

The spine should be flat and straight. A pilonidal dimple (dimple at the base of the spine) should have a closed skin surface. If there is an opening in the skin, the doctor and nurse will discuss this with you and will do further testing. It can be an indication of a problem with the baby's spinal cord, sensation, and movement.

Reflexes

Grasping reflex: The baby's fingers will grip when an object is placed in his hand or his hand is stroked. It is fun to watch a young sibling's face light up because, "The baby is holding my finger!" Some babies have such a strong grip that they can support their body weight, but the grip is not predictable, and a baby could be injured if allowed to hang from dad's fingers.

Moro reflex: This is also called the startle reflex. The baby will throw his arms out while drawing up his knees. Your baby will do this anytime he is startled. This reflex may not go away until the sixth month. This is a pretty funny reflex.

The Skin

Healthy newborns should have pink skin due to all the red blood cells circulating after birth. Even dark skinned babies should have a pink tinge to their skin. Your baby may not have normal skin tone for the first month or so. Sometimes Caucasian babies seem to be blue when they come out, then pink, then yellow (if jaundiced), and finally a normal color.

Newborn rash: Also called Erythema Toxicum, this normal finding usually occurs 24-48 hours after birth. It will go away on its own. Newborn rash consists of spots of one to three millimeters that may be white or yellow with red around the base. Basically, this looks like acne 14 years ahead of time. It will go away. If you are not familiar with the look of newborn rash, ask the nurse to check the skin. Babies occasionally have rashes that indicate an underlying abnormality and should be reported.

Acrocyanosis: The hands and feet appear to be blue, while the baby's face, mouth, and abdomen are pink. This occurs two to six hours after birth and is a normal finding, as long as the other areas remain pink.

Milia: These are small white spots on the baby's face. There is no need to squeeze them. These exposed sebaceous glands will resolve without intervention.

Vernix Caseosa: This substance may be present on your baby's skin at delivery. It was a protective moisturizer for the baby's skin while in the amniotic fluid. It is white and the consistency of a soft cheese. It will mostly come off with the newborn bath, and any part that is missed can be washed off later or even massaged into the baby's skin like lotion.

Dry skin: Many babies will have dry, peeling skin on their hands and feet. You do not need to put moisturizers on the baby's skin. However, if this bothers you, get a recommendation from your healthcare provider. The skin will eventually normalize, but dry skin comes from the vernix wearing off before the baby is born. This is most likely to happen to the hands and feet first, and then the rest of the body as the baby stays in the womb too long. Think two-week soak in the tub!

> Ronda: My first baby was born three weeks after the due date. Rob had dry skin all over his body. He looked pretty shriveled up for a while.

Stork Bites: Stork bites are pink or red spots usually found on the nape of the neck, but also on other parts of the face. They normally are gone by the second birthday.

Mongolian Spots: These spots, which are common in those with darker skin, look like bruises on the back and buttocks. They also normally fade by the second birthday.

Jaundice: Normal newborn jaundice is caused by the breakdown of excess red blood cells that make your baby such a cute, pink color at first. Most newborns have immature livers that are unable to process the bilirubin, which is the end product of red blood cell breakdown. The bilirubin escapes to the skin and gives the yellow coloration. This is called jaundice. Normal jaundice, also called physiologic jaundice, does not appear during the first 24 hours. The vast majority of jaundice cases do not need treatment except to monitor the levels of jaundice and continue frequent feedings for the baby.

Risk Factors for Jaundice

Cesarean babies have twice as many problems with jaundice than babies delivered vaginally, which may be because the birth canal pushes some of the extra blood out of the baby before birth and because vaginal delivery stimulates greater milk production in the mother (Rachlis and Petryshen 1992). The more milk a baby drinks, the more the baby will stool. Bowel movements are the main way that babies get rid of the extra bilirubin.

Ronda: Rob, my firstborn, was born by c-section, overdue, had some sleepiness from medications at delivery and was very large at 10lb, 5 oz. He developed jaundice and was monitored with frequent bilirubin blood tests, which required going back to the hospital every day or so. The purpose of the blood tests was to make sure his bilirubin level started coming down. Once the pediatrician could see that the level was going down, we didn't have to keep going back for more tests. His pediatrician was pro-breastfeeding, so she did not encourage supplementation; he nursed a lot in those first few days.

Other risk factors for high bilirubin and jaundice are preterm delivery (up to 38 weeks), Rh sensitization of the mother, babies with bruising, maternal diabetes, and greater than 10% weight loss of the baby after birth. It is helpful to know if the mom or baby has increased risk factors, because mothers can take actions to prevent or resolve the problem.

Symptoms and Treatment

If you go home and your baby is yellow, sleepy, and not eating well, call your healthcare provider for a follow-up check. The best way to get your baby over jaundice is to breastfeed as often as possible. Most authorities, including the American Academy of Pediatrics and the Academy of Breastfeeding Medicine, recommend that you breastfeed 8 to 12 times a day in order to treat and prevent physiologic jaundice (AAP 2004, 298; ABM 2010).

If your baby has a high bilirubin level, your healthcare provider may order phototherapy, in addition to frequent breastfeeding. This is often done in a pediatric hospital, and you will stay with the baby to breastfeed. Your baby will be monitored closely for bilirubin levels and will usually go home as soon as he is showing a safe downward progression in numbers.

Sometimes phototherapy can be done at home with a home health nurse. The baby can wear a vest with the phototherapy lights embedded inside. This makes the baby look like a glowworm. In the past, parents would be instructed to put their baby near a window for direct sunlight, but now windows have ultraviolet filtering which prevents this from working.

> Miriam: Rebekah needed phototherapy. Thankfully, we were able to do it at home. She looked like a little glowworm for a few days from wearing the phototherapy vest. Within a week all of the jaundice and most of the other newborn strangeness went away. She turned out to be a beautiful baby!

Preterm Babies and Jaundice

Babies that are born during late preterm (35-37 weeks) are at increased risk for jaundice. Babies born at this gestation have more immature livers that do not break down the bilirubin as efficiently as a full term baby's liver could. These babies often have delayed breastfeeding or poor weight gain and may need to be supplemented with expressed breast milk, donor milk, or formula after breastfeeding until they have gained adequate weight. The mother will need to work with the baby's primary care provider to assure that the baby is adequately maturing and gaining weight.

Breast Milk and Jaundice

Breastfeeding in the first 24 hours provides the baby with colostrum, a natural laxative. This helps them have more frequent stools and eliminate the bilirubin quickly. Some doctors have been known to encourage breastfeeding mothers to supplement with formula to clear up jaundice faster. Since formula is not as condensed as breast milk, the extra fluid/water is theorized to help clear the jaundice faster, but studies have not validated this.

God in His wisdom planned the formation of breast milk. Although it is more condensed than formula, it has natural laxatives. This allows the baby to have less fluid shifts, yet still have adequate stools.

Your milk should begin to change and you should notice fullness in your breasts before feeds by day three or four. If the baby is breastfeeding without problems and having four or more stools larger than a quarter by day five, the jaundice will begin to disappear.

If at any time your baby is too sleepy to nurse or is not nursing well, you should call the lactation consultant or take your baby to be weighed. The lactation consultant or healthcare provider may have the baby's blood tested for bilirubin levels.

Sometimes the mother is making plenty of milk but the baby is simply too sleepy or immature to nurse adequately. In this case, a lactation consultant can help the mother learn to help the baby nurse more effectively. The mother can also pump or manually express breast milk to feed her baby.

Jaundice Caused by Pathology or Injury

Some cases of jaundice are worse than others. Babies who have bruising on their heads are at an increased risk for jaundice, because their bodies have a hard time breaking down the extra blood cells in the bruise. Some diseases or incompatibilities between the mother and baby's blood types can cause a problem with blood cells. These cases of jaundice will require follow-up with the doctor and sometimes phototherapy and medicines to help the baby get rid of all the bilirubin.

Starvation Jaundice

Occasionally, jaundice is caused when babies are not getting enough to eat. In order to make sure that this is not the case for your baby, feed the baby 8 to 12 times per day in the first weeks. If he is not nursing well, or you doubt that your milk has transitioned to mature milk by day four, contact a lactation consultant. When your baby is satisfied after a feeding you may notice a zoned out look in his eyes, this is known as "milk coma."

Breastfed Jaundice

The final type of jaundice is breastfed jaundice or normal physiologic jaundice. This type of jaundice occurs when low levels of bilirubin are present in the baby for several months after delivery. Some doctors believe there is a component in the breast milk that hinders the breakdown of bilirubin, to allow the baby to benefit from its antioxidant effects. These low levels of jaundice are not harmful to the baby. The baby doesn't need to wean or supplement as long as he continues to gain weight appropriately.

Interaction with Your Baby

Gazing at your face and watching you move about the house will be one of your baby's favorite entertainments. When he leaves the newborn stage, he will become more interested in objects and toys. Your baby is learning that he is a human person and that his actions affect the environment. Playing with you throughout the day is crucial for his development. You may feel your baby is not responding the way you expect, but these interactions are a wonderful gift. Play sessions may not feel natural at first, but soon they will flow into your day. Interacting with your baby and meeting his needs for attention now will help him to feel secure in your love. He will have more courage as he grows and explores.

Here are some ideas for play.

- Smiling and talking while allowing your baby to gaze at your face
- Singing to your baby
- Reading to your baby
- Talking to your baby as you go about your activities
- Gentle massages
- Saying rhymes to your baby

How do Babies Think?

Infants do not have language, so they do not think the same way older children and adults do. Rather an infant's actions are based on his reflexes and needs. Newborns have very little working memory. This means that your baby cannot remember anything he is not immediately experiencing. For instance, if you are shaking a rattle for him and you move the rattle out of sight, he will not know that it still exists. This also means that punishing a newborn for unwanted behavior will not change the behavior. The infant is unable to associate the behavior with the punishment. An infant may be startled by your response, but there is no learning taking place. Because newborn behavior is reflexive and a result of needs, any punishment for unwanted behavior is inexcusable on the part of the parent. Infants do not develop working memory until six months (Gilmore and Johnson 1995). Even at six months the infant can only retain the most limited information for three to five seconds.

Until eight months or later, infants placed on a bed or other raised surface will crawl off and fall. Even if the fall is repeated the infant does not learn. It is only after weeks of crawling and practice that infants learn about their limitations. This process must be repeated each time your baby learns a new skill. The transitions from sitting, crawling, cruising, and walking all require weeks or months of practice before babies learn their abilities (Adolph 2000).

Parenting the Newborn

Much Christian literature has been written about morally correct and incorrect ways of child rearing. Using any infant parenting style, mom and dad can go on to make good or poor choices in other areas such as training, building character, and praise of achievement. Your overall manor of making choices is influenced by the way you see your responsibility to God for the children He gives you.

Many parents choose to nurture their infants by keeping them near all the time, wearing the baby in a sling during the day and co-sleeping with their baby at night. This parenting style is often called attachment parenting, and it has been used throughout much of human history. In some writings, this style has been lumped with all manner of permissive child-rearing choices. This is an inaccurate characterization of the style, which has a distinct meaning and does not incorporate all the parenting choices that have been assigned to it.

Attachment parenting can be a good way to parent a high-needs newborn, one who is colicky, cries often, or is sensitive to sound, light, and other stimulation. Some research indicates that this type of care is the most biologically appropriate for all infants, especially during the newborn period when the baby's physiological systems are regulated by the mother.

In some cultures, mothers feed their babies at least every hour. These babies do all of their non-nutritive suckling at the breast. They are worn in slings while their mothers work. These babies rarely cry and almost never have colic. The mothers are able to naturally space the births of the babies, and they rarely have problems with low milk supply. However, in many places where this is the norm, living conditions of these mothers require the baby to stay close.

If a mother chooses to follow the attachment parenting style, she should feel enabled to do so. Attachment parenting may not work for every mother. Other patterns of feeding and non-nutritive suckling can also be used, as long as the baby does receive a great deal of cuddling and holding.

Traditional or mainstream parenting is a style that incorporates the use of equipment like swings, cradles, infant carriers, and bouncy seats to hold the baby when the mother is not available. Mothers that favor this style will still hold their babies but will also allow the baby to have independent time. This style has become very common within the last century. Moms using this style are more likely to work and have other caregivers for the baby. Formula feeding and independent sleep are other characteristics of the style.

Extremes in parenting styles should be avoided. Attachment parenting taken to the extreme can result in a child that has trouble interacting with people and does not display appropriate exploring behaviors. To avoid this observe your infant closely. When he begins displaying more interest in his environment, encourage that by using a carrier that allows him to view his surroundings. Hand him off to family and friends as appropriate, and be sure to sit on the floor beside him as he plays with toys and explores a room.

Traditional parenting practices can be overemployed and result in negative outcomes as well. These babies may not bond well with their parents; they could have delayed development, and they tend to have more episodes of inconsolable crying. Moms who use a strict schedule and highly value independent sleep may comment, "It's so sad my baby will never let me rock him to sleep. He will only fall asleep in his bed."

Most parents find that a combination of styles works best for their family. Feel free to choose positive parenting behaviors or styles that work for you, your baby, and your home life. Some parents may tend to extremes and criticize others' parenting choices because the choices are not the same as their own. Romans 14 and 15 give us direction concerning our liberty in Christ. You are ultimately responsible to parent as God leads you.

Expectations

We all have ideas about what we expect babies to look and act like. Babies are newborns for such a short period of time! Newborns do look so differently than the image of a smiling, six-month-old. God is good to put all of those hormones in us to help us bond to these tiny and wonderful creations.

God made babies in such a way that adults are naturally drawn to them. Their big eyes and soft bodies entice us to love and cuddle. In many areas of life it can be the natural thing to focus on the outward appearance, but God has created each newborn with His image! What an amazing thought— each life is sacred to God, our heavenly Parent.

The information in this chapter can help you adjust your expectations. Your newborn will not be able to modify his behavior to accommodate your desires. He is simply too immature. The work you are doing now by interacting with him during your daily activities is increasing his ability to respond to you as he grows.

> *Isaiah 28: 9-10 [9] "Whom shall he teach knowledge? and whom shall he make to understand doctrine? them that are weaned from the milk, and drawn from the breasts. [10] For precept must be upon precept, precept upon precept; line upon line, line upon line; here a little, and there a little:"*

In Biblical times, children were weaned around three years old. The expectation was that they would learn a little at a time. The phrases in verse 10 repeats to emphasize the necessity that instruction be gentle, brief, and appropriate. How much more careful should we be with the infants entrusted to us? We should always be mindful of their innocent and developing minds. God has given us these babies to protect, love, cherish, and gently guide.

Summary

It won't be long before your baby's appearance will change and he will begin to look as most people expect a baby to look. Until then you should ask questions when you observe something that concerns you.

We live in an appearance and image based society and our expectations may be different from reality. But God has put many wonderful mechanisms in place so that we don't focus on the outward appearance but on the little person beneath. He helps us to see our baby through His eyes.

A Dutch Lullaby

Wynken, Blynken, and Nod one night
Sailed off in a wooden shoe —
Sailed on a river of crystal light
Into a sea of dew
"Where are you going, and what do you wish?"
The old moon asked the three.
"We have come to fish for the herring fish
That live in this beautiful sea;
Nets of silver and gold have we!"
Said Wynken, Blynken, and Nod.

Wynken and Blynken are two little eyes,
And Nod is a little head,
And the wooden shoe that sailed the skies
Is a wee one's trundle-bed.
So shut your eyes while mother sings
Of wonderful sights that be,
And you shall see the beautiful things
As you rock in the misty sea,
Where the old shoe rocked the fishermen three:
Wynken, Blynken, and Nod.

(Field 1891)

as soon as she is delivered of the child,

she remembereth no more the anguish,

for joy that a man is born into the world

John 16:21b

Chapter Four
Postpartum: Body, Mind, and Emotions

Postpartum Body

> Miriam: The only bad part about having a baby is the post baby body—no fun! You get to hear all the comments like, "Wow, it's like your head on someone else's body!" Or even better, "Gracious, you just blew up." My thoughts, "Uh thanks, how sweet of you to say that out loud, because that's exactly what I need to hear after laboring for hours."

Some women seem to bounce right back after having a baby, but this is the exception. It can take up to two years to fully recover from pregnancy and childbirth. A lot depends on how much weight you gained during pregnancy. Many women will feel back to normal within the first three months, but some may take longer. Everyone is different.

> Miriam: My mother-in-love (law) loves to say, "I wore my regular jeans home from the hospital after having my first baby!"

Unfortunately, waltzing out of the hospital in pre-pregnancy jeans isn't the reality for most women. You may find it easier to handle if you expect to look six months pregnant the first week. Getting back into shape may be at the top of your list and is important, but for the first weeks focus on breastfeeding and caring for the baby.

The first six weeks of breastfeeding, most of your breast milk calories come from the fat you put into reserve during pregnancy. Breastfeeding takes about 500 extra calories per day. You should not restrict calories below 1800 while breastfeeding. Counting calories is cumbersome; cutting out sugar, white starches, and all processed foods will get you off to a good start. This is a safe way to begin getting back into shape for most mothers.

Check with your healthcare provider regarding recommendations for the right time to begin exercising. Many providers will encourage you to begin walking and performing light exercise as soon as you return home from the hospital. Increased vaginal bleeding after activity is a signal that you need to slow down. Though extreme exercise can impair breastfeeding, routine exercise has many health benefits.

Everything Leaks!

Night Sweats

These full body sweats are the body's way of getting rid of excess fluids. They also may be caused by large changes in hormone levels. Round up a couple of old beach towels and sleep on them. They should keep the sheets reasonably clean from leaking nipples and night sweats. Some women will not experience night sweats. If you're running a fever with night sweats, call your healthcare provider because this could be a sign of infection. Night sweats usually stop after the first week or two; if they continue, let your healthcare provider know.

Leaking Milk

Leaking from your breast may decrease or even disappear after the first six weeks. Don't bind your breasts or lay on them. This can inhibit milk production and may lead to blocked milk ducts. Although it may seem helpful to use a breast pump to remove extra milk causing the leaking, this strategy will increase the amount of milk your body makes and result in more leaking.

Using breast pads to collect leaked milk is very helpful. Cotton or disposable pads without a plastic lining will allow the nipples to stay dry and receive airflow. A pad with a plastic lining prevents air exchange and can become a breeding ground for bacteria. You should replace breast pads when they become wet. Silicone breast pads (Lily Padz®) work for mothers with ongoing leaking, are reusable, and allow clothing to lie smoothly.

Urinary Incontinence

Some women experience urinary incontinence caused by the pressure on the perineal nerves during delivery. These nerves will normally heal without intervention. Urinary leaking can also be caused by the stretching of the bulbospongiosis muscles, which surround the urethra and vagina. These muscles are responsible for tightening the urinary sphincter at the end of voiding as well as keeping the vagina closed.

Performing Kegel exercises can return muscle tone and prevent leaking. Learn this exercise while sitting on the toilet. When you are in the middle of urinating, attempt to stop the flow. This will give you an idea of which muscles you need to exercise since the bulbospongiosis muscles stop the flow of urine. Kegel exercises can be performed at any place and time.

The recommended amount of exercise is to work up over four weeks to 300 contractions a day in three 20-minute sessions. It may take three months of exercising these muscles before you experience a significant benefit. If urine leakage is a problem, tell your healthcare provider at the postpartum check-up. The Resource section of this book has a web link to detailed Kegel instructions (Jelovsek 2011).

Hemorrhoids

Hemorrhoids are common during pregnancy and may appear for the first time after delivery. There is great pressure exerted on the anal area in the last months of pregnancy and during delivery. Hemorrhoids are veins filled with extra blood that can bleed. They occur in the last few inches of the digestive tract, just inside the rectum or the rectal opening. External hemorrhoids occur outside the rectum.

When they are swollen, hemorrhoids may itch. Witch hazel and Tucks pads can be soothing. There are also creams and suppositories that minimize internal hemorrhoids. Internal hemorrhoids may not be felt, but bleeding may still occur. If you have a hemorrhoid protruding from the anus, you can sometimes press the hemorrhoid gently to reinsert it. Hemorrhoids that cause extreme pain may contain a blood clot that needs to be removed. Contact your healthcare provider if there is an ongoing or painful problem with these.

Lochia (vaginal bleeding/discharge following pregnancy)

The bleeding after pregnancy is like a heavy period. This discharge is called lochia. Lochia will be red right after delivery and will gradually turn brown and then yellow. Discharge may last from two to six weeks. Lochia should smell like a normal period. A foul odor signals infection. Lochia should get lighter and lighter. If lochia begins to get heavier or you are passing clots, take a rest and decrease your activities. If resting does not decrease the flow, contact your healthcare provider.

Breastfeeding causes the release of oxytocin, which causes the uterus to decrease in size. The uterus contracts and becomes smaller over the course of several days/weeks after delivery. These contractions will feel like cramping from a period. The cramping may cause a slight increase in lochia during or just after breastfeeding. This is a healthy way for the body to return to its prenatal normal.

Musculoskeletal Pain

After delivery, you may notice aches and pains that you didn't expect. The hormones that prepare the body for and through the delivery process also have a great impact on joints, which can cause hypermobile joints and injuries for up to 12 weeks. It is important during this time to use good posture and positioning.

Carrying the baby close to the body is better for you than carrying him strapped in a car seat. Another preventive measure to protect muscles and joints is to be sure to hold the baby in a natural position for your hands, arms, and shoulders when breastfeeding or giving artificial milk. New mommies spend so much time nursing that it is very important to use a laid back or other very comfortable position while nursing; this helps avoid overuse injuries.

Often mothers have a tendency to lean forward and bring the breast to the baby, instead of bringing the baby back toward the mother's body to help him latch. This results in an uncomfortable hunched position that causes pain and aching in the shoulders, neck, and upper back. It is important to use positions for feeding and resting that are comfortable and require the least amount of muscle effort (Roberts 2011).

Intercourse

Healthcare providers encourage mothers to wait until they have no more vaginal discharge or until after the six-week postpartum check-up before resuming sexual relations. Follow the recommendations of your provider.

While breastfeeding, it is also normal for women to experience spraying milk during orgasm. You can apply pressure to the breast to prevent this from happening, or have a towel handy, if this is a concern.

If you had a repair from a tear or episiotomy after delivery, you may notice some pain or burning during intercourse. This may indicate scar tissue formation that your doctor or midwife may be able to release during an office procedure. Discomfort is not normal during intercourse. Get the help you need, so that you can enjoy your relationship with your husband.

Women who have been abused in the past may feel especially vulnerable or fearful during and after delivery. If you have experienced any type of trauma or fears that inhibit you sexually, seek skilled counseling. You should contact someone who has been trained; this person should be licensed or certified and should be experienced with trauma. A counselor can be very helpful. They may not have magic words that will instantly fix the problem, but it is amazing the difference a trained counselor can make.

You may experience a decreased sex drive while breastfeeding due to changes in hormone production that cause a decrease in the hormones that lead to sexual desire and ovulation. This may last for six months or longer in mothers who are exclusively breastfeeding and feeding at least every three hours.

Breastfeeding exclusively is the normal way to feed a baby; it also provides protection for your body and new infant, by limiting ovulation and providing natural spacing between pregnancies. This limiting of ovulation doesn't work for some mothers, even when exclusively breastfeeding.

Space between your babies allows your body to regain full strength prior to another pregnancy. The general recommendation is at least 12 to 24 months between pregnancies (Marston et al. 2007). These recommendations are not to discourage large families, but to promote the health of the mother and each baby that she carries and delivers.

> Miriam: Shannon and I didn't get the memo regarding safe spacing of pregnancies. I had Beka when I was in my early twenties, and I felt pretty invincible. We were thrilled to find out I was expecting a second baby when Beka was only five months old. We wanted a large family, and wanted to complete our family by my early thirties. The recommendations for spacing between babies reflect the ideal, but this is a very personal decision between you and your spouse.

The marriage relationship is sacred. It needs to be continually nurtured. The new father faces his own insecurities and challenges. A wife can help her husband fulfill his new role in many ways, however one of the most important things she can do is to continue supporting him emotionally and physically. When a postpartum mother becomes physically able, she should do whatever she needs to make her spouse feel loved. Regarding sexual relations within marriage the Bible says:

> 1 Corinthians 7:5 *"Defraud ye not one the other, except it be with consent for a time, that ye may give yourselves to fasting and prayer; and come together again, that Satan tempt you not for your incontinency."*

If you want a healthy marriage, make intimacy a priority. Having a baby is not an excuse for abstaining from sex unless there is a medical reason. Married couples with healthy pregnancies should enjoy sex during and after pregnancy.

God created sex for more than just procreation; it should be fun! Read the book, *Intended for Pleasure*, which is written for Christian audiences. You can find it and other resources in the Resource List at the end of the book.

Postpartum Mind and Emotions

Needing Extra Help

Taking care of yourself and a newborn is a big job. Your baby and your body need tender loving care. Try your best to keep at least one and preferably two other helpers with you those first few weeks. A helper could be your spouse, mother, aunt, sister, friend, older daughter, or father.

Miriam: I remember telling my father, "If you don't let mom come for two weeks you won't get another grandchild!" It was said with a hint of humor, but the point was that I needed help, and I was willing to ask for it.

Do not hesitate to ask for help. If your mother can't come or your relationship with her is strained, find someone who is able to be there for you. You will probably be surprised at the willingness of your family and friends to pitch in when the new baby arrives.

Talk with your helpers before the baby comes about what you expect. Discuss the way you want to care for your baby, and remember to be patient and gentle; they have not read the latest on baby care. The role of a helper is to help you. The helper should not force their ideas on you or your child and should not take over baby care. You are the mother, and you are the one who most needs to get to know your baby during this time.

Helpers can babysit older siblings, provide meals, and assist with housecleaning. Everyone who offers to help should be given an opportunity. If you have a baby shower after delivery, your hostess could pass around a meal sign-up sheet. This is a great way to get help, especially if your church or group of friends does not routinely provide care to women after delivery.

A thankful and gracious spirit is needed to remain in charge of your baby's care without offending your helpful, advice-giving friends and family. Tell your helpers how much you need, appreciate, and love them. Your sweet and thankful attitude will encourage your support network. The better care you take to establish this support network with the birth of your first baby the more likely it will be there for your next baby as well.

In many cultures, mothers take 40 days to recover from delivery. This is a great practice. If this is not something your friends and family do, you can begin with this baby, and as you have opportunities, help other new mothers. Make these first 40 days a time that is set apart for you and your baby.

Churches can be another great resource for support. Many women's ministries offer meals to new mothers. This is a great time for you to become closer to the women in your church. If no one offers, you can ask your pastor's wife or other woman in the church if help is available. It may not be available, but do not be afraid to ask. If this kind of ministry isn't active in your church, consider suggesting it to your pastor, or meet with some friends and volunteer to start it.

If help is truly unavailable, don't waste time stressing about it. God can give you the grace to get through the newborn period. If you don't have help, this is the time to let the housework go. You could purchase extra groceries beforehand and even make meals and freeze them so there is less work to do after the baby comes. Use your crock-pot and keep meals as simple as possible. Remember to focus on breastfeeding the first six weeks. Nothing else is as important as getting your baby off to a good start.

What if you feel awkward around the baby? It's okay. It will become more natural with time. Watching others interact with your baby can help. Mothering a newborn is not something that women were meant to do alone. Get as much help as you can for as long as you can.

> Miriam: I got over my feelings of inadequacy and learned a lot during the time my mother came to help me with, Beka, my first baby. When Mom left I realized that I still needed help. It would have been better to have help for the first six weeks. After my first baby, I told myself I would make sure to line up help for longer periods when the next baby arrived.

You may have been told, "Pregnancy and childbirth are a normal part of life and not a sickness. Women have been doing this for thousands of years. You should be able to do it by yourself." Although it is a normal part of life and women have been doing this for years, this quote doesn't take into account our current cultural setting and expectations. In the past, women expected to have family around to help with babies, and it was normal for families to come, stay, and take care of the mother and baby.

New mothers need a relaxed, uncluttered environment to do the best job of bonding with their new baby. They also need to have their own physical and emotional needs met; this allows the mother to focus on caring for the new baby. It will be some time before a new mother is able to resume her normal activities.

> Miriam: Even with my fifth baby I needed help! Although I am an experienced parent and a nurse, I still need my mother. It was such a precious time. Mom and Dad came for three weeks, and I was blessed to

have help for the first 12 weeks. With someone to help me, I had the time to hold baby Shannon for many hours every day. It was easy to respond to his needs. After all, he was right there in my arms where he belonged.

Needing sleep... Desperately

Almost every mother will be a little sleep deprived during the first week or two. The best way to cope with lack of sleep is to get more sleep! When your baby takes a nap, take a nap. This can be tricky if you always feel the need to do something, but taking care of your baby and yourself are most important these first six weeks. Getting through the first six weeks with a healthy body and breastfeeding relationship is a huge accomplishment! Push other things aside and be willing to suspend certain activities.

Naps are going to be a very important part of your day. Please take naps. Even a 20-minute nap, if taken at the same time every day, can make a big difference in the way a new mother feels. Take a nap with the baby or feed the baby, pass him off to a helper and take a nap, repeat until you feel rested. There may be times when you need to nap, wake up, feed the baby, and go right back to sleep.

If you have other young children at home, do your best to get someone to come in to help for even 30 minutes during the day while you nap. Remember that the sleep deprivation will not last forever. By the time the baby is 6 to 12 weeks old, you should be getting more sleep. It is amazing how much better a mother feels when she has had five continuous hours of sleep. Tips on ways to get four to five hours of sleep at night can be found in Chapter 7.

Baby Blues

Baby blues are common after delivery. Many mothers experience a day or two of sadness. This often occurs on the fourth or fifth day. You may feel helpless, sad, anxious, and have a difficult time concentrating. Remember, you cannot always control your emotions, but you *can control* your actions. Keep doing the important things. Feed and cuddle your baby. Take a shower. Continue your daily devotional reading, prayer time, and soak up some sun (Terman and Terman 2005).

The things that upset you during this time may be important or they can be somewhat silly. If you were in your "right mind," not whatever mind you have left after nine months of pregnancy, labor, delivery, and three nights of sleep deprivation, you would be able to handle these things. During the first several weeks after birth your resources are very low.

Miriam: I was taking a bath with my third baby when he was about four days old. This was supposed to be a relaxing time of bonding. I had just become really relaxed when he pooped in the water! Yellow poop! So gross! I cried. That ended the relaxing bath!

Later that morning dad noticed that I was upset, and he immediately left the house. He came back a few minutes later with two bags full of junk food! He said, "Honey, I noticed you seemed upset; ... here's some food." My mom turned on a Jane Austin movie, my husband rocked the baby, I took a nap, and by the next day, I was feeling much better!

I was pretty blessed to have such a mild case of the blues. It made a big difference that I had so many loving adults around to help me through that first week.

Usually these upsetting feelings will pass in a few days. Occasionally, a woman may have postpartum depression that lasts longer than two weeks. This can be very serious; please see Appendix B for more information.

When to Call your Healthcare Provider

+ Filling a pad an hour for more than two hours in a row
+ Bleeding that remains bright red after the first four days
+ Passing clots larger than a quarter
+ Foul smelling vaginal discharge
+ Persistent vaginal or abdominal pain
+ Fever
+ Red streaks or inflamed breasts especially if accompanied by fever or flu-like symptoms
+ Severe headache, seeing spots, or other visual disturbances
+ Pain or swelling in a leg
+ Feeling as if you may hurt yourself or your baby
+ Vomiting that is severe and frequent
+ Any other concerns (many times your provider's nurse or the labor and delivery nurses can answer other questions you may have)

Summary

Becoming a mother is a huge job. It is arguably the most rewarding and challenging task you will ever undertake. Embrace it all, the messy parts, the sweet parts, and the exhausting parts. God will give you all the grace and strength you need.

And Jesus saith unto them, Yea; have ye never read, Out of the mouth of babes and sucklings thou hast perfected praise?

Matthew 21:16b

Chapter Five

Breastfeeding Basics for the First Week

Breastfeeding is a learned skill for the mother and baby. Although you both have innate behaviors and reflexes that are helpful for breastfeeding, acquiring this skill will take more than "instinct." Like learning any new skill, breastfeeding takes time, help, and commitment. Knowledge and patience will be required to overcome the challenges that occur during birth and the first few days after birth. You will be on the fast track to successful breastfeeding when you understand the process of milk production, the normal nursing habits of newborns, and the ways your actions influence both.

Feed Early

Within the First Hour after Delivery

One of the best things you can do to positively influence breastfeeding is to take advantage of the first hour after delivery, because babies are primed for nursing during this special time. Hold your baby against your bare chest. The baby may be dressed in a diaper and possibly a hat; use a blanket against his back to keep you both warm. *Keep him against your bare skin until he has nursed for the first time.* To give both of you the best chance of breastfeeding, the baby should stay skin-to-skin for a full hour after birth.

> Miriam: My third baby was a little stressed after delivery. His respiratory rate was around 70, which is above the normal range and he was cold. The nurses were administering oxygen and keeping him on the warmer. It had been about 10 minutes since delivery when I insisted they bring him to me. I placed him skin-to-skin and held the oxygen close to his face. In less than five minutes, his temperature came back up to normal, his breathing slowed, and he no longer needed oxygen. He was able to latch well and breastfeed in the first hour.

If you have an uncomplicated vaginal delivery of a full term baby, do not allow him to be separated from you after delivery for routine care such as measuring, weighing, or giving the vitamin K shot. These routine interventions can be performed with the baby in your arms or at a later time after he has breastfed for the first time. If your baby is a nice pink color, breathing well, crying, and has no obvious defects, the nurse should be able to complete the initial assessment at the bedside.

If the baby is in distress, blue, or breathing poorly he may need an immediate assessment, but otherwise routine tasks can wait. Even if the nurse says, "I'll just take him for a few minutes," you should ask if this separation is necessary to the baby's immediate health or just part of routine nursery activities.

You will need to tell the nurses and your doctor beforehand, and possibly often, exactly what your expectations are. You may need your husband or other labor support person to help you in this area, as it is still common practice to separate mothers and babies right after birth.

You may have to say "Bring me the baby." Or "No, you may not take the baby. You may do your routine baby cares in an hour or two." Some nursery nurses can be very insistent and will resist changing their routine, but it is your right to delay routine tasks.

Sometimes you cannot breastfeed in the first hour after a c-section, because it may take the surgeon awhile to close the incision, and the recovery room may not have enough staff available to monitor the mother and baby. The good news is more hospitals are allowing mothers to have their husbands and babies in the recovery room right after the surgery. This is something you can ask about while you are choosing a hospital and healthcare provider.

Ronda: Rob was born on a Tuesday by planned c-section after two days (a week apart) of induction. He was three weeks late and large for his age. I was given some IV Demerol right before delivery, which caused Rob to be very sleepy at first. The pain from the incision site and his size caused difficulty achieving a good latch.

We were discharged on Thursday evening and got home about nine. Everyone was exhausted from work or travel. Rob finally woke up about midnight and wanted to nurse all night! This is not what I expected! We spent much of the night crying together.

On Friday morning, we made our way to the lactation consultant. She showed us the football hold, which we hadn't tried yet, and answered a lot of questions. She was a good resource for responding to my mother's concerns as well. My mother had three children from two deliveries, but hadn't nursed any of us. Every time the baby cried, my mom questioned whether he was getting enough to eat. It was helpful to have the lactation consultant verbalize again what I had been telling her about breastfeeding. Although I had a c-section, was a first time mom, and experienced some other challenges, with help I was able to breastfeed successfully.

Having the baby breastfeed within the first hour of birth is valuable and the normal course of events, but it doesn't always happen. If you and your baby do not get a chance to nurse during the first hour, you can still breastfeed successfully. Even babies who are born preterm and spend many weeks in the NICU with a feeding tube are able to learn to breastfeed. It does take more work and more help, but it can be done.

There are a number of strategies for helping your baby learn to breastfeed. The information later in this chapter on lying back to nurse can help a baby use his reflexes. Giving the baby an opportunity to lie on his mother's bare chest can often encourage him to use those reflexes, even if he is several weeks old (Colson 2010).

When the Baby Shows Early Feeding Cues

You can ensure that your baby has the best chance to learn at each feeding opportunity by responding to his reflexive early feeding cues. Crying is a late feeding cue. Once your baby is crying he may be too upset to nurse. You may need to spend time calming him before feeding.

Early feeding cues include:

Suckling: People often will say, "Look, he's eating his hands." Babies like their hands, because they like the taste of amniotic fluid, and that's what their hands taste like, at least until they get a bath and someone leaves soap in its place (Marlier, Schaal and Soussignan. 1998). Babies are used to sucking and smelling their hands. They suck for comfort as well, and hands are readily available. Their hands also help them find and adjust the position of the breast for a better latch.

Rooting: The baby does this by moving his head and mouth around looking for the breast. If you lightly swipe or poke your finger on the baby's cheek, he will often turn that direction. This is another instinct baby has for finding the breast.

Opening and closing the mouth, licking the lips: We can all understand this cue; we do it ourselves. Some of us are more active than others with these cues.

Fussiness: Again, we can relate to this. We can all remember being a little fussy when we had to wait too long for a meal.

Crying and frantic head movement: These are late feeding cues. Can you picture how the baby is feeling at this point? He is upset because he's hungry, and he is feeling unable to solve his very great need.

Many mothers discover that responding to their babies' early feeding cues prevents problems, and they get the satisfaction of having a happy baby. Responding to early feeding cues puts mothers on the fast track to a full milk supply, because milk supply is affected positively by regular, frequent feeding and sometimes negatively by listening to a crying baby.

A mother who does "one more thing" when her baby is showing these early cues is likely to end up with an unhappy baby and a low milk supply. We want to follow God's example of being sensitive and aware of our child's needs.

> Isaiah 65:4 *"And it shall come to pass, that before they call, I will answer; and while they are yet speaking, I will hear."*

How Long can Mom go without Feeding?

Going more than four to six hours during the night without emptying the breasts can affect the mother in several ways. Delayed emptying can lead to decreased milk production in most women. If you can produce more than four ounces in a feeding, it is probably safe to increase the length of your sleep time. Longer periods between feeds can also cause menstruation and an early return of fertility (Wiessinger, West, and Pitman 2010, 170). You need to weigh all the considerations when deciding how long to delay breast emptying at night.

You will learn about your breast capacity and rate of milk production as your milk supply becomes fully established, usually around day 40, and as your baby continues to grow (Mohrbacher and Kendall-Tackett 2010, 121). It is easier to maintain a large supply than it is to allow your production to fall off and then try to increase it later.

Feed Often

Establishing a Milk Supply

One of the biggest saboteurs to establishing a good milk supply is inadequate suckling (nursing) in the first six weeks, but you can support breastfeeding by offering frequent feedings. The more your breasts are emptied, the more prolactin receptors inside your breasts are activated. When prolactin receptors are activated, more milk is made. Your milk supply should grow from 1 ounce to 25 to 35 ounces per day by day 28 (Mohrbacher and Kendall-Tackett 2010, 100). Breastfed babies consume 25 to 35 ounces of breast milk per day from 1 to 6 months.

After birth, your baby's digestive system is learning to work in new ways. His body needs time to adjust to having oral nutrition. This is one reason why a newborn needs small feedings. You may be able to get two feedings in the first few hours after birth. After this, most babies sleep for several hours. Babies are much more awake by day two and will want to nurse very often until your milk transitions to mature milk. Your baby must eat a minimum of eight times per day, every day this first week. This will not be divided up evenly over 24 hours. The baby may want to nurse continuously for several hours, then wait three hours and want to nurse hourly after that. He may be thirsty and need a 10-minute drink or he may be hungry and need a 40-minute meal. These are all normal feeding patterns while your milk supply is being established.

Here are some little known facts about the first week. On the first day after delivery your breast may only produce a total of one ounce! Not one ounce at a time, but one ounce for the whole day! The first day your baby's stomach is the size of a marble. The most he can keep down is about one teaspoon. His stomach will not stretch the first day. Although you only make a small amount of colostrum the first day, that is all he needs.

Colostrum is packed with special antibodies that protect your baby. It is God's perfect vaccine program for your baby. Colostrum is critical to giving the baby passive immunity while his immune system is still developing. It also works as a laxative, helping your baby to pass the first black, tarry stools called meconium. The more stools your baby passes, the less chance he has of becoming jaundiced, so on day one, do everything you can to feed him at least 8 to12 times.

By day three, many babies can take an ounce at a time, about two tablespoons. By one week, your baby can handle one to two ounces per feeding. At two weeks, the amount is between two and three ounces. At one month, many babies can drink three to four ounces at a time. Most babies do well with four to five ounces every two to four hours even up to one year.

Milk supply is very simple. The more milk is removed from the breasts, the more your body will replace what was taken. This same process will increase your milk supply during your baby's growth spurts.

A Baby's Hunger is not Scheduled

If you can adjust to "Baby Time," breastfeeding can be easy and enjoyable. The need to eat will be especially frequent and unpredictable until the mother's milk supply is well established and the baby has regained his birth weight. If a baby's needs are ignored, he will experience poor growth and mother will have a poor milk supply. Thankfully, God made our bodies to enjoy breastfeeding, and that makes it easier to respond to our babies.

Try to be as laid back as possible when your baby wants to eat, even if it seems like you haven't moved from your chair in two hours. Get some water for yourself then feed him. There may be a few times when you feel like you haven't accomplished much more than feeding the baby, but that is a big job that only you can do! He will be past this stage soon, and you will have the joy of knowing that you met his needs in a special way.

Effect of Formula Use on Milk Production

You can ensure a good breastfeeding experience by only using formula if it is medically indicated. Formula use can hinder breast milk production. Every ounce of formula given to a baby is an ounce of breast milk the baby will not nurse for. That means the mother's body won't be stimulated to make that ounce for that feeding or the next one. Increasing formula supplementation will cause milk supply to decrease proportionally.

Babies have an intense desire to suck. When a baby is given a bottle, he is meeting his sucking needs. It is better for him to meet his sucking needs, when possible, at the breast to stimulate milk supply. Most perfectly full breastfeeding infants are willing to gulp down an ounce or two from a bottle right after nursing. This is not hunger, just a willingness to suck and an inability to control a bottle's flow.

Pacifier Use

You can use pacifiers in ways that support breastfeeding, if you take a few precautions. Some babies will lose weight or gain weight poorly if they use a pacifier too often or to hold off a feeding. When a baby sucks for ten minutes, a hormone, cholecystokinin (CCK), is released that makes him feel satisfied and sleepy (Uvnäs-Moberg, Marchini, and Winberg 1993). If your breastfeeding newborn is suckling and giving early feeding cues, you need to feed him. Pacifier use should be avoided till the breastfed baby is at least one month old to make sure breastfeeding is well established and the newborn is getting adequate feedings and gaining weight well. Some studies suggest that a mother who is committed to breastfeeding can allow her baby a pacifier at 15 days if he is feeding well and gaining weight (Howard et al. 1999; Jenik et al. 2009). Babies fed only artificial milk can be given a pacifier right away, because they are unable to achieve needed nonnutritive suckling with the bottle.

Using a pacifier too often in the early days can take too much of the baby's energy, especially for preterm and late preterm infants. A newborn needs his energy for breastfeeding. A pacifier is a great tool when a baby is full but fussy and his mother is unavailable, but it is a tool that should be used cautiously.

When babies are put to sleep in their own beds, pacifiers function as a protective mechanism to keep the airway open. Babies can use pacifiers to accomplish non-nutritive suckling, which is a normal and needed comforting behavior for babies.

Babies have to be taught how to hold a pacifier in their mouths. Often when a baby refuses to take a pacifier, it's because he hasn't figured out how to suck and hold the pacifier simultaneously. You can teach your baby to hold the pacifier in his mouth by holding it in place while he experiments with it.

Non-nutritive Suckling

You may notice that your baby will nurse for a few minutes, fall asleep for 20 minutes or so, wake up to nurse again for a few minutes, and fall asleep again. If your baby is gaining four to seven ounces per week and having the appropriate number of bowel movements, he is probably suckling for comfort and only taking in a few swallows of milk before falling back to sleep. Your baby can be soothed by suckling, even when he isn't hungry and doesn't need to be fed (Blass and Watt 1999). If your baby is *not* growing appropriately, this pattern of nursing indicates that you need to call your healthcare provider or see your lactation consultant.

Importance of Pumping to Maintain Milk Supply

Pumping can protect your milk supply. If your baby is having problems nursing or is too sleepy to nurse, at least, 8 times a day, pump to get the number of breast-emptying cycles up to 8 (10 to 12 would be better). This will maintain volume by stimulating breast milk production. However, the baby is much more effective than a pump and pumping is not nearly as rewarding as seeing your baby feed. Just like exercise, you may know it is good for you, but it's not always easy to make yourself pump every two to three hours, which is the frequency needed in the early days after delivery to build an adequate supply.

Indications of Good Breastfeeding:

+ The baby has four or more stools larger than a quarter's size each day after day four.
+ You hear the baby swallowing milk.
+ You see milk on the baby's mouth after a feeding.
+ Your breasts feel full, and after feeding that feeling is diminished or gone.
+ Your baby is gaining weight.

Most babies reach their lowest weight on day four. After day five, babies should begin gaining weight. They gain four to seven ounces per week or about an ounce a day after the first week. If you are concerned, have your baby weighed on a scale at your healthcare provider's office. Many hospitals provide weight checks with the lactation consultant. This can be very helpful as home scales will not be accurate enough.

The weight of the baby is the best indicator of adequate breastfeeding. However, all of your children will not gain weight at the same rate. Consistent weight gain is the goal. Even seasoned mothers struggle to avoid comparing weight gain between siblings.

Ronda: I struggled for months with the fact that my youngest child consistently weighed less than her siblings had at the same age. I had her weighed more frequently than her brother and sisters. I just couldn't understand why Kathy wasn't gaining a lot of weight. It didn't help that I was remembering my third baby, who was the heaviest of them all. It was a constant struggle to understand that Kathy was doing fine compared to her own previous weights, just not compared to her siblings. She remains proportionally smaller than the others, but is still at a normal weight at six years old.

Feel Good: The Latch is Key

Achieving a correct latch is one of the most critical aspects of breastfeeding. Latching is the way your baby puts his mouth on your breast. Take your tongue and feel your soft palate on the roof of your mouth towards the back. That's where your nipple needs to go inside your baby's mouth.

Your nipple needs to be so far back in the baby's mouth that it's between the baby's tongue and soft palate. This keeps your nipple from being pinched. It may sting when the baby begins to nurse, but that sensation should only last for a minute. When the baby has a good latch, his lips will be slightly flared outwards around your breast. Think duck lips, not the tight control needed for sucking a straw.

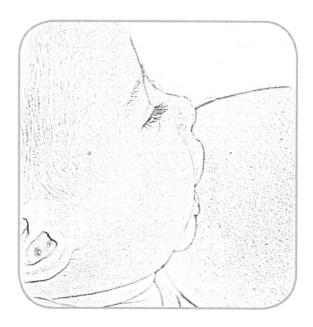

Now the big question is, "How does my newborn get that much of my breast in his mouth?" Get into a comfy position with lots of pillows for support, preferably reclined somewhat back on an angle as opposed to sitting straight up.

Latching Basics

1. Make sure your baby is awake and not screaming. If your baby is screaming, comfort him first.

2. Lay the baby across your chest with his face and mouth near the nipple. His entire body should be turned toward you (face, shoulders, tummy, and hips in a line). There should be no space between your bodies.

3. Bring the baby toward your breast when his mouth is wide open. The baby's chin should be close to the breast and the nipple pointing toward the roof of his mouth. This allows your nipple to be as far away from the baby's lower jaw as possible. He should have his head tilted slightly back as if sniffing.

4. When the baby is resting on top of you with your body in a lying-back position, his head will often bob as he positions himself and your breast to latch. You can assist latching by supporting your breast to make it more accessible to the baby, providing support to his head while nursing.

5. When you are helping the baby to latch, don't press on the back of baby's head to move it toward you. Just move his entire body closer.

There are a couple of websites with video clips that make this easier to visualize. One is an animated clip showing how to bring the baby onto the breast. This clip demonstrates how the mother's finger can flip the nipple into the baby's mouth (http://www.breastfeedingmadesimple.com/animatedlatch.html) (Breastfeeding Made Simple 2011).

Dr. Jack Newman's website offers videos of real babies latching and already latched, which can help the mother who has never observed a baby breastfeed (www.breastfeedinginc.ca then click on Online resources: videos) (Newman 2011). This information is also in the Resource List at the end of the book.

Never pull the baby off your breast. Always break the suction with your finger. Slip your pinkie finger into the baby's mouth at the cheek and break the suction before removing him from your breast. You will need to remove the baby if he has a poor latch. A single feeding with a poor latch can cause nipple trauma, which will lead to ongoing pain.

Breastfeeding Positions

Traditionally, women have been taught three basic positions for breastfeeding. These are the cradle/cross cradle, the football hold, and side-lying.

Cradle

The cradle hold is least helpful for breastfeeding a newborn. In that hold, the baby's head is in the crook of your arm. There is little control over the baby's head. Also, it is the most difficult position for adjusting the baby's distance from your breast, as the fixed distance from your shoulder to elbow can only be changed by an uncomfortable movement of your shoulder .

If a sitting cradle-type hold is desired, try the cross cradle, where the baby's neck is in your

Cross cradle

Football

hand and his legs are tucked into the crook of your elbow. You can open and close the gap between your breast and the baby's head much easier with this hold.

The football hold is great for larger babies and c-section mothers, because you support less of the baby's weight in your arms. Instead, use a pillow under your arm to support the baby.

The side-lying is a favorite hold for c-section mothers and mothers with large breasts or large babies as it requires holding less of the baby or the breast. There are many more ways you can hold your baby for nursing. As long as the baby has a good latch and his tummy and head are turned toward you, anything that works goes!

The laid back nursing position can be used with the mother lying back or reclined and the baby on top of her. Laying back can be used with the traditional positions as well. It is particularly helpful to encourage the baby to latch more deeply.

Side-lying

Laid back

Focus on Breastfeeding the First Week

Taking Time for Breastfeeding

This first week of breastfeeding is a very special time. You and your baby will be learning a great deal, and your body will be going through many changes. Treat this time like you would a vacation. Do not focus on work of any kind. This week your work is breastfeeding. You will be breastfeeding much of the time, and when you're not breastfeeding, you can be sleeping and recovering from delivery.

Learning to breastfeed takes time. New mothers and babies need plenty of privacy at the beginning. Your baby is learning to breastfeed just like you are. Give him many opportunities to practice. Allow your baby cuddle time and naptime on your chest during the first few weeks. This will encourage him to nurse more often, and with all of this practice you will both find that breastfeeding will seem easy and natural.

Avoid Distractions

It will be very helpful to surround yourself with encouraging people and to avoid those who would express negativity or would cause you to feel embarrassed while breastfeeding. Even someone who has a great chance of successful breastfeeding can be discouraged by receiving bad advice from the people in her life.

Some mothers may feel more comfortable using a cover-up during breastfeeding when others are present, but avoid this the first few weeks. You need to see your baby and your breast, so you can assess breastfeeding adequately. If you aren't aware of what is happening, your baby can change his latch and slide into a position that is more comfortable for him but damaging to your nipple. At least part of the time your baby needs to see your face while breastfeeding; this is important for bonding and his development.

It may be a good idea to avoid activities that take you away from your baby. The first week will be unlike any other. The key to this week is focusing on ensuring a good breastfeeding relationship. This may also mean that you need to seek professional help with breastfeeding if you are having problems.

Seeking Help

Getting emotional support and accurate information regarding breastfeeding is important this first week. If you need help, ask a friend or family member who has had a successful breastfeeding experience. If you are experiencing problems that are not easily resolved through the help of family and friends, don't hesitate to get professional help.

A board certified lactation consultant (IBCLC) is the best choice for professional breastfeeding help. If one is not available to you, there are other resources that mothers can access such as a WIC (Women, Infants and Children) peer counselor or a La Leche League leader. WIC peer counselors are available from many public health departments to help breastfeeding mothers. You may want to contact La Leche League and get support from other mothers who are breastfeeding. These professional breastfeeding advocates have many solutions that can help you breastfeed successfully.

Many hospitals have a lactation consultant available 24 hours a day who will be accessible to you after discharge. If your hospital does not employ a lactation consultant, you may call another local hospital, or find others available to outpatients in your area. Do not hesitate to call the lactation consultant once you get home, if you are having problems.

Nesting in Comfort

Make yourself a comfortable nest with diapers, snacks, blankets, music, and anything else you might need, and plan to stay there most of the day. This time of learning will make the first week and the rest of the postpartum period go smoothly.

> Miriam: When I had visitors with my fourth baby, I didn't even get out of my nest! I just covered up my pajamas with a blanket. I did not encourage visitors the first few weeks except my mother and other close female friends. I spent most of my time breastfeeding and watching movies. I took a long, relaxing bath every day. I spent some time outside and went for short walks with Lily in my arms when I wanted to stretch my legs. I didn't do any housework. I spent time loving on my three, older children and took at least one, usually two, naps a day. The results from all of this babying myself were fabulous! My baby was healthy and growing! Breastfeeding was going beautifully, and I wasn't exhausted. Lily woke up every two to three hours most nights for the first six weeks, but it didn't bother me, because I napped during the day.

Troubleshooting Early Milk Supply Issues

Two things solve almost every breastfeeding problem. They are the latch and time at the breast. It is uncomplicated. A good latch will treat and prevent nipple trauma. It also allows your baby to suckle in the most effective way. Adequate time at the breast releases the hormones that tell your body to make milk. If you get a good latch, and give the baby all the time he needs to nurse, you will be well on your way to a great breastfeeding relationship!

Increasing Milk Supply

An easy strategy for increasing milk supply is to position your baby skin-to-skin more often. Whenever life has become chaotic with other responsibilities and you notice a change in your milk supply, taking time to allow your baby to nurse skin-to-skin can help. It helps you to relax and get in touch with your baby. This will increase the baby's desire to nurse, which will in turn increase milk supply.

If you have to supplement with formula, you will need to stimulate milk production by pumping. You may only get a few drops of colostrum or milk at first. Even this small amount is very good for your baby, and you should give it to your baby with the next feeding. The primary reason for pumping in the first few days is to stimulate your breasts to make more milk. The milk that you actually get is a good secondary benefit.

Hand expression of breast milk can be done in addition to pumping. This is an especially effective way to remove colostrum. Hand expression is also referred to as manual milk expression. These are compression movements that help remove the milk from each section of the breast milk ducts in a systematic way. This prevents plugged ducts and increases milk supply. The Resource section includes links to several websites that demonstrate good milk compression techniques.

There are supplements, primarily over-the-counter herbals, which can help increase milk supply. Fenugreek and milk thistle are two herbal supplements that are often recommended. For more information read *The Breastfeeding Mother's Guide to Making More Milk* by Diana West and Lisa Marasco (2009).

Sometimes a mother might have a prolactin deficiency and need Domperidone, a prescription medication that is used off label to help increase milk supply. This is a condition that should be diagnosed and treated by a healthcare provider.

Transition to Mature Milk

Your milk starts out as colostrum, nutrient rich milk that is present from before birth to three to five days after birth. At some point after day two, your milk should change into watery, mature milk. This timing is affected by factors including your weight, number of pregnancies, and the type of labor and delivery you experienced.

It will take several days for your body to adjust to the new level of mature milk production. Some mothers experience such a change in milk production that they have engorgement, where breasts are swollen, hot, and very firm to the touch. If you are having problems with engorgement, your baby may only need to nurse from one breast per feeding. If you are having more problems you can try block feeding. Block feeding means that you would give the baby the same breast for a period or block of time. You would nurse only from one breast for two feedings (or three to four hours), and then switch to the other breast for two feedings and rotate back and forth. The block time may be increased if the engorgement does not resolve. This allows your milk supply to down regulate to the amount your baby actually needs.

Frequent nursing can decrease the symptoms of engorgement and protect you from breast infections and a milk supply that is too low. Hand expression of milk prior to nursing or using a pump to soften a hard breast can help the baby latch. Only express or pump enough for the baby to latch or to relieve discomfort. If you continue to have problems with oversupply contact a lactation consultant.

Delayed Milk Production

If your milk has not changed from colostrum to mature milk by day four, contact your healthcare provider. As mentioned, many things can cause a delay in milk production, but there are problems that should be evaluated by your healthcare provider right away. You may have a physical problem related to the birth that is affecting milk supply. You can work through the other possible causes of delayed production with the help of a professional breastfeeding advocate.

Your pediatrician may encourage you to supplement your baby with formula just until your milk becomes mature. This is likely to happen if your baby loses greater than 10% of his birth weight. If you follow the recommendations in this chapter, that is less likely to be a problem.

Going out Alone

If you will be gone for more than three hours (especially during the first three months) you will need to pump while away. If you wait longer to empty your breasts, the delay could cause engorged breasts, decreased milk supply, or breast infections.

Sleepy Baby

Some babies can be sleepy, especially at first. Wake your baby for nursing every two to three hours during the day the first week. You may allow your baby to go for one period of four or five hours at night between feedings. If he sleeps longer, wake him to eat.

The best way to wake him is to place him skin-to-skin (the baby in a diaper only against your bare chest) for 30 minutes. If that doesn't work, change his diaper. Lay him down and then gently help him do sit-ups. Stroke his face lightly. Take him to the busiest room in the house. Perhaps the bright light, noise, and activity will help to awaken him.

If you have tried all of these techniques and your baby still won't wake up, try again in half an hour. You can also watch him for periods of light sleep when you may hear him making noise or moving. Light sleep is a good time to try waking him. If your baby is sleepy and losing weight or growing thinner after day four, you need to contact a lactation consultant or the baby's healthcare provider. Even a phone call can really help.

Breast compressions can increase the amount of milk your baby gets with each feeding and can also increase the fat content of the milk. Breast compressions as you nurse a sleepy baby will help the baby become more interested because his effort is rewarded. They are done in several ways. Essentially, you compress the breast from the chest wall toward the nipple by pressing in and then toward the nipple with your free hand while the baby is nursing. There are several sites on the Internet, which give further information about this. Newman and Kerneman (2008) encourage mothers to do this process to help babies get more colostrum or mature milk in the early days when they are likely to fall asleep while nursing. Please refer to the Resource section for further links and useful sites.

The Baby won't Latch

If your baby won't latch and you have worked with a lactation consultant, you can ask her to show you how to feed your milk to your baby using a syringe, medicine cup or other small cup. Even preterm babies can feed from a cup. You should have a nurse or lactation consultant show you how to cup feed if you have a sleepy baby who also won't latch. It is very important that the milk is not poured down the baby's throat. The baby should control the rate of the feeding, just as God designed him to do from the breast. If milk is poured down the baby's throat, he can get the milk into his lungs and become ill.

Some mothers are more comfortable using a bottle, and this is a viable option, as long as you realize that getting the baby to latch onto the breast later may be more difficult. Babies get used to bottle-feeding, and breastfeeding is a different oral activity.

Nipple Soreness

If your nipples become sore, there are several strategies that can help. Hydrogels are absolutely wonderful to place on sore nipples, especially if they are kept chilled in the refrigerator. These silicone gelatin pads can be left on between feedings. While you are nursing, have someone place them in the refrigerator.

Ultra purified lanolin cream will keep nipples moist and help them to heal quickly. Apply a very tiny amount just to the cracked, damaged area of the nipple. Do not apply to the whole nipple or breast as it can cause the baby to have more difficulty with latching. Also, the lanolin causes the hydrogels to break down, so avoid using both of them at the same time. Hydrogels and lanolin can often be obtained at the hospital as part of your postpartum stay, but if you need to purchase more, they are both available in a store's infant care section.

Some women have slight nipple discomfort, but that should go away the first week. Cracks and bleeding are not normal! When nipples are so sore that clothing hurts, breast shells can be worn inside a bra to keep material off of tender skin. A mother with bleeding or intensely painful nipples needs to get professional help.

Thrush

Thrush is a fungus that can cause nipple burning and pain. When nipple pain begins after two to three months of breastfeeding, the cause is often thrush. For a baby, thrush will look like white patches inside his mouth that will not wipe away. Sometimes you may experience severe burning and pain without any visible patches in the baby's mouth. Topical antifungals and gentian violet are over-the-counter remedies that can be very effective. When the infection continues, oral antifungal medications may be prescribed by a healthcare provider. Both the mother and baby will need to be treated. You should not use lanolin or hydrogels if you suspect the pain is caused by thrush.

Nipple Shields

Nipple shields are often used with babies who are very tired and can't suck well, or when the mother's nipple doesn't match up to the size of baby's mouth. These can help your baby achieve a good latch when used correctly by applying the rounded part to the nipple first and then spreading the shield over the areola. Shields can be very helpful if nipples are flat or inverted, which means the nipples do not become erect when stimulated by sucking.

Many times, nipple shields only need to be worn the first few weeks. As the baby gets bigger and more coordinated, he will be able to breastfeed without nipple shields. The best time to try without the shield is when the baby is half asleep. If you think you need a nipple shield, contact a board certified lactation consultant.

If you are using a nipple shield, pumping several times a day after a feeding ensures that you develop an adequate milk supply. Babies who use nipple shields will need to be weighed more frequently, because some babies do not have adequate milk transfer.

Insider Tip: Not nearly as many nipples are flat or inverted as some people would have you believe. Many nipples that are diagnosed as such are quite capable of becoming erect when stimulated. There are solutions for this when there is a problem, so don't give up, seek help!

Breast Problems

Check your breast daily for lumps or bumps. A lump may be a plugged milk duct. Massage it as the baby nurses on that side. A painful or reddened area could be a sign of mastitis, which is inflammation of the milk duct that may become infected. This is a signal to go to the doctor immediately! Antibiotics that are safe for breastfeeding are available when needed.

Summary

The first few weeks after the baby is born are very busy for mothers. There are a number of important strategies used these first few weeks to make the breastfeeding experience successful. Feed early and often. Make sure that the baby is latching well when beginning a feed. Focus on breastfeeding for the first week and seek help for any concerns that you have.

Dear Jesus, Thank You for the amazing way you made me and my baby. The detailed care You give all of Your creations is breathtaking. You have said you care for the sparrows and the flowers growing in the fields; You have numbered all the hairs on my baby's head. Even when unexpected things happen, I can trust You. Give me wisdom to make good choices for my family when it comes to feeding my baby. Help me to be loving, patient, and responsive to the ones you have placed into my care.

In Jesus name, Amen.

Section Three

The Needs of the Newborn

Can a woman forget her sucking child,
that she should not have compassion
on the son of her womb? yea, they may
forget, yet will I not forget thee.

Isaiah 49:15

Need for Sustenance

Ronda and Miriam: We have chosen to use breast milk as well as artificial milk to feed our babies. Our choices were affected by many factors. There were times when Miriam had to use artificial milk due to medical indications. Both of us have used artificial milk because of an early return to work after the birth of our first children. We have also worked hard to provide human milk whenever possible and have found that to be easier with each successive child. We have found breastfeeding to be worth the effort but have experienced and certainly understand that there are times that artificial milk needs to be used.

There is a <u>lot</u> of emotion involved when women talk about breastfeeding as a choice of infant feeding. We assure you that we don't take lightly the problems of feeling pressured by your peers in favor of either artificial or breast milk feeding. We have read passionate statements from mothers on both sides of this choice.

*D*eciding how you will feed your baby is one of the first big decisions you will make, and this chapter will provide you with accurate information as you make your choice. No one should feel regret for the decisions she makes about breastfeeding and artificial milk usage. Both types of feeding will be discussed. To make the information less confusing and repetitive, this chapter will cover all general feeding information discussing it from a framework of breastfeeding. Toward the end of the chapter, differences that apply to artificial milk feeding will be discussed.

Information about the beginning weeks of breastfeeding is located in Chapter 5 in the section with other information that is vital to the immediate postpartum period. If you are breastfeeding, please be sure to read both chapters.

What: Human Milk versus Artificial Milk

Is Breastfeeding Worth it?

When it comes to breastfeeding, a valiant effort may be successful while a half-hearted effort may not. It will take perseverance to overcome some of the common struggles that occur in the first few days of breastfeeding. The first six weeks of breastfeeding will require more time and effort than artificial milk feeding, but the payoff is great after that. After these first weeks, breastfeeding becomes much easier than artificial milk feeding.

God's Plan for Baby Nutrition

There is good news! You were created to breastfeed, and most of you can do it very successfully! Some women spend a lot of time worried about milk supply and breastfeeding in general. God doesn't want us to worry about anything. He has promised to help us with everything and not give us anything that He won't help us with.

Let's think about this for a minute. Did you organize the development of your baby inside your womb by thinking about it? Did you, by your thoughts, make your body begin labor and give birth? No. God designed you to do those incredible things without your conscious thought! God has also created many intricate and amazing processes for breastfeeding that work without your direction or thought.

Not only has God placed mechanisms that assist with breastfeeding in your body, but your baby has many God-given reflexes (like those discussed in Chapter 3) and neurological programming that help him breastfeed as well! In fact, there are some fascinating videos of babies who are placed on the mother's abdomen immediately after birth, only to then crawl to the breast and latch without assistance (UNICEF Maharashtra 2007).

One recent finding, which has changed the way we think about breastfeeding, has to do with the mother's position. While breastfeeding in a reclined position, leaning back on pillows or in a reclined chair, the baby's reflexes are able to enhance breastfeeding. He uses his hands to change position and move the breast (Genna and Barak 2010).

In traditional breastfeeding positions, the mother must work against gravity to hold the baby up to her breast and the baby's reflexes actually move him away from the breast, which can hinder successful feeding. When the mother lies back, the baby's reflexes work properly to enhance breastfeeding, and both can relax and enjoy the breastfeeding period (Colson 2010).

The mother naturally strokes her baby in ways that stimulate his reflexes so that breastfeeding becomes a cooperative effort. For instance, in one study it was observed that mothers commonly stroked their babies' feet while nursing. When the feet were stroked, other reflexes were triggered in the baby, like the stepping reflex, which causes the baby to move up to the breast. The baby's mouth opened, his head nodded, and his arms worked to position him at the breast, enabling the baby to latch properly (Colson, Meek, and Hawdon, 2008).

Many mothers would prefer and sometimes even need to recline after delivery, due to residual pain or discomfort. Isn't it just like God to plan for babies to be more successful feeding in this position?

The Case for Breastfeeding

God designed human milk to meet all of a baby's needs for the first six months of life. Even more amazing is the fact that *your* milk is designed specifically for *your* baby. Your milk is unique to the specific needs and age of your baby. The composition changes as he does. This is easily understood in relation to aging, since a two week old has different dietary needs than a six month old.

What you may not know is that your body makes antibodies to help your baby fight off infection. If a baby picks up a germ that his mother hasn't been exposed to, his mother's close proximity will cause her milk to develop, within hours, a special component called an antibody that will kill that germ!

Not only does human milk protect babies from physical problems, but breastfeeding is healthy in other ways as well. Babies need skin-to-skin contact with their caregivers. Breastfeeding is a natural way of providing skin-to-skin contact many times per day. Babies relax and thrive when they are skin-to-skin with their mothers. This puts them in the hormonal state in which they can grow best.

When a baby is breastfed, he is at the perfect distance for his eyes to focus on your face, facilitating bonding. Babies can be held similarly when bottle-feeding, but it is also easy to hold the baby further away or to even prop up a bottle and leave the baby to feed himself. This isn't possible when breastfeeding.

The hormones released when you breastfeed influence the way you respond to your baby. When a breastfed baby cries, his mother's whole body undergoes changes that help her respond in loving and giving ways to her baby. This makes it much easier to choose to respond to your baby when you are busy doing something else, without feeling you are sacrificing to do so. A formula fed baby's mother can still respond to her baby in a loving and timely way, but her body will undergo fewer and less intense physical responses. Breastfeeding is one of God's ways of helping you make the choices that are best for you and your baby.

Recent research has also found that breastfeeding can help the mother. There has generally been a perception that breastfeeding moms get less sleep than those who use artificial milk. In a study of mothers who kept their babies in the same room with them at night, exclusively breastfeeding mothers actually report better sleeping, better daytime energy, and better physical health than mothers who used mixed or artificial feeding. Breastfeeding moms also reported less sense of depressed feelings, less feeling of no interest in life, and had lower scores of depression than moms who did not breastfeed exclusively (Kendall-Tackett, Cong, and Hale 2011).

The Risks of Formula

There are health concerns for both the mother and baby when artificial milk is used. Feeding babies artificial milk puts women at risk for various health problems. Women who do not breastfeed have a higher risk of breast cancer. Breastfeeding is associated with a 59% lower risk of breast cancer in women with a family history of the disease and a reduction of at least a 28% for those without a family history (Stuebe et al. 2009). Breastfeeding also lowers a breastfed baby girl's lifetime breast cancer risk by 25% (Ip et al. 2007).

Women who don't breastfeed also have increased likelihood of cervical and uterine cancers. Some studies show they are at an increased risk of osteoporosis, heart disease, metabolic syndrome, and diabetes, as well.

Feeding babies artificial milk puts babies at risk because all babies are designed for the benefits associated with drinking human milk. That doesn't mean babies fed artificial milk will conclusively have all the problems that may come, but throughout a population these problems will occur more frequently in formula fed babies. Some of these risks occur during the early months of formula feeding and some may not become evident until later.

Babies who are fed artificial milk have more ear infections and episodes of diarrhea. They are likely to have more serious colds and flu and have increased frequency of allergies. Artificial milk also puts a baby at risk for obesity, lower IQ, and osteoporosis as an adult. These risks are due to formula composition, which cannot match up to the composition of breast milk as there are live antibodies and nutrients in breast milk that can never be duplicated in formula.

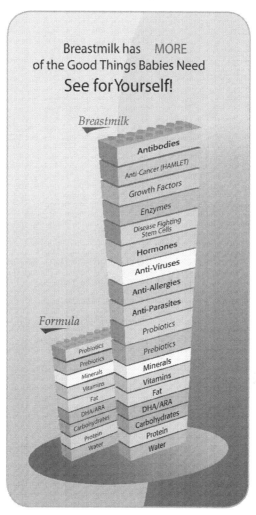

Developed by the California WIC Program. 2011. *How Does Formula Compare to Breastmilk?* Sacramento: California WIC Program.

There are also formula risks related to the way it is produced and reconstituted. There have been frequent instances of formula being contaminated during manufacturing, resulting in infant sickness and death. Since formula cannot be sterilized, it is important to choose a reputable brand of artificial milk to protect against some of this danger, as store brands and inexpensive brands are the most frequently contaminated.

When safe drinking water is compromised due to natural disasters, it is difficult to ensure the safety and availability of artificial milk and the water needed to reconstitute it. Mothers' bodies filter any harmful contaminants from the water they drink during the production of breast milk. The amount of water needed for a breastfeeding mother and baby is less than for an artificial milk-feeding mother and baby (Barrett 2006).

There is an inspiring story about a young woman who gave birth in an attic during Hurricane Katrina. She had been planning to formula feed, but she didn't have clean water or formula available. This new mom was able to breastfeed her baby and keep him alive (Brown, 2005, September 1).

Who: Usually Mom and Baby; What can Dad do?

Since breastfeeding can only be done by mommy, this may leave some dads feeling that they have fewer opportunities to bond with their baby. However, there are many other things they can do. Miriam's husband was the burper and changer. Ronda's husband did that as well as bathing and calming over-stimulated babies. The key is to include dad from the very beginning even if he is nervous. Babies need a lot of tactile contact, so encourage dad to hold the baby skin-to-skin.

Babies are able to tell that men feel different than women. Their bodies feel harder and their voices are deeper and louder. Let your baby go to his father early and often. A baby who becomes accustomed to his father right away will be very happy to go to him at the end of the day.

When Mom's not Available

If a mother is planning to return to work and will be gone through feeding times before the baby can drink from a cup, she will need to introduce a bottle. Some babies will take a bottle happily the first time and some will adamantly refuse.

If possible, it is best to wait until mom and baby love breastfeeding before introducing bottle-feeding. Ideally, a bottle should be introduced two weeks before work resumes. Sometimes it is best to have someone other than the mother give the bottle. Babies know something isn't right when the breasts are right there but mom is giving them something strange instead. Younger babies (under four months) tend to adjust to a bottle much more quickly than older babies will.

Miriam: My first three children had no problem going between bottle and breast. My fourth refused the bottle. In fact, she would drink maybe just a few ounces while I was gone for eight hours and then she would nurse every hour or two during the evening and several times during the night. This worked fine for us because I was working a few days per week and Lily was already nine months old when I returned to work.

This process of self-scheduling the long daily stretch while the mother is gone is called reverse cycling. It is the baby's way of adjusting to the new schedule. Most babies can go for one long stretch per 24 hr period. However, they cannot go all day and all night without eating (Wiessinger, West and Pitman 2010, 277).

Reverse cycling works great for some mothers. If you want to exclusively breastfeed for six months, allowing your baby to eat often when you are home can be very helpful. If you will be going back to work full-time and do not plan to feed your baby during the night, you need to help your baby accept a bottle happily from a caregiver.

Tips to Help your Baby Accept the Bottle:

+ Have someone other than you offer the bottle

+ Offer it when the baby is sleepy or just waking up

+ Some babies adjust best when it is as much like nursing as possible

  1. Warm the milk

  2. Place the bottle under your arm while you hold baby in a nursing position

+ Some babies adjust best when it is as different as possible

  1. Chill the milk

  2. Hold the baby looking away from your body

  3. Make it a game

This is one of those trial and error things. Keep trying until you find an approach that works for you and your baby. You can succeed at this.

Ronda: Whatever you do, don't forget to show your baby a bottle and teach him its purpose before going back to work! I forgot to do this with my second child, and it was a rough few hours for the babysitter that first day. Finally, on the advice of a postpartum nurse in the hospital where I was working, the babysitter put a small amount of corn syrup on the nipple of the bottle. By the time Sarah had sucked all the corn syrup off, she had figured out the process and was quite satisfied after that to take a bottle when needed.

When: How Often, How Flexible, and How Long?

The content in this section covers information that applies to many breastfeeding topics. Specific information pertaining to the first few weeks of breastfeeding can be found in Chapter 5.

Breastfeeding Timing for the Growing Baby

Human milk digests in 60 to 90 minutes. At that point it is *fully digested*. It isn't appropriate to expect a baby to wait three hours when he has a tiny stomach and digests his food in 90 minutes or less. If your baby nurses for 30 minutes and is eating every two hours, this means that you will have an hour and a half between the ending of one feed and the beginning of the next.

Milk Production, Breast Storage, and Baby Tummy Size

There are a number of variables that affect how often a mother must feed. Milk production varies among mothers. You may make milk at a fast rate, several ounces per hour or you may have difficulty producing one ounce an hour. Although the milk production rate influences the amount of milk available to the baby, availability is also affected by the mother's capacity for milk storage.

Breasts that are full make milk more slowly because hormone signals cue the brain to make less milk. Breasts that are empty make milk more quickly. The more the breasts are emptied, the more milk will be made. Some mothers are able to store more milk in their breasts than others. For example, some may store one to three ounces per breast, and others may be able to store up to six ounces per breast.

Moms who have a small storage capacity or a slow rate of milk production will need to continue to feed frequently as long as they are breastfeeding. This helps to keep the mother's milk production high enough to meet her baby's needs.

If a mother has a fast rate of milk production and large storage capacity, she is likely to feed her baby less frequently than every two to three hours. The differences in storage capacity and rate of production explain the reason that one mother may only need to feed 8 times per day while another may need to nurse 12 or more times per day. Most babies consume between 25-35 ounces of milk per day regardless of the amount of milk the mother has available at one time.

Another factor that affects how often a mother must nurse is the stomach capacity of the baby. Some baby stomachs can handle two ounces (after a couple weeks), while others can manage to hold three to five ounces rather early.

Ronda: I've had a baby with what must have been a five-ounce stomach and one with about a two-ounce stomach. The baby with the large stomach slept all night from eight weeks and was "fat." The doctor was concerned. The baby with the small stomach spit up large amounts of milk every time I let her nurse "too long." She rarely slept more than five hours at night. Her weight was in the 10-35th percentile. I was concerned about her. She is still thin at six years old and doesn't eat a full meal very often. But she is perfectly normal; she was just a different baby.

Milk Composition and Benefits of Frequent Nursing

A newborn has great difficulty regulating his body temperature, blood sugar, and hormone levels without the physical presence of his mother. A mother has the amazing ability to regulate her baby's temperature much more efficiently than a high-tech hospital baby warmer. Babies need to be near their mothers for these reasons but also because they need to nurse frequently. The composition of human milk has lower fat and protein concentration than any of the mammals. Babies must breastfeed often, in order to grow and feel satisfied. The physiology of the human body is very clear; your baby was meant to be kept close to you and fed often as a newborn (Kirsten, Bergman, and Hann 2001).

Milk composition tends to change during a feeding with the initial milk being greater in carbohydrates and the fat content increasing throughout the feed till it becomes the greater concentration. Because of this, it is important to encourage babies to nurse long enough at each breast to get a good supply of the fat content. This ensures the baby will continue to have adequate growth and development.

When babies nurse for a short period of time on one breast, they get more carbohydrates than fats in milk, which can lead to increased gassiness and colic. This is why mothers are encouraged to nurse for as long as the baby wants on the first side, and then go to the second side if the baby will take it.

Sometimes you will hear the milk described as foremilk— the initial milk the baby gets, or hindmilk — the milk toward the end of the feeding. It is actually the same milk with different fat compositions that transition gradually over the course of the feed.

A very interesting experiment conducted by a mother in England demonstrated this gradual transition by collecting breast milk samples every few minutes during a pumping cycle. Just by looking at the milk samples in test tubes, you can see the way the milk changed. She had the samples analyzed for concentrations, which highlighted the differences (Ablett 2011). Another amazing feature of the wondrous creation of our bodies!

Length of Breastfeeding Periods

How long does it take a baby to empty a breast? Babies vary widely! Sometimes a two month old can eat in 10 minutes. Another baby, or even the same baby at another time, will take 30 minutes.

It is *very normal* for a week old baby to nurse, fall asleep for 20 minutes and nurse again. If this is happening, it may mean that he needs a bit more milk. Sometimes a baby will nurse, then sleep for an hour, then wake and want to nurse again. Some babies will go two or three hours between feedings.

Growth Spurts

Your baby may be trying to increase milk supply because he is having a growth spurt and wants to cluster feed. Generally cluster feeding occurs when the baby is two days old, then again at growth spurts which occur around two to three weeks, six weeks, two to three months, and six months of age. Cluster feeding is a time when the baby wants to eat very frequently, possibly 30 minutes of nursing, 20-30 minutes of break, then 30 minutes of nursing, followed by another short break. This pattern goes in cycles off and on for a couple days because the baby is trying to increase the milk supply to match his increased appetite due to growth. After a few days, the frequency and length of nursing periods will return to normal. Many babies will sleep for longer periods in the days following a growth spurt.

Common Concerns

Unless your baby is experiencing a growth spurt, constant nursing after the first week may signal a problem. Most babies should be able to go an hour and a half between feedings much of the day. If the baby is frequently feeding more often than that, he may not be getting adequate milk transfer. *Milk transfer* refers to the amount of milk that goes from the mother's breast to the baby's stomach. One frequent cause of inadequate milk transfer is improper position on the breast, which is is called a poor latch. Another indication of poor milk transfer is that the baby tends to "snack" by only nursing for 3 to 5 minutes every 15 to 30 minutes. If you notice this pattern, contact your healthcare provider or lactation consultant.

If the baby is falling asleep after just a few minutes of nursing, you can try various methods to encourage more suckling: breast compressions, skin-to-skin contact, talking or singing, stroking the baby's feet, or helping the baby do gentle sit-ups in your lap.

Many moms say their babies stopped being interested in nursing at about four months. When your baby pops off every few minutes because he is too distracted to breastfeed, it does not mean that he doesn't want to breastfeed anymore or that you should wean him. It is common for babies to go through a stage where they are just discovering the world and are too busy to nurse.

> Ronda: My children all became disinterested in nursing at about four months, even in a room by ourselves with low lighting and no sound. They were just too interested in what was around them. It is very frustrating when you are taking a break from work to go feed your baby, and they are not on your schedule!

You can encourage several good feeds a day by going into a darkened and quiet room. Sometimes even a quiet room does not work, so you can try waiting until the baby is drowsy. If you don't think breastfeeding is going as well as it has in the past, or like it should, please seek out help from a local lactation consultant, peer counselor, or from a La Leche League leader in your area.

Weaning Your Child from Breastfeeding

When should a mother wean her child from human milk? The American Academy of Pediatrics recommends breastfeeding for at least one year and as long after that as the baby and mother desire (AAP 2005, 2012). In traditional cultures, it is common to breastfeed to age three or later. Many sources suggest the age as late as five.

The Bible Encyclopedia writes, "When Samuel was weaned, he was old enough to be left with Eli for the service of the tabernacle (1 Samuel 1:24). As no public provision was made for the children of priests until they were three years of age, it is probable that they were not weaned sooner (2 Chronicles 31:16; 2 Maccabees 7:27)" (McClintock and Strong 1894, 892).

> 2 Chronicles 31:16 "Beside their genealogy of males, from three years old and upward, even unto every one that entereth into the house of the LORD, his daily portion for their service in their charges according to their courses;"

This passage discusses how King Hezekiah was to distribute the tithes and offerings to the priests and their families. McClintock and Strong indicate the reference in this verse to "males from three years old and up" as a reference to the age at which children were weaned.

There are benefits to giving your child human milk long past the first year. Human milk provides the young child with concentrated antibodies that help him fight illness. It seems that children wean naturally sometime after the age of two and a half, but many young children prefer to breastfeed much longer. Your child is growing rapidly and human milk is designed to support that growth.

The Talmud, a Jewish commentary on the Law of Moses, states that children have the right to be breastfed for at least two years. In fact, breastfeeding is encouraged for longer periods, and mothers were given special rights and privileges if they breastfed their children up to five years of age (Eidelman 2006).

Miriam: I have friends with healthy, well-adjusted, older children who have admitted to me with hushed tones and a sheepish grin that they breastfed through the fourth year.

This may not be for everyone, but if this is something that works for you, wonderful! We expect young children to drink lots of milk. Some families encourage drinking milk at every meal. It only makes sense to offer human milk when possible. Human milk continues to be better for a young child than cow's milk. Choosing to wean should be a personal decision.

Ronda: I weaned my first three children somewhere between 18 and 22 months of age. When it came to the last baby, Kathy did not want to wean. We decided to continue longer and actually weaned at three years of age. There was family pressure at that point, so we set the date and talked about it every day up to her birthday. On her birthday, we had one final nursing then pronounced her officially grown to a little girl age. She hasn't yet outgrown the snuggles and cuddles that the other children quit before her age.

Where: Modesty and a Baby's Rights in the United States

Babies need human milk. It is their only food and drink. Human milk is usually fed to a baby from a breast. When we think about feeding a baby in public it may help to think about it this way—how would you feel if you were only allowed to eat in the car, a bathroom, or at home? It would be weird and leave you feeling left out of things. Well, we're not suggesting that your baby feels left out, but if you are a people person, you surely will, unless you become comfortable feeding your baby in public.

Some mother-baby pairs may only need to nurse every three to four hours. If that's you, nursing in public may not be necessary, but for the mother and baby who need to nurse every two hours, having to run to a private place for every feeding might be close to impossible.

There are many ways to nurse in public while maintaining modesty. You can use a blanket or cover-up. You can wear a loose t-shirt and an over shirt or jacket. You can use a book to cover up while you latch your baby. You might be surprised at how clueless people will be. With a little practice no one will even know what you are doing. Many moms wear their baby in a sling and nurse while they shop.

Some mothers may be too nervous to nurse in a public place; that's fine. This will probably change over time with more children. There are many places such as a dressing room where a mother can feed her baby. Many malls now have lactation rooms for feeding babies. Some communities are providing window clings to businesses that designate the business is committed to encouraging mothers to breastfeed on their premises.

We should be accepting of others who do choose to breastfeed in public. It is really sad to hear of a Christian mother who goes up to another mom quietly breastfeeding in public and tells her she should go somewhere else because she doesn't want her children exposed to "images of breastfeeding in public." We need to extend grace to other mothers about their feeding choices, no matter what those choices may be.

There is actually much to consider about the consequences of the United States cultural norm of seeing breasts solely for their sexual function. The stigma that moms have faced with breastfeeding in public has hampered our view of breastfeeding in this country (Wolf 2008).

All but five states have laws that allow a mother to breastfeed in any public or private location. For further information about the State Breastfeeding laws a good site to reference is the National Conference of State Legislatures (www.ncsl.org) (Breastfeeding State Laws 2011). Also, lawyer and breastfeeding advocate, Jake Aryeh Marcus J.D, has a website of this information with interpretations specific to the individual state laws (www.breastfeedinglaw.com) (Marcus 2011). Babies legally have the right to nurse anywhere they are allowed to be.

As a breastfeeding mother, it is important to be sensitive to others and to be as modest as the situation demands while still providing for your baby. When Miriam visits in a new home, she always asks, "Will I make you uncomfortable if I feed my baby?" She has done this many times! Most people are comfortable with a mother discreetly nursing her baby.

How: Techniques, Hints, and Pumping

Feel free to use whatever position is comfortable for you and your baby. You may be comfortable lying down, lying on your side, sitting straight up, reclining, or standing. Breastfeeding positions are discussed in more detail in Chapter 5. The important thing is that your baby's body is facing you. His ears, shoulders, and hips should be in alignment. The position should feel comfortable to you, and the baby should be getting milk. You can tell your baby is feeding if he is swallowing with each mouthful and having at least three stools or bowel movements the size of a quarter every day (Wiessinger et al. 2010).

Overabundant Milk Supply

Sometimes your milk supply can become overabundant. This may be caused by over stimulation (pumping often to get ready for a return to work) or a God-given ability to produce great amounts of milk. If you have so much milk that you truly need to decrease your supply, the best way to resolve this problem is to allow the baby to take from just one breast per feeding and leave the other breast till the next feeding (as much as six hours later).

You may need to express or pump the other breast just a little, so that you are comfortable; this will prevent painful engorgement. It will take a couple of days for your body to adjust to the new level of production. You can even give the baby the same breast more than one feeding in a row if your supply is much too high. Again, pump or hand-express the other breast just until you are comfortable.

There are herbs and teas that can help reduce supply in extreme cases. We recommend that you check with a lactation consultant or other breastfeeding support provider before using any medications or over-the-counter products to decrease supply.

Pumping and Work

If you will be at work when it is time to feed the baby, you will need to pump the same number of times that your baby would normally nurse at home or ideally every three to four hours. A new (2010) federal law requires many employers to give you breaks to pump. Certain employers (those with less than 50 employees) do not have to follow this new law (Fact Sheet #73, 2010).

You should plan to pump a minimum of 15-20 minutes per session. Milk can be stored at room temperature for four to six hours. It is safely stored in a cooler for eight, in a refrigerator for a week, and in a stand-alone freezer for six months. When milk is bad… it tastes and smells sour just like sour cow's milk.

While pumping, it may be helpful to call someone and talk about your baby or look at the baby's picture. Some new pumps have a way to record your baby's sounds, so you can listen while you pump. You may also bring something that smells like your baby, like a blanket or onesie. Doing these things can allow your milk to come out or letdown more quickly and increase the amount of milk obtained. Each pumping session can get varied results and there are measures you take to get more milk during a session. Here are some ideas:

+ Pump for 15 minutes then take a break for a few minutes before resuming pumping.

+ Play with the settings on the pump. Many newer pumps have a fast and slow setting. Switching between settings every 10-15 minutes can help obtain a second letdown.

+ You can also compress your breasts to help more milk to come out. Breast compression is exactly what it sounds like. You place your hand on your breast and squeeze with very firm pressure. Keep this up for a few minutes. Release the pressure for 30 seconds and then compress again.

+ Make sure to read the manual that comes with the pump and make sure that you are using the appropriate flange size.

If you are not pumping enough milk to cover your baby's needs while you are away from him, contact a lactation consultant, La Leche League leader, or peer counselor. Get the help you need. You can find lactation consultants through your local hospital, through several websites (see Resource List) and through the La Leche League.

Feeding Twins or Other Multiples (by Jennifer Roy)

The primary issues with breastfeeding multiples are positioning two babies at the breast at one time, scheduling/nursing frequency for each baby, milk supply, and your own nutritional intake. Breastfeeding twins or multiples requires sheer determination and commitment, but it can be done! You may have to "blaze your own trail" as you determine what works for you. A nursing pillow designed for twins is an excellent tool for positioning two babies to nurse at once. The Anna Pillow and others like it allow two infants to nurse in the football hold but with your hands free to feed yourself or hold a glass of water.

If you do not have the luxury of a nursing pillow or your babies have outgrown it, you may find the following position useful: sit down with the babies on each side (or have someone hand them to you one at a time). Hold the first baby in the classic cradle hold to your left breast and get him latched on comfortably. A regular pillow placed under your elbow is helpful for support. Make sure your right breast

Twin football

Twin cradle football

is ready for nursing. Now with your right arm, scoop the baby on the right up into the football hold to nurse at the right breast. Your left hand will be somewhat restricted with the first baby but still able to reach around and help the second baby latch on if needed.

You can also attempt to hold both babies in the football hold with a pillow under each arm or hold both babies in the classic cradle hold with one in each arm, one crisscrossing over the other. The size of your twins will determine which positions are comfortable for the babies and you.

Should twins nurse from both sides each time or develop his own supply at his own designated breast? You can do either if your method is working. However, many mothers produce more milk from one breast than the other, which can lead to one less nourished baby should you allow designated sides. You may also develop a "lopsided" chest by assigning a certain breast to a certain baby.

Twin cradle

Twin crisscross

For these reasons, a more useful pattern is to have each baby switch sides from one feeding to the next. At the first feeding of the day, Baby A is at the right breast and Baby B is at the left breast. At the next feeding, Baby A is at the left breast and Baby B is at the right breast. You can use a bracelet as a tool for remembering. Baby A always nurses on the side with the bracelet if you switch the bracelet to your other wrist accordingly after each nursing.

Should the babies always nurse at the same time? They don't have to. However, it can get very confusing and completely consume your day if both babies are fed only on demand. This can add up to a lot of stress. A recommendation is that if one baby is hungry, feed both if possible. The hungrier twin can nurse longer.

You can nurse simultaneously or one right after the other. This way you know that both babies were fed. Usually the twin who wasn't fussing is rather hungry and happy to eat. It is also good to avoid the experience of being a few minutes into nursing Baby A when suddenly Baby B begins yelling insistently to be fed too. Instead, you have two contentedly suckling babies and less stress for yourself.

For additional babies like triplets or quadruplets, feeding the babies in a rotation will ensure that each baby gets some human milk. Essentially you would feed Baby A and Baby B, while C gets a bottle, then be sure Baby C gets to feed from the breast at the next feeding time, along with A or B. As mentioned for twins, it is easier to keep everything straight if all babies are fed at nearly the same time and if one is hungry feed them all. Of course with triplets or quads, you will need help much of the time to be able to keep the babies fed and cared for.

With two or more babies relying on you for all their nourishment, you can wonder if it's possible to produce enough breast milk. The good news is that it usually is. If you dedicate your time during the first few weeks to nursing the babies, your body will produce an amazing milk supply. If you feel unsure about how much you are producing, use a breast pump every two to three hours for twenty-four hours and total up the amount.

Remember that babies are able to extract a bit more than a pump can at each session. If you do not seem to be producing enough, don't give up! Do what you can to increase your supply. Keep nursing the babies but consider adding a couple ounces of formula at the end of the feeding, if the babies are not gaining adequate weight. You should only supplement with formula if you have genuine cause for concern about their intake. Starting formula can be heading down a slippery slope to not breastfeeding at all. Use it judiciously and keep in mind your goal to breastfeed. Try increasing the minutes spent breastfeeding rather than increasing the amount of supplemental formula.

Your own increased nutritional intake is absolutely essential if you are going to be able to feed multiples. You may need an additional five to seven hundred calories over your usual amount. To get those calories, you may find yourself eating six or eight times a day. If you are hungry, you need to eat. Your body is rapidly burning those calories manufacturing milk! Make wise choices to consume plenty of protein and calcium-rich foods. Your fluid intake has to be kept up as well. You may find yourself consuming water almost constantly. You should drink water and other healthy, non-caffeinated beverages, whenever you are thirsty. It's a great idea to have a water bottle for yourself sitting next to where you nurse your babies. Your body is relying on you to drink the fluids it needs to produce enough milk for your babies (LLLI 2008).

What to Know about Artificial Milk

The Purpose of Formula

Artificial milk does serve a purpose in situations when the mother is not available or for the very small percentage of women who cannot physically breastfeed. God has given man the intelligence to solve the problem of what to do when human milk is not available. Some mothers have more problems with breastfeeding than others. That does not make them less of a mother or even less of a loving mother. God provided the resources to develop artificial milk, and it should be used when necessary.

Artificial milk comes in three levels of preparation: ready to use, concentrated, and powder. Ready to use is just that; ready to pour into a bottle and feed to the baby, so it is the most expensive. This type is best to use in an emergency, possibly while traveling or when you are going to be out running around. Concentrated formula is liquid and only requires water added. It is less expensive than ready to use, but more expensive than powder. Powder formula is the cheapest form and requires the most mixing, but many products are available to make this easier to use while traveling. All three preparations when used according to the directions and diluted correctly, if required, are equivalent to each other.

Artificial milk also comes in a dizzying array of nutrient combinations. The biggest distinction is between cow milk-based formulas and other bases like soy, goat, or partially hydrolyzed bases. Most babies are started on cow milk formulas and then moved to one of the other formulations if there is a problem with the baby's formula tolerance. This can happen with lactose intolerance or whey allergies.

Often soy-based formula is used when a child has a temporary intolerance of cow's milk or ongoing allergy to cow milk protein. Goat milk formula has less lactose, so is better tolerated by babies with lactose intolerance. It has much less folic acid naturally than cow milk formula, so you will need to choose a brand that is fortified with folic acid.

Partially hydrolyzed formula is used for babies with significant allergies and requires a prescription. There are several other specialty formulas for babies with specific problems. If you need further information, you should discuss this with your baby's healthcare provider.

There are two fairly new formulas, AR (anti-regurgitation) and DHA/ARA, which try to improve the use of artificial milk. AR formula has an additive that makes it thicken in the stomach and make the baby less likely to spit up; it doesn't always work and there are mixed reviews on whether this product is useful.

DHA and ARA are fatty acids that have been added to formula, purportedly to help with babies' development, particularly of the brain and eyesight. There has not been adequate research to substantiate that adding these plant-based acids provides the same benefits as the acids that naturally occur in breast milk. They have not been proven to be safe or effective.

It is generally safest to use the well-established, brand-named formulas, since the generic or store brands are more often recalled. However, major formula brands have also been found to have contaminants, since formula can not be sterilized. There are multiple choices of formula even within a given brand. You should choose a formula that has iron included. Ask your doctor which formula he recommends and why that particular brand is recommended.

You will need bottles and nipples. Although a breastfed baby rarely takes over five to six ounces at a time, a bottle fed baby can tolerate up to eight ounces and you will want to get full size bottles. Nipples should be purchased based on the age of the baby and you may have to work with a few different shapes and flow rates of nipples. There are a lot of variations of bottles and nipples; you can get advice from friends about what works well.

Who is Involved in Artificial Milk Feeding?

When feeding formula to babies, it is possible for dad and others to feed the baby, so that mom has time to do other things. It is important that the baby be held close and can still have the benefit from skin-to-skin contact when bottle-feeding. Hold the baby in a comfortable position for both the feeder and the baby. Don't give in to the temptation to prop the baby with a bottle. This can cause him to get too much milk, which can settle in the back of the throat and cause him to gag. This position can also cause the milk to get into the middle ear causing ear infections and damage baby teeth causing cavities.

Stop and burp the baby about every five minutes during a feeding to help him relieve gas build-up in the stomach. It is much better to get the gas to come back out the mouth, than to deal with it passing through the whole digestive system. Burping also provides another opportunity for interaction. Another tip: formula stains fabric. Be sure the baby has a bib and have plenty of burp cloths available. Also, any formula stains need to be pre-treated before washing.

When and Where does the Baby need to be Fed?

Formula does not digest as easily as breast milk, so formula-fed babies can usually go three to four hours between feedings. They should be given up to three to five ounces of formula every three to four hours and can usually manage a longer six to eight hour break at night. As they get older you can move up to six to eight ounces at a time. Babies on artificial milk are generally able to go longer between feedings, so they can often handle a schedule better than a breastfed baby in the first few weeks. Formula can be given wherever you and baby are.

How is Formula Feeding Done?

It is important to be sure baby's bottles and nipples are cleaned with warm, soapy water, then rinsed and sterilized each day. Babies are more susceptible to infection in the first six months, before they build up their immune system.

Fluoride-free, filtered water should be used to mix formula. This water is available near the formula at the store. It is usually called nursery water. Tap water may have additional minerals that are not recommended for babies. Always follow the directions on the formula container carefully. Water should be boiled first, add the powder and mix thoroughly, then allow the formula to cool before feeding the baby. Formula can be used when lukewarm or cooled, depending on your baby's preference. Babies can become very ill and require hospital admission if the formula is too diluted or concentrated, so always measure the scoops accurately and follow directions carefully

Summary

Method of feeding is a personal family choice; having the best information to make your decision is important so you will feel good about the choice you make. Breastfeeding has many benefits for the mother and baby, but there is a great initial investment of time and determination. While mom is the primary feeder with breastfeeding, dad has very relevant responsibilities in caring for the new baby.

There are many things to know how to successfully breast and/or bottle-feed. For more information, please see a lactation consultant or healthcare provider. Feeding is one of the primary activities of babies for the first few months. Moms can be successful and enjoy feeding their babies, no matter how they choose to feed.

for so he giveth his beloved sleep

Psalm 127:2b

Chapter Seven
Need for Sleep

Psalm 127:2-3 2 "It is vain for you to rise up early, to sit up late, to eat the bread of sorrows: for so he giveth his beloved sleep. 3 Lo, children are an heritage of the LORD: and the fruit of the womb is his reward."

*I*t can be challenging to get enough sleep with a new baby! Here's some good news: this time of frequently interrupted sleep will not last forever, and implementing the information in this chapter will help moms and babies get more sleep and feel more rested.

How do Babies' Sleep Patterns Differ from Adults?

At birth, babies and sleep don't fit together the way we would like, because babies' sleep cycles are much different than adults' sleep cycles. A newborn simply is too immature to sleep through the night consistently.

In the womb, a baby experiences very little difference between day and night. Babies experience their mother's cortisol (the hormone that makes you feel awake) and melatonin (the hormone that makes you sleepy) while inside the womb (Mirmiran, Maas, and Ariagno 2003). Adults produce more cortisol during the day and more melatonin at night. As a protective mechanism, your newborn produces equal amounts of these hormones throughout the 24-hour period, so it should be no surprise that your baby has his days and nights confused.

Newborns spend more time in active sleep, and their sleep cycles are about half as long as adult cycles. The lighter phase of sleep protects against SIDS (Sudden Infant Death Syndrome), and the frequent awakening allows the baby to feed and obtain the calories necessary for growth.

Circadian rhythms are the internal governors for adult sleep and wake cycles. It will be several months before a new baby develops a working circadian rhythm (Pantley 2002, 43). The baby is likely to develop more stable sleep patterns between 8 and 12 weeks when their hormone release patterns become closer to adult patterns (Pantley 2002, 43).

Sleeping Through the Night

"Is your baby sleeping through the night?" This may be one of the most frustrating questions asked of new moms. We have all heard it, usually from people who do not have young children. It is frustrating, because it feels like people are measuring your mothering skills. In reality, this is probably a way for an experienced parent to commiserate with the new mother.

It is the rare and unusual baby who sleeps through the night before eight weeks. Remember, when your newborn sleeps four to five hours at night he has reached the major "Sleep through the Night" milestone!

An infant, who bed-shares with his mother, will be less likely to sleep through the night. He will remain in an alert sleep pattern, rather than progressing to a deep sleep pattern. This occurs when he is in contact with the mother's smell, sound, and touch. Having an alert sleep pattern is actually a positive behavior, since this active sleep can result in greater brain development for the newborn (Siegel 2005).

Miriam: All of my babies were between eight and nine pounds. I produced about three ounces of breast milk per feeding. Even though each of my babies was quite willing to sleep through the night by 10 weeks, I had to wake them up or their weight gain would slow. I also fed in the middle of the night to keep up my milk supply. Co-sleeping and bed-sharing allowed me to be successful with breastfeeding.

My sister, on the other hand, has a large storage capacity. Her baby weighed six pounds at birth and voluntarily slept through the night at seven weeks. My sister pumps in the early morning and gets 11-12 ounces. She then waits an hour, wakes her baby, feeds him, and sends him to grandma's house until she is home from work at 4pm.

She pumps once or twice at work and empties her breasts at most six times per day, yet she has all the milk she needs for the baby. Her baby is exclusively fed human milk and is gaining weight at a very good rate. Nursing during the night is not necessary and she chooses to have her baby sleep in a separate room.

Here are two people from the same parents with vastly different breastfeeding and "sleeping through the night" experiences. This emphasizes why it is important not to compare yourself with others.

Miriam: Both my sister and I were able to exclusively breastfeed. Obviously, our mother/baby routines were very different. If I tried to follow a routine similar to my sister's, I would have needed to add formula. I chose exclusive breastfeeding instead of time at work or uninterrupted sleep at night. Other women with small storage capacities may choose differently. If my sister had tried to follow my routine, she would have had chronic oversupply issues and needlessly been up at night. It was very important that neither of us pressured the other to follow a specific routine.

Sleep Training

Sleep training is a term used to discuss how to teach your baby to sleep on his own. Following the recommendations for calming the baby and laying him down drowsy or just as he falls asleep will help the baby to learn to fall asleep on his own and return to sleep when he wakes during the night. This must be done daily from birth. If you have an older baby who has never learned to sleep independently these techniques will work, but it will take more patience. Teaching babies to sleep as just described is a gentle yet effective method of sleep training.

Some authors recommend a specific method of sleep training that has come to be known as "crying it out." It is generally meant that you leave baby in their crib in the room alone and close the door. If the baby starts crying after you leave, you don't respond even if the baby cries for 20 minutes or longer. The general purpose of not responding is to let the baby understand his need for attention will not be met, so he will give up and go to sleep. This method of sleep training is not best.

The term "crying it out" has also been inaccurately ascribed to a method of sleep training that encourages you to let your baby cry or fuss quietly for a few minutes in the process of learning to settle down and go to sleep. This type of sleep training has the objective of allowing a baby to learn to settle down on his own, rather than teaching him to give up or that the mother is unavailable. If your baby is fussing or talking quietly for a few minutes that is fine.

If you choose to allow your baby to cry for longer than a few minutes, you should wait until the baby is out of the newborn period and at least 12 weeks old. When your baby is screaming, go to him and meet his needs, even if that need is for comfort and your presence.

Young babies have limited ability to self soothe. If your baby is escalating his cry after he is laid down for a nap, you need to calm him. Gentle crying that occurs because the baby is in the process of settling down does not escalate to full-throated screaming. Newborns that have escalated their cry to screaming will likely continue to scream until they are exhausted. Screaming, sobbing, and crying cause a dramatic increase in heart rate, increased stress hormones in the brain and blood, and increased pressure in the brain. Crying until exhausted is physiologically distressing and unhealthy for the baby.

Babies sometimes cry when they are sleepy. Many babies will be happy to be rocked, nursed, or patted to sleep, but some will not. Occasionally, babies will cry themselves to sleep; this happens most often when the baby is overtired from extra stimuli like visiting family or a long outing. Limit stimulation by laying him down in a quiet, darkened room to help him go to sleep.

If your baby is tired and crying from loneliness and he stops crying when he sees you, he might need your presence. You don't have to leave him alone. You can lie down on the adult bed beside him in a co-sleeper or stand beside his crib to stay with him until he falls asleep.

When your baby cries before sleep, make sure all of his needs are met, especially that he is fully fed, clean, and not in discomfort. If the baby is crying because he is tired, then the best thing you can do is help him go to sleep.

Miriam: Somewhere close to four months I began laying the baby down for regular naps. These regular naps occurred when he was naturally tired. The baby had developed a rhythm, and sometimes I guided that rhythm so natural tiredness would occur at a convenient time for me.

I would do this by feeding at a time calculated to encourage the baby to sleep at the desired naptime. For instance, if I wanted him to nap at ten each morning, I would offer a feeding at eight thirty and another feeding at nine forty-five. As the baby became used to sleeping at ten each morning, I encouraged SNAP cycles. By the time each baby was leaving the newborn period, naps were a recognizable part of our routine.

Elijah, my third, would sometimes cry or whimper for three minutes before falling asleep. I would time it by the clock. It was comforting to have his sleep routine so predictable. If he cried for longer, I knew he probably was not ready for a nap.

Since we began sleep training on day two, it was the natural next step to put him down for regular naps. For my babies, falling asleep and sleeping well was easy. We still enjoyed special times of rocking and nursing to sleep, but I wanted the baby to have the ability to comfort himself and fall asleep on his own. I have friends that choose to rock their babies to sleep for every nap throughout childhood and that is wonderful, but it may not work for every parent.

Influencing Sleep

There are many factors that influence sleep. Here is a table listing many of these factors. You have influence over some of these, but others are beyond your control.

Factors that Influence Your Baby's Sleep

Factors you may change	Factors you cannot change
✦ Baby's sleep space location	✦ Baby's personality
✦ Baby's feeding routine	✦ Volume of milk storage capacity
✦ Baby's daily environment	✦ Volume of baby's stomach capacity
✦ Baby's napping habits	✦ Baby's rate of milk digestion
✦ Rate of breast milk production*	✦ Baby's digestive system maturity

*Mothers who nurse more make more milk and make it more quickly unless there is something physiologically wrong with the mother.

Changing Sleep Cycles

Your baby's sleep patterns will change rapidly during the newborn period. Almost all babies will have one stretch of sleep lasting 3-5 hours during a 24 hour cycle. The first step to regular night time sleep is gently moving this nap to night. Here is a list of simple yet effective strategies.

Moving the Long Nap to Night

1. Feed your baby a minimum of every two to three hours during the day. This helps your baby get the majority of his calories during the daytime. If your baby is sleeping, undress him down to his diaper and place him skin-to-skin while stroking and talking to him. You can try some gentle sit-ups or a diaper change. If he still is very sleepy, put him back on your chest and try again in 30 minutes. Waking your baby every three hours during the day to nurse is one of the most important techniques for establishing longer sleep cycles at night. It is a lot of work, especially when you are already very tired, but it is worth it.

2. Feed your baby more often in the evening hours. Most babies will nurse frequently in the evenings, because that is when your milk supply decreases.

3. For most of his naps during the day, place your baby in a different sleep space than the one he uses at night. Using the main living area in your home will help ensure that he is exposed to daytime levels of light and sound.

4. Keep everything dark and quiet at night. A noise machine may be especially soothing. Use a soft nightlight when attending to nighttime needs.

5. Include the baby in your daily activities. Take your baby on an outing to grandma's house or the park.

6. You do not need to respond to every noise at night with a feeding, if your baby is growing well. Wait until you are sure your baby is awake to eat.

7. You can ask your spouse or helper to comfort the baby at night, so that he goes three to five hours without nursing. It is best to wait until the baby is a month old, gaining five to seven ounces per week, and breastfeeding is going well before using this technique. Your helper can take the baby to another part of the house or you can go to another room. When you are nearby your baby can smell your milk, so he will be more likely to continue wanting a feed.

8. Share these techniques with your husband and helpers, so that all of you can implement them.

Usually by the third night the baby will have moved the long nap to nighttime. Be aware that you will have to feed more often during the day to ensure the baby gets the same number of calories. Nighttime helpers can use the soothing techniques in Chapter 11 and should follow all safety precautions for infant sleep.

During the first few weeks, newborns may sleep up to 18 hours a day, but the short stretches of sleep can be frustrating to parents. These strategies for moving the long nap to nighttime may take several weeks to work, but little habits begun now will make a difference later.

Breastfeeding and Sleep

Breastfeeding often makes mothers and babies feel sleepy. The skin-to-skin contact and the hormones released when your baby suckles cause sleepiness. Many mothers take advantage of this time (at lease, during the newborn period) by encouraging their babies to nap after a feeding while catching a nap themselves. This is a great way to sneak in the sleep you aren't getting at night. This is a way that God created your body to provide for your need for sleep. Napping is critically important to moms and babies during the newborn period.

Some mothers will choose to nurse their babies to sleep for every nap. This tends to work for moms who are not as concerned with a schedule. The downside of using this technique for every nap is that some babies begin to wake more and more frequently to suckle for comfort, and will not develop longer nighttime sleep patterns.

Nursing your baby to sleep for some naps can be very helpful even for moms who prefer a schedule. This is particularly true when your baby is ill, over-stimulated, or ready for nighttime sleep. Your breast milk contains tryptophan, a hormone that makes your baby sleepy. Breast milk contains more tryptophan in the evening hours (Cubero et al. 2005). Breastfeeding is a valid technique for encouraging the baby to sleep, and you may choose to use it, especially during the evening.

Offering a feeding before sleep can be helpful during significant times of development such as, the fourth and eighth month when babies are commonly difficult to nurse and often experience sleep regression. Mothers who prefer schedules do not need to be afraid to use this technique; these times will pass, and moms can gently encourage a routine while still meeting the infant's needs.

SNAP

The acronym SNAP stands for Sleep-Nurse-Activity/Play. Many mothers have found that ordering the baby's day this way helps him develop manageable rhythms and helps her predict the child's next activity. According to this pattern, after the baby has slept you nurse him, encourage him to play and be wakeful for a period of time, and then let him fall asleep. The SNAP pattern encourages babies to go to sleep independently without needing to nurse and also helps some babies suckle for longer periods and take more milk at one time. Some babies will be better satisfied at each feed, so many mothers find this pattern to be very helpful.

Sleep: The most important piece to SNAP is that the Sleep comes before Nurse and after Activity/Play. This allows the baby to go to sleep without associating feedings with sleep.

Nurse: Nursing should take place after the nap. This gives the baby energy for being alert for a short period of time.

Activity: The Activity portion of SNAP includes activities like changing or bathing your baby. Perhaps he will spend a few minutes in his swing or bouncy chair near you while you are busy with dinner. It is the time your baby spends awake when you are not intentionally interacting with him; it also includes routine care you give him like diaper changes or burping. It may seem like your baby only nurses and sleeps, but don't worry; even a bath or change of clothes counts as the Activity portion of SNAP in the first few weeks.

Play: Many parents find that their baby is rarely awake in the first few days, so they want to spend every wakeful moment engaging the baby in Play. This is the perfect way to help your baby develop, and although he may not seem to comprehend everything, you can be sure that he is growing and developing as you interact with him. Literally trillions of neurons are wiring in the first few months alone!

As much as your baby needs your presence, there will be times when he needs less direct interaction, so that he is not overwhelmed. He also needs time to process all of the new sensory input. He will cue you by looking away, closing his eyes, or fussing. He may need some quiet time such as gentle, quiet rocking in your arms, skin-to-skin, or some time in his swing or bouncy seat. When your baby begins giving sleepy signals such as yawning or fussing, go ahead and put him in his sleep space. It is time to begin the SNAP cycle again.

The SNAP pattern is very helpful, especially for high needs babies, but *establishing a routine does not relieve a mommy of her responsibility to respond to her baby's cues.* This attempt at a routine should be gentle and allow your baby to grow and change in a healthy way.

Sleep Beyond the Fourth Month

In just a few short months, your baby will not be as sleepy during the day. He will probably transition to three or four naps per day by the fourth month. At 8 to 10 months most babies will be ready to drop the third nap, but will continue to have a morning and afternoon nap throughout the first year.

You can plan for this earlier by encouraging him to take those longer naps at times of your choosing. If you would like, you can put him in his room or turn off artificial lighting and decrease the noise level for those two or three naps that you think will be a continued part of your routine. The quiet of his bedroom may encourage deeper sleep and prepare him to move to his bedroom after the sixth month.

Observe your baby's patterns; think about when you would like for those routine naps to occur. Once he reaches the fourth month, instead of a SNAP pattern, you can use a SNAP-N pattern (Sleep, Nurse, Activity/Play, Nurse), so that the baby will be awake longer, then will sleep longer with a full tummy. The length of the SNAP or SNAP-N cycle will increase as your baby grows older.

In the first months, the baby's bedtime will be closer to yours, but as he grows it will move to an earlier time. By the fourth or fifth month, most babies will be happiest if they are put to bed for the night by seven or eight in the evening. You can feed the baby again before your bedtime. Some people refer to this feed as a dream feed, because the baby does not even wake up while nursing. At night the quiet and darkened room will signal that nighttime is different. Your baby's body will respond to dark and quiet with hormones that help him sleep. Some families may choose to avoid an early bedtime, so that the baby can spend time with his parents after their long day at work. This is okay. Remember this is your baby.

Where Should the Baby Sleep?

The American Academy of Pediatrics (AAP) recommends co-sleeping, where young babies sleep in the same room with their mother for at least the first six months of life (AAP 2011). We recognize that some mothers may not follow this recommendation. Although many health organizations discourage sharing a bed with a baby, they do encourage mothers to co-sleep with their babies.

Reasons for Baby to Share Your Room

Concerns with Long Sleep Cycles

SIDS is the sudden death of an infant from an undetermined cause even after investigation and autopsy. Responsible for over 2,300 deaths in the United States each year, SIDS is the most common cause of death in healthy babies over one month of age. Although the SIDS rate has fallen by over 50% since 1983, much of that is due to better recognition and classification of situations. Over 4,500 Sudden Unexpected Infant Deaths (SUID) occur in the United States each year. These are babies who died suddenly from no immediately explainable cause (CDC 2011b). Some of these deaths are from SIDS, while others may be from malnutrition, suffocation, neglect, or unknown health problems.

The risk of SIDS is highest during the first six months. This is why the AAP recommends that babies up to six months should co-sleep in the parent's room. SIDS is associated with deep, abnormal sleep patterns that occur when babies are left undisturbed for long periods of time.

Babies who sleep with or near their mothers are aroused by the movement, sound, and smell of their mothers and have more regular breathing and body temperature. Babies sleeping in the same room as their parents for the first six months have less incidence of abnormal sleep patterns that can lead to SIDS (Scragg et al. 1996).

Babies, especially small or premature ones, who are allowed or encouraged to sleep for a long period during the night may have problems maintaining their growth. If your baby's growth slows after he begins sleeping through the night, you may need to add more feeds during the day and possibly a night feed (Mohrbacher and Kendall-Tackett 2010, 129).

Modifiable Risk Factors for SIDS

1. Smoking during pregnancy: This is the primary risk factor for babies to die from SIDS.

2. Consistent exposure to second hand smoke: This doesn't mean when someone is smoking near you at the family reunion picnic, but when smoke is present in the home, car, and baby's environment.

3. Drug and alcohol use by the mother: These items impair the mother's judgment, decision-making ability, and alertness to the baby's needs.

4. Overheating: Babies should not be dressed too warmly. In hot climates be sure to provide good ventilation in the room, possibly a fan or air conditioning that doesn't blow directly on the baby.

5. Feeding the baby artificial milk products: Breastfed babies have a lower risk of SIDS, because breastfed babies sleep for shorter stretches and are less likely to go into the deepest levels of sleep (Vennemann et al. 2009).

6. Placing the baby on his tummy to sleep: If the baby usually sleeps on his back, you need to consistently place him in that position. If you place your baby on his back and he is able to roll back and forth and lift his head, don't worry if he rolls onto his tummy.

7. Blankets: You can use long sleeved pajamas or a sleep sack, instead of covering the baby with a blanket. Blankets can become loose, entangle the baby, and cover his face. Even when swaddling, it is important to be sure the baby cannot work his way loose.

8. Pillows or other objects in bed: Keep all soft objects away from a baby's face during sleep. There should be no stuffed animals, pillows, or extra supplies left in the baby's sleep area. Babies look very small placed in the middle of this big empty surface, but it's amazing how far they can scoot themselves.

9. Waterbeds, couches, and recliners: These sleep surfaces have been identified as suffocation risks for babies. Babies can become wedged between the parent and the back or sides of this furniture.

10. Cords (blind cords, wires, curtains): Keep your child's sleep surface clear of any object that could entangle him. Any curtain or blind cords should be tied away from the baby's reach. You can avoid this completely by placing the crib on an inner wall or away from the window. Some baby nightgowns may still have a cinch drawstring to tighten the bottom, but that design has being phased out to prevent entanglement.

11. Soft sleeping surfaces: Babies must sleep on firm surfaces only. Examples of soft surface include fleece pads in the baby's bed, water mats, duvets, or any surface on which you can leave a handprint. The baby's mattress should be firm with minimal extra padding.

There are other risk factors for SIDS over which parents have no control. Some of these are ethnicity, season of birth, premature birth, and gender. These are things we need to leave in the Lord's hands.

What about Bed-sharing?

It is important to state at the outset of this section that this book does not make a recommendation for your family regarding bed-sharing, which is defined as the baby sharing the same sleep surface as the mother. Information is provided to enable you to evaluate the risks and benefits. The AAP and many other healthcare organizations recommend against bed-sharing, and there are good reasons for this. There are many qualifying factors that must be met to make bed-sharing safe. Mothers who do not take their complex role as mother seriously may not value meeting all the criteria necessary to make this a safe experience for the baby. There are other sources that recognize, for the committed mother who is willing to follow the guidelines, bed-sharing can be a safe alternative (Ball 2009).

Benefits of Bed-sharing

It has been demonstrated that a mother's body regulates her baby's breathing and heart rate (McKenna 1996; Gettler and McKenna 2010). To be effective, the baby should be close enough to be heard, seen, and touched by their mother. Other benefits of bed-sharing include ease of breastfeeding, since babies are fed more often during the night and mothers often feel they get more sleep. Mothers who work during the day and bed-share at night have an exceptional way to reconnect with their infant. This also increases the duration of breastfeeding when mothers work during the day. Many mothers are able to return to sleep more quickly after they breastfeed when they bed-share (Quillin and Glenn 2004).

Risk of Bed-sharing

Although the benefits of bed-sharing are extensive, there is a serious risk of overlay and suffocation. It is more dangerous for the baby to sleep with someone other than his primary caregiver. Other dangerous ways for a baby to sleep are with a mother who smokes, has had alcohol or other drugs, or is sleeping on a couch or chair (McKenna and McDade 2005).

Decisions about Bed-sharing

This is a decision you need to evaluate carefully. If you choose to bed-share, you must follow all safety precautions. Many studies have been done to evaluate the safety of bed-sharing in various populations (McKenna and McDade 2005; McKenna 2011). "There is no published evidence of any increased risk to a baby from sharing a bed with a firm mattress with parents who do not smoke and have not consumed alcohol or other drugs providing the bedding is arranged so that it cannot slip over the baby's head, and the baby is not sleeping on a pillow, or under an adult duvet" (McKenna and McDade 2005).

As adults, we make decisions every day that can result in serious harm if we don't consider all the possible ramifications. Taking a chance with our own safety can lead to heartbreaking situations, but the loss of a baby through a bad decision can be devastating for a lifetime. Parents need information to make wise decisions. Whatever choice you make about where your baby sleeps should be made after prayerful consideration.

Everyone should know by now to not drink, text, or take narcotic pain medications and drive. We expect people to be able to recognize when they are impaired and refrain from driving. We don't have the same expectation when it comes to sleeping with a baby. The message to "Never sleep with your baby" is more succinct and memorable than a list of the many precautions that must be taken to do so. Advisory groups know that some parents won't bother with the precautions, and the cost is so great!

According to population statistics and research studies, many parents do choose to bed-share despite recommendations from doctors and other groups. *Because it is clear that some parents will bed-share, it is important to discuss ways to make this activity as safe as possible.*

Precautions for Bed-sharing

1. No one but the parents can be in bed with baby. It is safest to place the baby on the outside of the mother, not between the parents. You should sleep facing your baby, with one arm above baby's head and your knees drawn up around him (Baddock et al. 2007). Put him on his back to sleep.

2. You and your spouse cannot have used alcohol, cigarettes, or any substance (even cold medicine or herbs) that could make you extra sleepy or impair your judgment in any way. This is possibly the most overlooked precaution.

3. It is *safest* to sleep with the baby on a firm mattress placed on the floor.

4. If a mother has extremely large breasts or either parent is significantly overweight, bed-sharing may not be safe. The baby should not be able to roll into a valley between a parent's body and a sunken mattress.

5. The bed should not have any gaps that could entrap the baby. The standard type of waterbed is off limits, as well as foam-type mattresses, or wooden frames that can create a gap where baby can get wedged. If you can leave a handprint in a foam-type mattress, it will not be a safe sleep surface. A mattress with a pillow top can be flipped to the other side, or you can place a yoga mat under the sheet to prevent the mattress from molding around the baby's face.

6. Babies should never sleep on a sofa or be held by a sleeping parent in a recliner.

7. Make sure the father always knows when the baby is in the bed and is willing to take responsibility for him, especially if you choose to place the baby between the parents.

8. If you choose to place a railing on the side of the bed where baby sleeps, make sure that there is no possibility of a gap forming between the railing and the mattress or any other part of the bed. The mattress pushed up against a wall or other furniture pushed up against the mattress will not provide a safe sleep surface, since a gap may form.

9. There should be no strings attached to any bed occupant's clothing, such as drawstring waistbands.

10. No pillows, stuffed animals, or fluffy bedding should be in the baby's sleep space.

11. If the mother has long hair, it should be tied back.

12. No heavy bedding; if the room is cool, dress the baby in a sleeper

13. Only breastfeeding babies should bed-share. Bottle-fed babies are safer in a sidecar or co-sleeper, because of the differences in the physiological responses of breastfeeding versus bottle-feeding mother/baby pairs.

14. Do not swaddle the baby during bed-sharing (Baddock et al. 2007; McKenna 2011). Babies need their arms and legs free.

If it is not possible to assure that all of these criteria are met, then bed-sharing will not be a safe experience. Following these precautions does not guarantee your child's safety. The heartache and guilt of losing a baby by suffocation is horrific. Do not discount the seriousness of following these precautions.

Miriam: My husband and I did more bed-sharing and co-sleeping with each child. When baby number four came, I finally bought an official sidecar (an arm's reach co-sleeper). It was the best piece of baby equipment we ever bought. I didn't even need to get out of bed, yet she had her own secure sleep surface less than 12 inches from me. I would often sleep with my hand touching her. It was the perfect solution for us.

Ronda: My husband and I used modified bed-sharing with all our children. I would have my husband bring the baby into the bedroom when she was hungry. Then after nursing on one side, I'd move the baby to the outside side of the bed and roll over to nurse on the second side.

We might continue through a couple cycles of nursing and sleeping. At times, I found it hard to rest fully with the baby in the bed. I would have my husband return her to her crib for the remainder of the night.

Some mothers may find bed-sharing intolerable. It may feel like you can never really sleep well with the baby in bed with you. Some mothers feel like they are on alert even when the baby is in the same room. You should always feel confident in your decision to do what is safest and best for your family. Consider the options available and make decisions that provide a safe and healthy experience for your baby. Further resources on co-sleeping and bed-sharing are included in the Resource chapter.

Moving Baby to His Room

You may choose to transition the baby to his own room at the end of six months. This can be done by nursing the baby in his room once a day, then placing the baby in his crib for one or more daily naps. Leave the door open and an overhead fan on or perhaps a white noise machine or music. As the baby becomes comfortable in his crib at naptime, you can add in the nighttime sleep period. Begin these crib naps sometime during the newborn period. This will make it much easier for an older baby to adjust to spending time in his room.

Common Sleep Remedies

Independent Sleep: Many parents plan to have their baby sleep in a crib or bassinet at least part of the time. If that is what you expect, it is best to lay him down some during the day. Begin this napping process soon after birth. If you hold him all day long for the first few days or weeks it will be more difficult for him to become used to being away from your body during sleep.

Some mothers will hold their babies all day, but then want the baby to sleep separately at night. This usually results in very poor sleep for both mom and baby. From day one lay the baby down for some daytime sleep.

Sleep without Props: In the first few weeks babies may need some help with sleep as they transition to the outside world. Sleep props are pacifiers, swaddle blankets, bouncy seats, swings, the parent's chest, or anything that the baby uses to help him get to sleep. Parenting advice usually presents sleep props in a negative light but present sleep routines in a positive light. The difference between a sleep prop and a sleep routine is that the sleep routine should end slightly before the baby is asleep, but a sleep prop is used until the baby is asleep and during sleep.

If a baby comes to rely on a sleep prop, he will have trouble going back to sleep at night without the prop. Any mother who has had to get up 10 times to put the pacifier back in the baby's mouth knows how frustrating this can be. A sleep routine might include rocking, singing, or nursing the baby to sleep, but then he wakes up slightly as he is placed in his sleep space; so he is learning to get to sleep on his own.

Newborns sometimes need sleep props and sleep routines. The key is to gradually wean the newborn from the sleep prop, and only use the sleep prop when needed. The best way to teach a baby to go to sleep without props is to lay him down slightly awake. If you choose to nurse your baby to sleep, his eyes may blink open when you move him to bed. You might even encourage him to stir slightly.

Miriam: Shannon and I have used sleep props (pacifiers, swings, swaddle blankets, our bodies) for each of our babies in the newborn period. We've

In Review:

Here are some helpful steps that will encourage good sleeping habits for your baby.

1. Implement the SNAP cycle, but modify it when your baby needs an extra feed.

2. From the first day, keep things boring and dark at night.

3. At night, only change baby if he is soaked or soiled. Some babies are sensitive and will cry if their diaper is slightly wet; if this is the case, change it.

4. Feed the infant every time he is awake during the day the first two to three weeks.

5. Wake the baby every two to three hours during the day in order to feed.

6. Encourage the baby to eat often during the evening hours.

7. The before bed feed should be a full feed. If your baby takes only one breast, see if you can gently awaken him to nurse from the other breast as well.

8. If the baby has an early bedtime, get him up and feed him before you go to bed or to sleep.

Following these steps consistently can help you avoid many sleep problems and give your baby an easier transition to sleeping on his own.

been careful to use them only when needed, always encouraging the sleep routines and props we planned to use beyond the newborn period. There is a balance that needs to be found for each baby by doing what needs to be done to get some sleep and preparing for good sleep habits on down the road. Much of our newborn care isn't focused on "fixing" the baby's immaturity, but rather putting up with it in a loving manner—just like God puts up with our immaturity! (Colossians 3:13)

Sleeping at an Incline: Many newborns sleep best when they are not laying flat. The concern with allowing your baby to sleep at an angle is that he does not become slouched in a way that hinders his breathing. Many parents allow a newborn to sleep in an infant swing or other seat marketed for infant sleep. Check with your healthcare provider about this choice.

> Miriam: I bought an inclined sleeping device for my fifth baby that I used during the night. We used a newborn swing during the day. By the fourth month he was used to laying flat. I just transitioned him a bit at a time during the daytime naps.

Summary

Those first few months when your baby is developing his rhythms can be challenging. Many, but not all, babies will sleep five or more hours through the night by the time they are between 8 to 12 weeks of age, but there is a wide variety of reasons why this may or may not occur. Remember that each baby is different and respect the way God made him.

Co-sleeping is recommended for all parents and babies to protect the baby from deep sleep cycles, which have been related to SIDS. Choosing to bed-share is an option that requires serious and prayerful consideration of the required safeguards, possible benefits, and consequences. This time will pass, and for now while you are enjoying your sweet newborn through an exhausted haze, you can call out for help from your Heavenly Father who longs to hear and answer your prayers.

> *Hebrews 4:15-16* [15] *"For we have not an high priest which cannot be touched with the feeling of our infirmities; but was in all points tempted like as we are, yet without sin.* [16] *Let us therefore come boldly unto the throne of grace, that we may obtain mercy, and find grace to help in time of need."*

The steps of a good man are ordered by the LORD: and he delighteth in his way.

Psalm 37:23

Chapter Eight

Need for a Schedule

God's Grace for a Newborn's Needs

*Y*ou and your baby are unique individuals. This means your parenting style will be reflective of your personality and needs. If you are a person who enjoys structure and thrives with a schedule, then you may use more of a schedule than other mothers. If you are very unstructured and creative, then a schedule may seem impossible and stifling. You may, however, need to adjust your natural parenting style for the best interests of your baby, who may have a different personality than your own.

In order to develop a gentle routine that works well for your family, you need to understand how babies eat and sleep. Please be sure to carefully read the chapters on sleep (7) and infant feeding (5 and 6) before reading this chapter. A good understanding of your baby's needs helps you to understand the type of gentle routine needed.

The High Needs Baby

Your baby may desperately need a schedule. This may be the case if he is very sensitive to excessive noise at naptime or needs a certain amount of sleep and cannot tolerate random naps. Babies who are frequent criers will often do better if they are placed on a schedule and kept in a predictable, quiet environment close to their mother.

Baby-wearing can help you manage a high needs baby without being tied to his schedule. This works because the baby who is often worn in a sling or wrap becomes very comfortable being with his mother. Because he has you, he doesn't need a crib or swing to take a nap. Many high needs or sensitive babies may not easily nap in public or fall asleep at a friend's house in a crib or pack 'n play, but many do sleep in public places if worn by their mother.

Miriam: My sister has a sensitive baby that likes to be at home. Even as a four-month-old, he could easily discern the difference between his home and his grandmother's. At five months, he saw my sister with wet hair for the first time. She went to pick him up out of bed, but because he had never seen her with wet hair, he cried and cried.

He consistently reacts with crying to unexpected events and notices everything in his environment. My sister enjoys being at home and being on a regular schedule. Her baby has done very well and does not have extended periods of crying. It is possible that he would have been a difficult baby for a mother with a different personality.

The Laid Back Baby

Some babies are more laid back and prefer a gentle routine. Having your baby on a gentle routine means he follows the schedule, but you aren't required to do the same. For example, if your baby routinely naps in the afternoon at two for two hours and you want to go shopping, you may drop the baby off at grandma's house while you shop, or carry the baby in a sling.

If you want to go to the gym, but the baby will need to eat while you are gone; pump before you leave (if you plan to give him bottles of breast milk occasionally) or take the baby to the gym nursery and feed him when it is time. The important thing is making sure your baby's needs are met. You can be creative in the way you meet those needs.

To Schedule or Not to Schedule

Your Responsibilities

> *1 Timothy 5:14 "I will therefore that the younger women marry, bear children, guide the house, give none occasion to the adversary to speak reproachfully."*

This verse tells us that younger women are to be guiding or managing their homes. In order to manage your home, you will need to understand your baby's needs. As you begin to understand his activities, patterns, and routines, you will be able to manage your other home and family responsibilities. However, during the newborn period, you may delay some types of endeavors like planting a big garden, starting a side business, or spring-cleaning, but you can attempt to meet the daily needs of your family. This doesn't mean you need a showplace for a home, exquisite meals, or perfectly dressed children.

The rest of the verse says, "...give none occasion to the adversary to speak reproachfully." Fulfill your basic responsibilities and focus on the love and attention your family members need. Do not be caught up in frivolous pursuits, especially gossip, instead focus on your family responsibilities.

Demand and Scheduled Feeding

In some baby books, you will find information advocating either demand feeding or scheduled feedings with times chosen by the parents. Demand feeding seems to work very well for some mothers but schedules helps others cope with the new tasks that come with mothering. Find a way that works for your baby and for you!

Demand feeding can mean you feed the baby when he gives hunger cues, but it can also mean that you approach each day without any type of plan, simply reacting to each cue from your child. You should respond to your baby's cues, but having no plan can result in an unpredictable day that is not ideal for your sanity or your baby's development.

On the other end of the parenting spectrum are mothers who use a strict three or four hour schedule. Newborns have significant needs that will not always be predictable. A strict schedule will not be conducive to meeting your baby's needs in a gentle way. Understanding your baby can help you predict his needs and make it easier to discover the routine that works best for both of you, even in times of unexpected need. A baby's valid needs should be attended even if that means ignoring a schedule.

Most babies need familiarity and routine but will not be able to stay on a strict schedule long, because newborn babies grow and change faster than any other age. Not only are their bodies growing but their brains are growing as well. As the brain grows and develops, the need for stimulation, sleep, nutrition, and physical contact change. You may have a few days in a row that are the same, but expect your baby to be in a state of rapid change.

It's hard to know what will work best until you try, and it doesn't give you a sense of security to be told you have to figure it out for yourself. God has given us a lot of grace and freedom to follow our Mommy Sense when finding a balance between the baby's needs and our desires. Many mothers find that a combination of scheduling and following cues works very well.

A Gentle Routine

Using aspects of each style leads to the mother and baby finding a gentle routine. A gentle routine is a loose plan for your day; it is flexible and allows for you and your baby's needs to be met. It also helps you to anticipate needs, so that you can be prepared to meet them. The routine is made up of various activity patterns that occur during the day. This is a bit like the way music has themes that repeat in various ways. Your baby's day has highs and lows, calms and higher energy times. It flows in better harmony, when you can understand the patterns and play along in tune with your baby.

There are several different approaches to following a gentle routine. You may have a mental list of activities you have planned for that day and another mental list of your baby's needs. For instance, every two to three hours your baby will nurse, need a change, and play. For the first three months he will also take a nap. If you know that these events will take place every two or three hours you can expect and plan for them. This is the SNAP cycle. You can work in your list of activities, like a shower, when the baby is napping.

Miriam: I realize it would be nice if we could recommend a specific schedule. I remember wanting everything planned out when I had my first baby. I felt that having the whole day planned would help me be the best mother possible. Unfortunately, the schedule that I read about (a three hour pattern of feeding, playing, and sleeping) did not work.

My daughter's feeding pattern was only two hours for some of the day, and if I dropped a feeding as was recommended by a certain age, my milk supply dropped. I was afraid to disregard "expert" advice, especially because I didn't have other breastfeeding mothers around me to ask. Unfortunately, the advice recommended that babies who needed to eat more often than every three hours be given a formula supplement. I look back now and realize how ill-advised that was!

A Common Routine

Newborns repeat the same activities all day long. These activities occur in patterns and the patterns make up the routine. Mothers can gently guide the order of activity to adjust the routine in ways that help her and the baby.

The majority of newborn babies will naturally complete a daily routine that repeats the SNAP pattern every two and a half to three hours. Some babies will need a routine of patterns that are one and a half to two hours long, and a few babies after eight weeks may use a routine of several patterns lasting three and a half to four hours long during the day. Your baby's routine should not be considered a schedule to be timed by the clock. Instead, it is made up of predictable activity patterns.

As you probably have guessed, the length of your baby's patterns will depend on the size of his stomach, the quality and quantity of milk, and the storage capacity of your breasts. Other factors like a growth spurt, teething, illness, and stress will affect this as well.

You can help your baby move to a three-hour pattern length by offering feedings every three hours, even if your baby does not give you hunger cues. If you wake the baby at seven in the morning, and he nurses for 30 (or 40, or 60) minutes, you will plan to feed him again at ten. A pattern that is longer than three hours during the day can negatively affect nighttime sleep and may decrease your milk supply. Babies younger than eight weeks should not have any four-hour patterns during the day.

When the baby does wake up to nurse, encourage him to eat a complete meal. Every baby is different in the amount of time they take to get a good feeding, but many newborns will nurse for 30 minutes or more, especially the first few weeks. Breast compressions are the primary technique you should use to ensure a full meal. Other techniques are discussed in Chapter 5.

The routine will likely be more predictable with formula fed babies, since the composition of artificial milk is always the same. It is much easier for mothers to assure that the baby has taken a specific amount of formula every time a feeding is offered.

Common Patterns

The three-hour patterns will change at different stages of the newborn period. Some mothers handle the baby's routine differently than others. There are several different patterns of activities that babies can do during this routine. Most mother/baby pairs will use a combination of these routines.

Nurse – Sleep – Nurse – Sleep

During the first few weeks, your baby may only be awake a few times a day. His routine will mostly consist of the pattern of nursing and sleeping. Those times when he is awake you can encourage a SNAP pattern.

SNAP

This routine will be very useful towards the end of the newborn period and throughout the first year. It will be very common for your baby to nurse first thing in the morning, play for an hour or two, and then be ready for a morning nap. This is the routine that mothers use when they want the baby to fall asleep without nursing.

SNAP-N

This routine consists of feeding the baby, keeping him awake for a while and then feeding him again before a nap. Some mothers choose to nurse the baby to sleep for comfort. In this case, the baby may only nurse for a few minutes while drifting off to sleep. This routine works very well for mothers who have small capacity breasts or a slow rate of milk production. It allows the baby to get in the most milk possible.

Nurse – Sleep – Awake Time

After the first month, your baby will be awake more. Some mothers prefer to nurse the baby right before sleep. Nursing makes both the mother and baby feel sleepy. If you choose to nurse your baby to sleep and you are happy with your routine, that's great! The only caution about this pattern is that it tends to make the overall routine less predictable than a nurse-awake-sleep pattern, and it may be more difficult to lay the baby down to sleep, if that is what you are planning to do.

Miriam: When my son was 11 weeks old, I didn't feel the need for a schedule, but I did pay attention to his routines and patterns. This allowed me to predict his needs. I used SNAP and SNAP-N patterns, depending on his needs and my daily activities.

Many mother/baby pairs follow the same three-hour pattern all day long except at night, right before bedtime. As you get to know your baby and become better at predicting his needs, the actual times of activities and length of patterns will become less important to you.

What to Expect as Your Baby Grows

It's great to be able to predict what our babies will need. In the newborn period the baby's needs change rapidly. These are good tips for each time frame of the newborn period that will help you prepare to meet your baby's needs.

The First Two to Four Days

The first few days you will need to focus on recovering from delivery and feeding the baby. Even though you won't have great quantities of milk, the more times your breasts are stimulated the more milk you will produce and the better your baby will do. You should not be doing anything besides resting and feeding your baby.

The baby may be very sleepy the first two days and then suddenly be more awake and nursing very frequently, as often as every hour or two. Learning to breastfeed in a reclined, relaxed position can make a huge difference. Eat good food, watch some old movies, and think of this as a vacation with a purpose—recovery for your body and nourishing your baby.

From Milk Transition to End of the First Two Weeks

When your milk transitions into mature milk you will notice a change in your routine. Your baby will probably sleep for longer times, may begin spitting up, and he will begin stooling and voiding many times per day. He may be content to nurse every two to three hours.

You will need to continue to *feed your baby every time he is awake, and do this until he has regained birth weight.* If you fail to respond to his feeding cues or do not feed a minimum of 8 to 12 times per day, he will not grow well and you will not develop a full milk supply. Babies should gain a half an ounce to one ounce per day.

The Rest of the First Month

Your baby may continue to sleep many hours each day this month. Expect a growth spurt during week two or three. He will want to nurse more often. This may last for a day or two until your supply increases.

You can plan for these growth spurts by choosing some books to read or DVDs you have wanted to see, something you find really absorbing. Get some yummy snacks and curl up for your mini vacation with a purpose.

Some parenting advice tells mothers to expect to add in an extra feeding or two during a growth spurt. Growth spurts would be better described as a time when your baby nurses continuously for long periods of time. It is much more than an extra feeding or two.

Your routine will continue to develop. A great way to help your baby begin a gentle routine is to encourage him to nurse, then play, then sleep once or twice per day. Of course, if you want to nurse or rock your baby to sleep, that is fine, too.

Some mothers enjoy taking advantage of the natural sleepiness that babies feel after breastfeeding. However other mothers, who are planning to return to work, are concerned that they will make the transition to daycare very difficult for their baby if they always nurse him to sleep. If you are concerned about this, you can help your baby go to sleep without nursing. However, babies are very adaptable.

When the mother is not around the baby cannot smell her milk. He may have a little bit of difficulty, but the caregivers will be able to help him get to sleep, and when you are home with him, he will know you're nearby and you can nurse him to sleep. By this age, babies know when their mother is near.

The Second Month

If you do not want to nurse the baby to sleep, you can begin giving him a pacifier to help him sleep as long as breastfeeding is going well and baby is gaining five to seven ounces per week. This month your baby may be a little more awake. Continue to use a SNAP pattern when possible. Your baby may sleep and nurse without a wakeful period for much of the day. Often babies will sleep during the morning hours and then have a wakeful period in the late morning and then again in the late afternoon and evening.

Expect a growth spurt sometime between six and eight weeks. You'll know it is happening because your baby will cue for more feeding time. Again, this may last for a day or two until your supply increases.

You may find that by this time your baby is using a predictable three-hour pattern. Many babies are able to maintain a consistent three-hour pattern and that is wonderful for their mothers! Sometimes babies will be able to go three hours and other times need to be fed more often. This is especially true for babies of mothers who have small capacity breasts.

Some parenting advice suggests that mothers and babies who cannot go three hours between feedings have a problem with either the quality or quantity of milk.

This does not take into account the differences among mothers and the differences among babies. If your baby is gaining a half-ounce to one ounce per day, there is nothing wrong with your milk or your baby's growth! If you have concerns, take your baby in to be weighed. Formula fed babies are able to go three to four hours between feeds because cow's milk is more difficult to digest than human milk.

The Third and Fourth Month

These two months are times of change. Your baby will be more alert and for longer periods. He may be awake through two feedings, so his complete pattern may be four hours. He may need a SNAP-N routine to accommodate the longer pattern, but many babies are able to continue a SNAP routine without problems. Now is the time to observe the baby for appropriate weight gain and to observe any decrease in milk supply.

At this age, some babies become distracted by everything. You may be in the habit of putting your baby down for a nap in the middle of a noisy room, but all the sudden he can't sleep because the noise keeps him awake. You may need to move a couple of his naps to his own room.

Babies during the fourth month often go through a period when they show very little interest in nursing, because they are fascinated by discovering everything they can about their world. Most babies will lose interest around four months, even if they then go on to breastfeed till they are two or three years old.

It may be helpful to nurse your baby right before naps and bed even if this has not been your habit. Sometimes this is the only time when a baby who is just discovering his world will nurse. This is also why a late night feed just before you go to bed and an early morning feed are still important. These feeds allow you to make sure your baby is still getting adequate nutrition.

If you are able to get in a good feed before the morning and afternoon nap, another at the baby's bedtime, another at your bedtime and an early morning feed, you will still be getting five good feeds a day. Even if he is only snacking at the other nursing sessions you will still be able to maintain an adequate supply.

Helping Your Baby's Sleep Cycle

Help your baby by nursing frequently during the evening. Newborns tend to nurse the most between nine at night and one in the morning. A great technique for the first two weeks is to become a bit of a night owl. Stay up late while you nurse the baby then sleep in until nine or ten in the morning, at least while you are on maternity leave.

Try different things until you find what works. Figure out how to get the sleep you need. Remember that your schedule will be constantly adjusting the first six weeks, because your baby's needs and your ability to produce breast milk are changing rapidly.

How Babies Fall Asleep

Babies naturally fall asleep at the breast the first few weeks. It is very sweet and one of the best parts of breastfeeding, however many mothers will want to teach their babies to fall asleep independently. From the very first day, try to rouse him just a little bit (get his eyes to blink, for example) just before you lay him down to sleep. If you are consistent about this, he will naturally learn how to go to sleep on his own. As he gets older (over two weeks) and you know when he is done eating, lay him down while he is still awake, but drowsy (maybe his eyes will be closed). You want to barely wake him before putting him down for a nap.

If he wakes and begins to cry, comfort him. This might be gently rubbing or patting his back, rocking him, or nursing him until he quiets and is ready to sleep. Again, lay him down before he is completely asleep. You may have to do this several times, but all of your work will pay off many times over! *It is much easier to teach a newborn good napping habits than it is an older baby.*

Putting it all Together

Once you are able to predict your baby's needs with some accuracy, you will probably be able to guide him into a gentle routine that suits both of your needs. *The key to a gentle routine is planning the feeding times, because feeding is the activity that drives sleep and wake cycles.* A successful way to ease a baby into a pattern that suits you is to offer feedings that will encourage the routine you want. For instance, if you enjoy taking a walk every morning at eight, feed the baby at a quarter after seven. If he doesn't wake for that feeding, try again the next day, perhaps begin at a quarter till seven attempting to wake and feed him. Almost all newborns will respond to this gentle way of getting them into a routine. If the baby does not wake up to eat, don't leave him hungry or crying while you complete your activity. Remember to be gentle and respond to his needs.

If you want your older baby to go to sleep at seven nightly, you can feed your baby at six-thirty and then put him down to sleep. In the beginning, you can expect him to wake up at eight or nine and be ready to eat and play again. This is normal, but if you want your baby to begin nighttime sleep at seven, when he wakes at eight, meet your baby's minimal needs and put him back to bed. If you are patient and consistent, your baby will adjust to bedtime at seven. Of course, if you attend two evening church services a week; you may want your baby to become used to a later bedtime. A fussy baby two nights a week is no fun.

You may offer the baby a feeding right before you run to the store even if it isn't his normal feeding time and he isn't cueing for a feeding. Many times a baby will take a full or partial feeding and then you and your baby can go to the store and have a pleasant time.

Choosing a morning nursing time to start your day can be very helpful to developing a predictable routine. At this feeding you would expect you and your baby to be awake for some time afterwards. This might be a feeding at ten the first few weeks because the mother and baby are sleeping in. Later in the newborn period the first morning feed may be at seven. If you desire a predictable routine to begin your day, simply offer a feeding at the time of your choosing. It may take several days before your baby begins to expect this feeding, but if you are consistently offering it, he will eventually begin to request it.

What if you want to begin your day at seven but your baby requests to nurse at six? There are several different ways to handle this. You can nurse at six and offer another feeding at seven. You can wake the baby at five for a feeding and then again nurse at seven. Or you can give a partial feeding at six and then offer a full feeding at seven. When giving a partial feed, try not to keep your baby awake. If your baby falls asleep after taking only a partial feeding, you will allow him to sleep until seven when you can encourage a full feeding. Keep in mind that an early morning feed (between four and six) is a normal need for a breastfed baby.

Breastfed babies will sometimes begin to sleep for long stretches of time, especially if they are not sleeping in their mother's room. This can be dangerous for the baby in terms of increased risk of SIDS, and it can decrease the mother's milk supply. Some mothers with large capacity breasts can go eight hours or so between feeding, but many mothers will eventually notice a decrease in milk supply, if long stretches of time become routine. It may be tempting to make night feeding easier by pumping and then offering a bottle of pumped breast milk to the baby. In some cases this works out to be a good way of dealing with nighttime feedings, but in other cases this can lead to a decreased supply, since babies empty the breasts much better than a pump.

Topping off the baby with a bottle, instead of nursing right before you go to bed is another technique that mothers use to increase the sleep stretch. This is counterproductive to a good milk supply. Young, healthy mothers who are staying at home with their babies should find other ways to get adequate rest, like sleeping when the baby sleeps, and making provision for feeding the baby when he is hungry.

Some babies do better in the comfort of their own homes and beds, and will be out of sorts if something out of the ordinary occurs. This does not mean that you need to avoid all unusual events such as vacation, a wedding, or a party. Remember that all actions have consequences. If you keep the baby up through a naptime to see the family members at a reunion, you may end up with a cranky baby, and it shouldn't be a surprise.

Make some time the next day for the baby to get extra sleep and special attention. It is better to plan ahead to allow you to meet your baby's needs for feeding, playtime, and sleeping. Every new parent will learn that planning and babies should go together, but they often do not. In other words, expect the unexpected! Any type of schedule that causes you to stretch out feeding times, drop feeds by offering a bottle of water, ignore the baby's cry, or delay feeds is not recommended. This is not a gentle routine. *A gentle routine rests on the mother planning activities by anticipating and meeting needs. She may even offer an activity before the baby cues for it.*

The Formula Fed Baby

There may be a circumstance where you will need to use artificial milk instead of breast milk. If, for whatever reason, a consistent four-hour schedule is necessary to your life, breastfeeding may not be the best choice.

Miriam: I was able to exclusively breastfeed my second baby, Jac, until I returned to work. My employer was wonderful and allowed me to pump often, up to three times per shift. The problem was that working the night shift and an early return to work after delivery drastically reduced my milk supply.

Even with prescription medication, supplements, and lots of hard work, it was necessary to add formula. It was upsetting when I couldn't exclusively breastfeed, but I did have the satisfaction of giving my baby as much breast milk as possible and knowing I had tried my best.

Tips for a Gentle Routine

1. Attempt to get your baby outside, possibly for a walk or a trip to grandma's, for a few hours every day.

2. Several times per day attempt to keep the baby awake and interested in playing with you; do this after breastfeeding.

3. As the baby grows, attempt to move him to a SNAP pattern. This pattern may only work part of the time. This is not a rigid formula but can be used as a guide.

4. Put the baby down in a bed or bassinet for some naps. If he nurses to sleep, wait until he has fully breastfed, and then move him to a safe sleep surface in your living area.

5. If you choose to bed-share or use a co-sleeper and plan to transition the baby to his room during the first year, feed him in his room once a day and put him in his room for one or more naps per day.

6. Treat sleep times that you plan to make part of his routine after the newborn period differently. These nap times may be enhanced by a before nap feed, a noise machine (ocean waves, white noise, etc) and by turning off artificial lighting.

7. Offer a feeding right before you retire for the night, this may help the baby move the four to five-hour stretch to a time that will be more convenient for you.

8. Begin your baby's morning at the same time every day.

Planning to meet the needs of a formula fed baby can be easy. Many formula fed babies are on very predictable four-hour routines and sleep all night long. On the other hand, formula fed babies do tend to get more illnesses and nothing throws off a schedule like an illness.

Summary

A baby's routine is gradually created during the newborn period as he becomes able to internalize the difference between day and night and follow his body's circadian rhythm. As patterns build, you may notice more things that happen at the same time on most days. These events become part of the baby's routine. Some mothers are perfectly comfortable listening to the baby's cues and balancing their needs with the baby's needs.

Other mothers, especially first time ones, may need a schedule for security. Many of us have followed a rigid schedule for most of our lives. We may not go to sleep at the same time every night, but we are at class or work the same time every morning. We eat lunch at the same time every day. Schedules are comfortable. Soon your baby will also follow a gentle routine, but during the first few months remember to meet your baby's needs as you ease him into daily rhythms.

Unfortunately, there are men and women with good intentions who believe their personality and style of parenting is the only right way. Choosing to use a flexible schedule, follow cues, or use a gentle routine is an area of preference. The Bible says much about a parent's responsibilities to lovingly meet their child's needs even if it does not outline different parenting styles. The best way to deal with others who may be critical of your parenting is to have patience with them, take their advice with a grain of salt, and rely upon the Spirit to help you forgive their criticism.

Babies have special needs. Anticipate those needs and realize that as your baby passes the newborn stage, it is likely that he will rely on the gentle routines that you have initiated for feelings of security and comfort. You will experience the joy of a baby who feels secure and is able to focus on growing and developing. Watching your baby grow and learn new things is one of the most rewarding parts of mothering! You and your baby are unique. As you follow the principles of love and responsiveness to your baby, you will find the rhythms and routines that work best for you.

A Morning Hymn

Awake, my soul, and with the sun
Thy daily stage of duty run;
Shake off dull sloth, and joyful rise
To pay thy morning sacrifice.

By influence of the Light divine
Let thy own light to others shine.
Reflect all Heaven's propitious ways
In ardent love, and cheerful praise.

In conversation be sincere;
Keep conscience as the noontide clear;
Think how all seeing God thy ways
And all thy secret thoughts surveys.

Wake, and lift up thyself, my heart,
And with the angels bear thy part,
Who all night long unwearied sing
High praise to the eternal King.

Praise God, from Whom all blessings flow;
Praise Him, all creatures here below;
Praise Him above, ye heavenly host;
Praise Father, Son, and Holy Ghost.

(Ken 1674)

The eternal God is thy refuge, and underneath are the everlasting arms:

Deuteronomy 33:27

Chapter Nine
Need for a Safe Environment

*E*ach of us has a strong, God-given instinct to nurture and protect our babies. Mothering can be an anxiety-producing endeavor when we consider the many daily activities that could result in injury if safety concerns are ignored. Accurate safety information can help us make decisions that protect our children from needless injury.

As we approach this topic, we should keep in mind that God is the only one who can guarantee a person's safety. How comforting it is to know that our children belong to God, who is sovereign over the events of life. Although we must exercise appropriate caution, we can rest in the fact that He loves our children and has their best interests at heart.

> *Matthew 18:10 "Take heed that ye despise not one of these little ones; for I say unto you, That in heaven their angels do always behold the face of my Father which is in heaven."*

Clothing

Miriam: When Lily was about three months old we had a major ice storm complete with power outages. A thick layer of ice covered everything and under its weight and strong winds, tree branches fell on top of power lines. The electricity was out with no hope of a speedy return. The parsonage didn't have an alternate heating source, so we chose to flee to the city.

All the children were bundled up and buckled in the Suburban with the heat going full blast. My babies were not going to become popsicles! As we pulled out of the drive, I turned around to check on the screaming baby. "She is probably freezing. I have to get my children to civilization fast!" I thought. I took my glove off and put my hand under her blankets. Lily was soaked in sweat! Her whole body was covered. She was warm, way too warm. Oops!

I was in survival mode; unfortunately, I had overcompensated for the weather. It can be difficult keeping a baby the appropriate temperature, especially when the mom is focused on escaping a natural disaster.

This example brings up the question, "How can we appropriately dress the baby? How do we know if he is too cold or too warm?" Healthy term babies usually need to be dressed in the same amount of clothing as anyone else in the same environment. Are you cold? Then the baby may be a bit chilled as well, but if you only need socks and a sweater, don't put a hat, jacket, and blanket on the baby.

If you are warm in a long sleeve shirt, the baby might be too warm as well. Your baby's tummy should feel warm, but his ears should feel fresh or slightly cool. Follow your healthcare provider's advice when it comes to keeping a hat on your baby, but be aware that hats can contribute to overheating. Again, do the ear test. If his ears are warm, your baby is probably too warm.

Babies are too cold when their arms and legs are cool to the touch. A cold baby's skin may be a little blue and he may shiver. If the baby is cool, add a layer. It can be a little tricky keeping a newborn the right temperature, but with some practice you will become an expert.

Safe Transportation

Babies need to be securely transported. Newborns have yet to develop the good head control of older babies. Mothers often carry babies in infant seats, car seats, and strollers. An alternative method of carrying is to use a wrap or sling; this is particularly helpful for new mothers after cesareans. Using a wrap allows your baby to be securely nestled in his favorite place, and you will have your hands free allowing you to carry the diaper bag, carrier, or other objects.

Many mothers find that they can shop, dine out, visit with friends and do pretty much anything with their babies wrapped securely against their chest. There are comfortable front and back infant carriers that the baby's father can use. A popular wrap, the Moby wrap, comes in many colors and patterns so both parents can be happy with their infant carrier.

If you do choose to carry your baby in an infant seat, be sure to strap the baby in completely as soon as you put him in the seat. Most veteran mothers have stories of babies falling out of various swings, bouncy seats, carriers, and car seats. This often happens with the help of a toddler sibling or cousin. It is easy to forget that he isn't strapped in and transport the baby unsafely.

Infants need to have good head control and meet age or weight requirements before they can be placed in certain carriers like backpacks or bicycle toddler seats. Most strollers and pull-behind bike trailers are safe for infants—if the equipment is designated for that age. Be sure to read the instructions carefully on any equipment you plan to use.

While being transported in a vehicle, infants should be secured in a car seat. Infants carried on the driver's lap can be injured by the airbag, become a projectile flying through the car, and nearly always suffer serious injury or death during an accident.

Children need different types of car seats depending on their age and size. Choose the appropriate seat and install it correctly. There are places in most cities that offer car seat testing. Many police departments offer this service, and there are certified car seat safety experts that may be available in your town.

Safe Eating

In the first four months of life, infants should be given nothing to eat besides breast milk or artificial milk. Babies being fed artificial milk often start on infant rice cereal after the fourth month. Artificial milk does not provide adequate nutrition and that deficit becomes more pronounced after the fourth month, so infants need the additional nutrients in the cereal. Breastfed infants do not need additional supplementation, and most recommendations suggest they should not start any kind of complementary foods before six months (AAP 2005, 2012).

The World Health Organization (WHO) recommends that all parts of a bottle including the nipple be sterilized in boiling water before use. All of the parts must be completely covered in boiling water. They should be left in boiling water with a lid on the pot, until the feed is being prepared. Unused prepared formula should be discarded after two hours. WHO has prepared a pamphlet with this information that can be downloaded from their website (WHO 2007).

Water should be boiled prior to use. Some community public water supplies may be too high in fluoride for an infant (CDC 2011a). Also, too much fluoride can be toxic to a baby's developing brain (Grandjean and Landrigan 2006). It is important to mix formula with sterilized fluoride-free water. You can contact your local water supplier for this information or you can go to the CDC website to check your local water supply (apps.nccd.cdc.gov/MWF/Index.asp). If you are using well water, you will need to have it tested to make sure it is safe for a baby.

Safe Play

Your infant may be small now, but it won't be long until he's mobile. This can be a cause for concern in a home that has not been baby-proofed. There are several guidelines to keep in mind in order to protect your child.

Babies need to be safe when they are not being held. They should not be left on elevated surfaces unattended. A blanket on the floor provides a safe place for babies. Even tiny babies are able to roll and fall, but they can't fall off the floor. If you place the baby on the couch, even for a few minutes, the baby can fall. It is also important not to place the baby in his carrier on an elevated surface like a kitchen counter or table. If the baby rocks or shifts enough to move off the elevated surface it could result in a serious accident.

Once a baby is able to roll, any area where he is placed needs to be baby-proofed. This means removal of small objects that could be put in the baby's mouth, padding of sharp corners, and removal of plants and any items that could be damaged, particularly if damage to the object could result in the child being cut or injured as well. As they grow older, you will be able to teach your children to refrain from touching decorative items, but until then, be sure to provide a safe environment for the child.

You can restrict your baby's area of exploration by using gates and play yards, especially when you have to leave the baby to go to the bathroom, answer the door, or check the oven. There are many different baby-proofing items to help you achieve a safe environment.

Safe with Pets

Dogs and cats are often part of our households before a baby comes. It is very common for companion animals to struggle adjusting to the new baby. Pets should never be left alone with access to the baby. Infants can be seriously injured by even small dogs and are not ready to learn how to interact safely with them.

You must teach the dog that the baby belongs to you and you alone. You do not want your dog treating your baby like a puppy. While some dogs may be tolerant of babies, it is important to think about the way that dogs socialize with puppies. If the puppy gets too rambunctious and annoying, the older dog will nip at it, growl, or pick it up and shake. These behaviors could have disastrous results if practiced with a baby.

One of the baby's belongings should be brought home before the baby is. It should be laid in a prominent place and the dog should only be able to smell the object from a respectful distance—the distance that you would expect a well-mannered dog to stay from a guest.

When the baby is brought home, his parents should walk around with the baby into every part of the home showing the dog that this is now the baby's home. The baby should be held above the dog's head and the dog should never be allowed to jump up to the baby's level. The dog should never be allowed to bury his head into the baby's tummy or approach the baby closely.

Whoever is carrying the baby should enter the room before the dog. The dog should never be allowed to walk ahead of the stroller. These simple behaviors reinforce that the baby is above the dog in the pack. The dog will learn to ignore the baby.

> Miriam: We have always had dogs. Some of my earliest memories involve being comforted by a big lab in bed with me when I was afraid of the dark. My husband and I are dog people. When we brought our fourth baby, Lily, home we had a European Great Dane. He was my dog, and he was jealous of Lily. We had to be cautious with him. He was so tall that the baby was accessible to him everywhere but in the crib. It was a challenge teaching him that the baby belonged to me. It took a couple of days.
>
> What seemed to help the most is that I began spending ten to fifteen minutes alone with the dog every day, away from the baby. We also took opportunities to reinforce the baby's status. By the end of the first week it was old news. The dog ignored the baby, except for looking at me when she cried. By the time Lily was six months old, the dog was very tolerant of her; however, we were very careful never to leave them alone together.

The best way to keep a cat out of the baby's space is to shut the door. During the pregnancy begin teaching the cat that the nursery, or your room if the baby will be sleeping there, is off limits. Cats like soft, warm places. Babies are soft and warm. Because a young baby cannot move his head, it is quite possible that an infant could be suffocated from a cat in his bed. Cats may also like to lick the milk off of a baby's face or bat at a baby's wispy hair. Do not leave a cat unsupervised with a baby. It is an old wives tale that a cat "steals the baby's breath," but it is unsafe to allow a cat in the baby's sleep space.

Safe Sleeping

One of the biggest fears that parents face is sudden infant death syndrome (SIDS). SIDS is not the same as suffocation. Suffocation or strangulation occurs when a baby's air supply is cut off by an object such as a blanket, pillow, or cord. It occurs when a baby cannot get enough air or his air way is occluded. SIDS occurs when a baby dies from no known cause.

Sometimes babies stop breathing even though their airway in not occluded. Keeping fluffy blankets and pillows away from your baby will protect him from suffocation but not SIDS. It is important to differentiate between the two, because suffocation is essentially preventable. The two become confused because suffocation can look like SIDS. At times, it is hard for medical examiners to determine the difference.

Many sources discuss swaddling a newborn as a soothing measure and routine practice. If done safely, swaddling can be a reasonable alternative when you are not available to hold your baby. The main concerns with swaddling are that the baby's hips will not develop correctly, be too loose in the socket, or even dislocate. This can occur when the baby's legs are swaddled too tightly for him to flex his hips and assume the position that baby's normally have when laying without a swaddling blanket. A normal posture for a baby is different than an adult's normal posture. To avoid this problem, be sure that your baby's legs are not restricted when he is swaddled.

There are several other concerns with swaddling. The blanket should be tight enough that it doesn't loosen and pose a suffocation hazard but not so tight that it restricts breathing. Once babies can roll over they should not be swaddled. They can roll over onto their faces but then they are unable to use their arms to keep their airway clear. Another concern is that when a baby's arms are swaddled tightly to his sides he will not cue normally for feedings (Mohrbacher 2010). The baby's arms can be swaddled in a flexed position near his face. Infant mitts can prevent the baby from scratching his face, but they also prevent normal cueing and development, and they should not be used routinely.

Swaddling is best used as a soothing measure for an upset baby when the mother can't have skin-to-skin contact with the baby. It can also be used to prevent a newborn from startling himself awake, particularly when he is beginning to establish sleep cycles. Swaddling should not be used for an overly sleepy baby, and skin-to-skin should be used instead of swaddling especially when a baby is not gaining weight well.

Double swaddling, the practice of using one piece of cloth to restrain the baby's arms and another to wrap the baby's entire body, should not be used. This type of swaddling restricts the baby's movement even more than the uterus did. Mothers may be tempted to double swaddle a baby who wriggles free of a swaddle or does not sleep as long as the mother desires, however this type of swaddling can lead to many problems.

There are blankets that are marketed for swaddling. These blankets have Velcro to help make certain that the blanket will not come undone. Some of them are designed in a way that makes it easy to swaddle the baby with the legs and arms flexed. If your baby does not enjoy swaddling or you choose not to use it, a sleep sack is a good alternative. This is a one-piece, gown-like garment that closes at the bottom so the legs stay covered, but it doesn't restrict movement. See Chapter 7 for more information on sleeping.

Safe in Crowds

It can be very tempting to try to take your new baby to church, the store, and other places. We understand that stir-crazy feeling, but it is very important to listen to your healthcare provider's advice and keep the baby away from groups of people for the first six weeks.

The seriousness of a newborn getting an illness must be considered. Even breastfed babies have little immunity built up. When a small baby less than six weeks old becomes ill, it can be very dangerous. Babies who are born prematurely, have spent time in Intensive Care, have had surgery, or have had respiratory syncytial virus (RSV) are at even greater risk and may need a longer time away from crowds.

While a trip to grandma's house and a mostly empty park are probably okay, large family reunions, stores, and even church should be avoided. It is your job to protect your baby; this includes his health. The first six weeks will fly by and you will soon be able to share your favorite activities and places with your baby.

Women with newborns in Old Testament times were expected to take time away from sacred and secular obligations. Breastfeeding women were excused from much of the ritual fasting. God knows that newborn babies and postpartum women have special needs.

Choosing a Caregiver

Most of us would like to be the only caregiver our child ever needs. However, a large portion of new mothers will return to work within the first three months after the baby is born. Although many Christian mothers value staying at home, they often return to work early as well.

We all have different ideas of what a good caregiver looks like. Some might prefer an individual who only cares for two to three children and is able to give the child very flexible, personal attention. Others may prefer a large facility that has more caregivers and a scheduled way of organizing the day. Cost for childcare will be another factor that needs to be considered. You may be fortunate to have childcare provided by your work.

Finding safe, affordable childcare can be a challenge. No one feels comfortable leaving their baby with a stranger. It can help to get recommendations from others who use childcare. Some childcare providers provide a live webcam, so that, parents can observe the facility from the Internet during the workday. A licensed daycare is one that is routinely checked by the state for safety and cleanliness. This is not a guarantee it will be a good place for your baby, but it is an indicator of a healthy environment. You may consider running some type of background check on those involved in the care of your child.

Your child will need to form a close attachment to the person that cares for him during the day. This is critical to his development. Many parents experience jealously when the baby is happy to go to the caregiver or cries when he is picked up from daycare. It can be helpful to understand that this attachment is normal, necessary, and should be encouraged by the parents.

If your child has a marked change in behavior or is more fussy or withdrawn than normal, you may need to make a change with caregivers. If your Mommy Sense is telling you that something isn't right, you need to investigate carefully and be willing to find a different arrangement.

Criteria to consider when selecting a caregiver:

1. Clean facilities: Whether in a private home or another facility, there has to be a level of cleanliness that gives you confidence in the caregiver.

2. Demonstrated kindness and interest in the children: The caregiver(s) should take pleasure and pride in their work. You need to observe at various times while you are trying to choose a specific caregiver. If you become concerned

about the caregiver's attitude, you should watch carefully while reevaluating the situation. You need to meet each person who will be caring for your child.

3. Willingness to follow your specific instructions: This willingness should be evident even if your instructions differ from what the caregiver prefers. For example, if you want your baby fed after his nap and then allowed to fall asleep in a bed when he is tired, the caregiver needs to do this. It can be problematic if your caregiver is not willing to follow your instructions. Of course, there may be things that you do at home, that would not be feasible to do in a setting with several babies.

4. Each child has their own safe sleeping space and supplies.

5. For an out of home daycare facility, ask about turnover rate for workers.

6. For an in home daycare, find out who will be in the home.

7. Will your child ever be taken out of the home or facility? Are you confident that this person will have adequate help with multiple children in other environments?

8. The childcare provider needs to share your philosophy of childrearing and support your efforts as a mother. Does this person share your faith, morals, and ethics? Is this the type of person you would be comfortable lending your car to? Would you be comfortable with this person house sitting for you? Do you trust their overall judgment?

Our children are our most precious possessions entrusted to us by God. We must be prudent to do everything in our power to make sure that they are cared for in safe, loving environments.

Childcare can be very expensive, especially young infants and families with multiple children. Unless a parent's income is significant, it can be less expensive for a parent to stay home with the children. When your commute, wardrobe, lunch money, and childcare costs are subtracted from your paycheck, the take home pay may not be worth all of the effort, even for mothers bringing home an average income. This is particularly true if there are multiple children needing childcare.

Miriam: I have been able to use limited childcare because I have worked hard to ensure that my schedule allows either myself or my husband to be available to care for the children. I have worked full-time, part-time, occasionally, and stayed home full-time with my children. Coordinating childcare and my work with my husband's work has been a juggling act at times, but it is worth the effort to make sure that the children have safe and loving care.

Ronda: My husband and I were blessed to have daycare provided in an on-site facility for all our children. This well-maintained facility provided a wonderful staff of women who clearly cared for each child. Although the facility cared for a number of children simultaneously, there was always adequate staffing to meet the children's needs. Specific instructions were welcomed and followed. It provided great peace of mind to know that our children were being cared for safely.

The decisions regarding childcare should be made prayerfully, with consideration of everyone's needs. Some families decide that one parent should stay home or work part-time, in order to provide care for the children. This decision can be difficult financially since many benefits are not available for part-time workers. Parents may decide to forgo extra debt, a car payment, and fancy vacations in order to make this a possibility.

Sometimes it simply isn't possible for a parent to provide all childcare. Consider what Hannah did with Samuel, her firstborn, long-awaited son. She sent him as a young child to live with Eli the priest and his family. She was doing what she knew God had called her to do, nevertheless, what an act of faith! God protected Samuel in Eli's house (1 Samuel 1: 1-28).

Moses was taken from his mother as a young child and reared as a prince of Egypt (Exodus 2:1-10). Boaz's firstborn son was nursed by Naomi, not Ruth (Ruth 4:16). We see several instances in the Bible when a caregiver other than the biological mother took good care of a child.

There is always concern when mothers need to leave their young babies with caregivers. This is natural and part of the way that God created mothers to respond to separation from their babies. You need the peace that comes from knowing that you are doing what God wants you to do. This peace can be obtained through prayer, careful weighing of your options, finding a good caregiver, and trusting God.

Sometimes a scripture verse, song, or hymn can bring us peace when our minds begin to stray to troubling thoughts. After we have dealt with valid concerns, we need to focus our minds on good things (Philippians 4:8). The hymn, *I Need Thee Every Hour*, and others that assure us of God's sufficiency for all areas of life can bring comfort.

I Need Thee Every Hour

I need Thee every hour, most gracious Lord;
No tender voice like Thine can peace afford.

I need Thee every hour, stay Thou nearby;
Temptations lose their pow'r when Thou art nigh.

I need Thee every hour, in joy or pain;
Come quickly and abide, or life is vain.

I need Thee every hour; teach me Thy will;
And Thy rich promises in me fulfill.

I need Thee every hour, most Holy One;
Oh, make me Thine indeed, Thou blessed Son

Chorus:
I need Thee, oh, I need Thee;
Every hour I need Thee;
Oh, bless me now, my Savior,
I come to Thee.

(Hawks and Lowry 1872)

Summary

This chapter has covered a number of topics related to safety for your newborn. It is difficult to be vigilant every minute of time, but your newborn is very vulnerable, and it is important to be aware of his surroundings. Making safe choices about clothing, nutrition, and environmental safety issues also gives you the ability to enjoy your newborn while you are together.

Safe sleeping choices will help you both get the rest you need so that you can do it all over again the next day! Choosing the right caregiver when you are not with your infant allows you to relax and perform the other responsibilities of your life, without having to worry about your child while apart. Trusting in God and His goodness is necessary as we face all the challenges and worries of motherhood.

But whoso hath this world's good, and seeth his brother have need, and shutteth up his bowels of compassion from him, how dwelleth the love of God in him? My little children, let us not love in word, neither in tongue; but in deed and in truth.

1 John 3:17-18

Chapter Ten

Need for Love

God made a promise to the righteous in Israel that one day they would experience peace, joy, comfort, and material blessings. He compares their reward to what a child experiences when loved by his mother.

> *Isaiah 66:10-14* ¹⁰ *Rejoice ye with Jerusalem, and be glad with her, all ye that love her: rejoice for joy with her, all ye that mourn for her:* ¹¹ *That ye may suck, and be satisfied with the breasts of her consolations; that ye may milk out, and be delighted with the abundance of her glory.* ¹² *For thus saith the LORD, Behold, I will extend peace to her like a river, and the glory of the Gentiles like a flowing stream: then shall ye suck, ye shall be borne upon her sides, and be dandled upon her knees.* ¹³ *As one whom his mother comforteth, so will I comfort you; and ye shall be comforted in Jerusalem.* ^{14a} *And when ye see this, your heart shall rejoice, and your bones shall flourish like an herb: and the hand of the LORD shall be known toward his servants,*

One of the sweetest experiences of motherhood is rocking our babies to sleep; those serene moments we spend inhaling the baby's scent and rubbing our cheek against their soft head. These invaluable moments bring a sense of peace and love.

> Miriam: In the early days, when babies sleep so much, I remember waking each of them just to look into their eyes and win a smile. My mom tells the story of my dad trying to have special times with me when I was a newborn. He worked near the house and frequently came in to watch me sleep. He couldn't seem to catch me while I was awake. Finally my mom told him, "You know, you can wake her up and play with her." Dad was delighted.

Parents and babies need intimate moments of shared love like these. Love is one of the most basic needs we have as humans. Parents do not need to "have it all" in order to rear a loved child but they must give and receive love in healthy ways. If a baby does not receive love, he will not develop properly. Loving a child sets him up for a successful life. In this chapter, we will first look at the different ways of showing love and then at the tools available for providing love.

We tend to idealize motherhood. We think of those beautiful portraits of Madonna and child, and visualize having those perfect moments for ourselves. We want to feel the right emotions at the right times and have it all together. Here is a secret; even the best moms only have it "together" part of the time.

Sometimes our expectations are unrealistic. We each experience special times, but those moments do not make up life. We also have messes to clean, tears to wipe away, illnesses to pray through, and all the other challenges of life.

We need to focus on what God requires of us as mothers. What God requires of you may be different from what He requires of another mother. Your baby is a unique individual. His needs may be very different than other babies. Your mothering style will be different as well. After all, there is only one you!

God designed you distinctively and His love for you is great. You will succeed, as long as you follow the principles of love, grace, and mercy in parenting. Your individualism brings glory to God!

> *Isaiah 43:7 "Even every one that is called by my name: for I have created him for my glory, I have formed him; yea, I have made him."*

God is infinitely creative and active. He glories in the special way that He made you and the unique way that you reflect glory back to Him. As you seek Him, you will become more like Him. But He is infinite, so this means you will also become more your unique self!

You don't have to "have it all together" in order to love your baby the way God intends. Remember, the goal is to please God, and He never asks anything of us that we cannot do in His grace and strength. The problem many of us have is that we confuse pleasing God with pleasing ourselves or others. This is when life can become impossible to deal with. We often put expectations on ourselves that are not from God. It is helpful to refocus on what God requires from us.

> *Micah 6:8 "He hath shewed you, O man, what is good; and what doth the LORD require of thee, but to do justly, and to love mercy, and to walk humbly with thy God?"*

If you are giving love to your baby in healthy ways, it is pleasing to God.

Matthew 22:36-40 [36] *"Master, which is the great commandment in the law?* [37] *Jesus said unto him, Thou shalt love the Lord thy God with all thy heart, and with all thy soul, and with all thy mind.* [38] *This is the first and great commandment.* [39] *And the second is like unto it, Thou shalt love thy neighbour as thyself.* [40] *On these two commandments hang all the law and the prophets."*

In order to love our babies properly, we must first consider this question: "How do babies experience love?" Babies experience love when their physical, emotional, intellectual, and spiritual needs are met.

Physical Needs

How do you know that you are loved? If your husband was sitting on the couch and you went to him for a hug and he refused to touch you or hug you when you asked, would you feel loved? If he refused to stop the car and get you a drink, because you *just ate* two hours ago, would you feel loved? What if your husband didn't speak your language and you couldn't understand a word he said, would it be difficult for you to feel that he loved you?

Think about your baby. Some infant guides suggest that babies only be fed every three to four hours. Perhaps you only eat every three to four hours, but as a breastfeeding mother, you probably drink often throughout the day to get all the water you need. Do you think your baby might be thirsty more often than every three to four hours?

When mothers insist on a regimented feeding schedule and ignore the baby while he cries, the baby will not understand her love. Babies understand love when their needs are met. Parenting literature often maintains the dangers of instant gratification and the need to teach babies patience. This is not appropriate in the newborn period, since the newborn does not have the mental capacity to understand that concept. Mothers should take the time to understand the baby's needs in that moment and then promptly meet them.

If your baby is crying because he is lonely, but you ignore him to teach him patience, it is not showing love to the baby. What if your husband said, "You know, you want to hold my hand whenever we are out driving, but you just need to be patient and wait." Would you wonder about his love for you?

You know your husband loves you when he demonstrates his desire to be with you; he hugs you and holds your hand. He would never keep you from getting a drink when you needed it or keep you from eating when you were hungry. He loves you in very practical ways. This is how we love our babies: in very practical ways by meeting their need for touch, cuddling, food, drink, warmth, and rest.

It will be appropriate as your child grows to help him learn patience, but we need to be sensible. If you don't routinely make your older child wait for more than an hour for a drink of water when he asks for one, why would you make your newborn wait for a drink? There will be many opportunities to teach delayed gratification as your child grows.

Touch

The need for cuddling and touch is as critical as the need for food. Extensive research shows this to be true. Touch can literally mean the difference between life and death. Your baby physically needs to be rocked and held.

Miriam: When I was a nursing student, I had the opportunity to spend a day in the NICU. They sent me to what was called the "feeders and growers" room. The nurse was caring for five babies. Several times throughout the morning a couple of the babies had a bradycardic episode when their heart rates dropped too low and they stopped breathing. The nurse would walk over to the baby, rub his back, and talk to him. Immediately, his heart rate would increase and he would begin breathing again.

One time the nurse was very busy with a baby and another baby had a bradycardic episode. The nurse asked me to go to that baby. After just a second or two of feeling me gently rub his back and talk to him, his breathing and heart rate returned to normal. I was amazed at how needy those babies were for loving touch and the stimulation of another person.

Dr. Nils Bergman, in his work with mothers in Africa, found that when premature babies were placed skin-to-skin with their mothers that the death rate was dramatically reduced. This became the basis for a method of premature infant care called Kangaroo Mother Care, which emphasizes skin-to-skin contact, early breastfeeding, and lots of encouragement and support for mom and baby (Bergman and Jürisoo 1994).

Miriam: When Lily, my fourth child, was six weeks old she became very ill with respiratory syncytial virus (RSV) and was placed on a ventilator. When she was weaned from the ventilator her respiratory effort was significantly better when I stood next to her isolette, talked to her, held her hand, and cuddled her. In fact, the nurses would report, "She stays within parameters only when the mother is in immediate contact." If I stepped away even for a moment, her oxygen saturation decreased. The effects of my presence were profound and we were thankful that we had the opportunity to be with her all day and night.

Skin-to-skin is not only for preterm babies. Even full-term babies receive benefits from skin-to-skin contact. Separating mom and baby carries significant risks. A baby that is not in contact with his mother is likely to have more problems maintaining blood sugar levels and staying warm. Another risk that can arise is an abnormal heart rate and breathing rate when away from the mother. "Skin-to-skin contact between mother and baby at birth reduces crying, improves mother-baby interaction, keeps the baby warmer, and helps women breastfeed successfully" (Moore, Anderson, and Bergman 2007). Not only do many research studies show that regular, loving, physical contact needs to be a part of your baby's day, your own Mommy Sense will as well.

> *Matthew 19:14-15* [14] *"But Jesus said, Suffer little children, and forbid them not, to come unto me: for of such is the kingdom of heaven. 15 And he laid his hands on them, and departed thence."*

Every mother and baby is a unique individual. God in His amazing creativity planned these differences. You can be the mother God made you to be. This means you may wear your baby in a sling all day or you may utilize an infant swing or other safe place at times. These are both okay. An important aspect of this book is to let you know about needs of your child. When you are meeting your child's needs and following the principles of compassion, love, and mercy, you have a great amount of Christian liberty. It is important to not compare yourself with others in this area.

Other Physical Care

> *Matthew 7:9-12* [9] *"Or what man is there of you, whom if his son ask bread, will he give him a stone?* [10] *Or if he ask a fish, will he give him a serpent?* [11] *If ye then, being evil, know how to give good gifts unto your children, how much more shall your Father which is in heaven give good things to them that ask him?* [12] *Therefore all things whatsoever ye would that men should do to you, do ye even so to them: for this is the law and the prophets."*

Your baby needs to be safe, warm, fed, and clean. Providing for these needs promptly is the most basic way of telling your baby, "I love you."

Matthew 6:8b "Your Father knoweth what things ye have need of, before ye ask him."

God often compares Himself to a parent. Just as you will become very adept at anticipating your baby's needs, God knows what your needs are. We can look to His example in preparing to meet our baby's needs.

There is an amazing hormone in your body called oxytocin. This is the hormone that helps you to feel love for your baby, spouse, family, and friends. It is released especially during breastfeeding. Each time a mommy feeds her baby, oxytocin is released. This means every time you respond to your baby's need for food or drink, you are strengthening your love.

Oxytocin helps you to feel deep connectedness to your baby. Breastfeeding gives your body many opportunities every day for oxytocin to work its magic in the relationship. If you choose to feed your baby artificial milk, you will miss out on one of God's designed blessings. This is not meant to say that mothers who use formula do not love their babies. It simply means that breastfeeding mothers have the extra physiologic help of oxytocin.

Babies do not have extensive material needs. A baby is just as happy in a used infant carrier as a brand new one. Your baby will be happier in your arms than in any bouncer, activity center, or swing. A baby does not care what he is wearing as long as it is warm and soft. Your baby has yet to identify a desired brand or color scheme. He is happy with your face, your body, your milk, and your voice. God will provide for you, so that you can provide for your baby.

Philippians 4:19 "But my God shall supply all your need according to his riches in glory by Christ Jesus."

Emotional Needs

Just as an adult longs for companionship and love, so does a baby. Adults often need the comfort that God gives through His Word. Babies do not understand the concept of God or trusting in God, but they do understand the comfort they receive from the ones who rock, sing, cuddle, and feed them. A baby's need for love is just as valid as his need for food, warmth, and shelter.

2 Corinthians 1:3-4 [3] "Blessed be God, even the Father of our Lord Jesus Christ, the Father of mercies, and the God of all comfort; [4] Who comforteth

us in all our tribulation, that we may be able to comfort them which are in any trouble, by the comfort wherewith we ourselves are comforted of God."

As a new mother, God will give you the ability to comfort your baby. This does not mean that your baby will never cry or will easily be consoled by you, but it does mean that God promises to meet your need when you ask Him for help. You won't be able to provide for every need immediately, but babies are quite resilient. It won't alter a baby's personality if he has to occasionally wait for his needs to be met. However, we should be sure this is the exception and not the norm. Just as God provides for our needs, we should strive to meet the needs of our babies.

There are times that we have to allow the baby to cry, while we do something he doesn't like. You may have to restrain the baby during a shot or a blood draw. Or, you may choose to continue driving home while your baby cries, knowing that you will be home in a couple minutes and be able to meet the baby's need. At other times you may choose to stop and console the baby, knowing you don't have a better location to stop just down the road. God knows the pain that comes from listening to your baby in distress, and He will give you the wisdom to know when to allow the baby to cry and when to comfort the baby. He will comfort your heart with the ability to comfort your baby.

Ronda: We did a lot of traveling from Florida to Indiana when our children were babies. I can still pick out places along the way where we had to stop, just to console a baby. Once when we were parked along the interstate, a man stopped to see if we needed help. At that point, we really wished that he could help. On another trip we were traveling without air conditioning and took pictures of our furious son, Rob, when he had had enough. Those will probably come in handy some day!

Intellectual Needs

Babies have complex brains that are developing at an amazing rate. In order to develop properly, a baby's brain must receive appropriate types and amounts of stimulation. It seldom takes much to stimulate a newborn's brain appropriately. Consider the kind of environment from which a newborn has just emerged. While a baby in the womb can taste, see, smell, and feel, the input is much less than they will experience after birth.

A newborn who is cuddled by a family member in the middle of a noisy living room receives ample stimulation. Have you ever noticed how tiny babies often fall asleep at the mall or in a noisy restaurant? That is a coping mechanism for infants. Their bodies shut out some of the input by sleeping. This is also why small babies scream in these types of environments. The screaming shuts out all the other input, too. Sometimes babies will scream hysterically and then suddenly fall asleep. It is much easier to cope with those behaviors once you understand the underlying cause.

Infant swings, mobiles, and bouncy seats provide many different types of stimulation, although the best way for your baby to learn is by being held in your arms. Babies enjoy looking at contrasting colors, wavy lines, and spinning ceiling fans. Your baby is hard-wired to look at human faces, especially mom and dad's. Hearing your voice, tasting your milk, feeling your skin are perfect sensory experiences for your newborn to four month old.

Spiritual Needs

Newborns are spiritual beings too. By meeting your baby's physical and intellectual needs in a loving atmosphere, you are preparing your baby to accept that there is a loving God who desires a personal relationship with him. Feeling desired or wanted by his parents makes it much easier for someone to believe that God desires him.

Initially, your baby learns that his needs will be met. At the very beginning, he won't even know that *you* are taking care of all of his needs. Of course, he won't be thinking, "Oh goody, all my needs are met." Babies do not think in words, but rather in feelings. As he gets older, he will recognize that his needs are met by you, which builds trust and helps your baby learn what love is. You will be rewarded by his smiles, coos, and laughter. Our babies learn to trust us just like we learn to trust God, one step at a time.

As you build a relationship of trust with your baby, he will prefer you above anyone else. He'll begin to gaze deep into your eyes and respond to the sound of your voice, even from across the room. He will know that his mommy fixes all those problems that babies have. When he is older, he will learn that you, too, have needs. As you walk with God and reflect Him in your life, your child will see that God meets your needs. You will have the opportunity to teach him that it is ultimately God who provides for us all.

> *Isaiah 28:9-10 [9] "Whom shall he teach knowledge? and whom shall he make to understand doctrine? them that are weaned from the milk, and drawn from the breasts. [10] For precept must be upon precept, precept upon precept; line upon line, line upon line; here a little, and there a little:"*

These verses recognize that small children must learn lessons one piece at a time and then repeat them, just like verse 10. You will have the opportunity to teach your young child about God a little at a time. As a baby, these lessons are very rudimentary; you are teaching your baby what love is! A tiny bit as each need is met, a little more each day. The care you give your baby now will count for eternity. None of your love, time, and sacrifice, is wasted if it is offered in worship to God. If you meet your baby's needs to the best of your ability, that is accepted by God and pleases Him. Are you thankful to God for your baby? He accepts sacrifices of praise and thanksgiving as worship. We have the wonderful privilege of worshipping God as we love and appreciate our baby as His gift.

> *Psalm 107:22 "And let them sacrifice the sacrifices of thanksgiving, and declare his works with rejoicing."*

Do you praise Him because your baby is fearfully and wonderfully made?

> *Hebrews 13:15 "By him therefore let us offer the sacrifice of praise to God continually, that is, the fruit of our lips giving thanks to his name."*

God cares about you and your infant. He has provided for your baby's spiritual needs through you now and ultimately through the sacrifice of His own son, Jesus. Pray for your infant now: for your baby's present and future. Pray that as soon as he is old enough to understand the gospel that he will believe in Christ alone as his personal Savior (John 3:16). Many children are capable of understanding and responding to the gospel by age five or six and some are ready even younger.

Do you understand salvation well enough to explain it to a five or six year old? If not, begin preparing now. The book, *The Lamb*, is an excellent resource for parents of five and six year olds (Cross and Mastin 2004). Work on keeping your explanation simple.

What must be believed in order to receive eternal life? What constitutes saving faith? "Saving faith is the belief in Jesus Christ as the Son of God who died and rose again to pay one's personal penalty for sin and the one who gives eternal life to all who trust Him and Him alone for it" (Hixson 2008, 84). Saving faith does not require a complex understanding of theology. God reminds us that we should have the faith of a little child (Luke 18:17).

Another way to meet your newborn's spiritual needs is to surround him with beautiful music. Singing or playing music for your baby is a great way to minister to his spirit. Music can bring an atmosphere of peace and tranquility to your home.

Spend some time looking for worshipful music. Music can be a big help in getting you through your day as well. There are many resources available that provide a wide selection of free music. Lullabies and other songs that you sing to your baby are a fantastic way of connecting with him.

Relational Needs

Strengthening the network of relationships in your life allows you to meet your need for relationships and paves the way for your baby to have relationships with others. The most important networks consist of your immediate family, your parents, siblings, and your extended family. Other networks may include your church, friends, and work.

Primary Caregiver

The family is the primary unit God designed for giving your baby love; no substitute can do it like you can. A newborn recognizes his mother's scent from the first moments after birth and can respond to the voice of their father. Your baby is ready from day one to join your family's network.

A baby is designed to deeply bond with one or two primary caregivers. A primary caregiver is the person who spends the most time providing care for the baby. If you go back to work full-time when your baby is six weeks old, frequently get a weekend sitter, and put the baby to sleep in his own room all night, that leaves very few hours a day to spend quality time with him. At that point, you are not the primary caregiver; grandma or the daycare worker is. Sometimes it is hard to accept the reality of our situation. You cannot fit a baby into the corners of your life (early mornings and early evenings) and have the same level of bonding that comes from spending hours day and night with your baby.

If you must work, it is important to spend the majority of time away from work with your baby, in order to keep that connection strong and viable. As we have said, we all have to make healthy choices and take responsibility for the outcomes.

Along with a consistent, loving presence during the day, a baby needs routine. The consistency of a cheerful environment will bring the security that your baby must have in order to develop properly. When you are truly unable to stay home with your infant, you can find a loving, committed caregiver who can provide for the baby's needs while you are working. It is important to allow your baby to form a close, emotional attachment to that person. She needs to be a consistent presence in your baby's life. If you work full-time, make an effort not to resent your infant or toddler's preference for this person. It reflects a normal and desired response in your baby.

A word of caution, if your husband works nightshift and needs to sleep during the day, it is almost always a bad idea to have him care for the baby during the daytime hours while you are at work and vice versa. This will put severe stress on all of the relationships in your family, especially as the baby is awake more during the day.

> Miriam: When my first baby, Beka, was a year old, we had the opportunity to have a trusted friend and her daughter care for her in our home during the two or three days a week that I worked. I was so relieved when Beka would run to greet her when she walked in the door. There was a small part of me that wanted all of my child's love, but I was really overwhelmed with gratitude that we had a caregiver who truly loved our child and was someone we could trust.

Balancing the Primary Caregiver Role and Work

The working mother can employ other strategies to retain the role of primary caregiver. She might choose to avoid overtime hours or choose to run errands once a week and keep her evenings free for the family. She can ask that the baby be brought to her or go to him on her lunch break. She can awaken him in the early morning hours or adjust the evening schedule to allow more time together.

If you work until 4 or 5 p.m., putting the baby to bed in the early evening is probably counterproductive to building a strong relationship. By keeping him up longer, you will have more time together, and he will adjust his sleeping patterns. Your relationship is more important than a routine. You may choose to sleep with your baby at night while following all recommended safety precautions or using a co-sleeper, so that you each can hear, feel, and smell each other all night. This can be a very successful way to reconnect with your baby and maintain the role of primary caregiver.

> Miriam: When I had Jac, my second child, my husband was in seminary full-time. We needed to get through one more year of classes. Shannon and I were focused on the long-term plan for providing for our family. We knew we had to get through this difficult year, in order to serve God to the best of our abilities. I had the opportunity to train as a labor and delivery nurse, if I would agree to work full-time for one year on the night shift.
>
> We prayed and fasted about this decision; we both believed that this was God's plan for us for a short term. I took the job. I was able to train in

a specialty that I loved, and Shannon was able to complete his master's degree. He also worked a part time job. Every minute I wasn't at work, I was with my babies. During the day while I slept, college girls came over to my home; they took care of the children, cooked meals, and cleaned the house.

I could feed Jac anytime he needed it. He took many of his naps in my arms as we both slept. If Beka was having a rough moment, I knew about it. It certainly wasn't easy, but we made it through. Even though it was not what I would consider the ideal situation, it was the best we could do, and God in His mercy made up the difference.

If you are working, days off and weekends can be spent with your spouse and baby. Do not employ a sitter unless you must have one. You may choose to keep your newborn with you during church and take your baby to run your errands. It is important to make choices that work best for your family, since God has given the responsibility of your family to you and your husband.

Miriam: The sweet ladies at church really wanted to keep Beka in the nursery, but I couldn't stand to put her in there. I knew that they would take good care of her, but I wanted to be with her. She was my baby. I remember when family would come to visit and feeling relieved when it was time to feed her, because I would finally get her all to myself.

It is critical to allow time to nurture the relationship with your spouse, not only for your mutual happiness but also for the security of your baby. While your baby is so young, it may be helpful to go on dates taking the baby along.

Some couples may live away from family or close friends that they would trust to watch their baby. These couples may choose to have a date night with the baby or at home while he is napping. As your baby transitions out of the newborn period, it will be easier to get out together more regularly. It may be encouraging to remember the newborn period only lasts 12-16 weeks.

As a side note to the suggestion of date nights, couples are at different places in their relationships. Some parents may not feel that they can "date" with the baby around, and some parents would not even consider leaving the newborn with a sitter except for work. You do not need to leave the baby for a date night unless you or your spouse feels that is needed. There is nothing in Scripture mandating a date night without the children every week, although it is a healthy practice that helps many couples with their marriage.

There are many aspects to your married life, and you should experience personal fulfillment stemming from the relationship with your husband. However, that fulfillment is not the goal of your marriage but a byproduct of your relationship. Your marriage is to be a picture of Christ and the church. Your responsibility as a Christian is to advance the kingdom of Christ.

A large part of this responsibility is accomplished through the rearing of godly children. In this path, you will find joy and fulfillment. As a parent, you are called to become mature and to take on the roles of wife and mother. You need to focus a good portion of your life on rearing your children in a way that directs them to lead godly lives.

Dad's Role

It is important for dads to feel connected to their babies too. Give him the baby to hold and cuddle right away. He may not be able to feed the baby, but he can connect in other ways: bathing, burping, rocking, massaging, dressing, and diapering. Don't underestimate him. He may be awkward at first, but if you are careful to encourage, you will have an able helper.

Your baby needs his dad. Fathers generally provide different kinds and intensities of stimulation for the baby. This masculine presence is important for development of a healthy child. Unless he is doing something truly dangerous (like throwing a young baby in the air or rough housing with a newborn) do not correct him. It is your responsibility to maintain the safety of your child. If he puts the diaper on incorrectly, ignore it. Thank him for his help. Of course, if it falls off or creates a problem, he'll figure out there needs to be some re-working.

> Ronda: My husband, Bob, was a wonderful caregiver with all our babies. He would take Kathy outside to sit on the front porch for a change of scenery whenever she was grumpy. She loved it and would always quiet down for him. He watched each of the kids from an early age if I had to go somewhere. He enjoyed the playtime, but also the more mundane tasks of bathing and rocking them.

For Single Mothers

If you are rearing your child alone, you are experiencing additional challenges and perhaps some suggestions in this book will seem unrealistic. The reality is that your situation is more common than any of us wish. Here are some suggestions for sharing the experience of your baby with your family.

If it is possible, keep grandpa close to your baby. Perhaps you have a brother who is willing to be involved with your child and is a safe person for your child to be with; encourage that involvement. Consider moving close to family who will help you give your child all the love he needs.

Protect those relationships that will enhance the life of your child. This is the time to draw family, church family, and friends close to you. Find people that you can trust to help you love your baby. Although it is natural to feel love for a baby, it is not easy to make all of the sacrifices that must be made on a daily basis to meet a baby's needs. Consistently showing love is difficult, and becomes more difficult when you have the full responsibility for your child's care. You will need help. Be sure to ask God for the wisdom He promises to give.

Extended Family

Extended family is an important part of your newborn's world. Not many people care how many times the baby pooped today or if he smiled, but your extended family probably will. Many of us live far away from our families, but do your best to keep your family in the loop. Your extended family is possibly the only other people who will love your baby close to the way you do.

One day your newborn will grow up, and your family will be a part of your child's support system. You will determine a large part of that relationship. You may not always be available to your child. One of the best gifts you can give your child is a good start to healthy relationships with extended family members. This process begins in the newborn period.

Grandparents, aunts, uncles, and cousins will be excited to see the new baby. Do what you can to encourage those visits and interactions. This is more for the family than the baby, but if they connect solidly with this tiny, new person now, they will be more likely to desire interactions (read "babysitting") and give support later.

Ronda: Extended family events have been an important part of our family's life. We live twelve hours away from most of our family, but we have made the effort to take trips home for vacation times nearly every year of the 23 years we've lived in Florida. That is a significant commitment, but we have been there for almost every family reunion, many weddings, and even funerals.

Our children have good relationships with our brothers and sisters, some cousins, aunts, and uncles. We believe this has bound our children closer to each other and to our extended family and given them a sense of who they are. We have fun reminiscing about family camping reunions that happened years ago, because we were there to experience it firsthand.

Summary

Babies experience love through the senses: cuddling in your arms, suckling from your breasts, skin-to-skin contact, sounds from your voice, and sights of your face. You are meant to sustain the life of your newborn with your physical body, intellect, emotions, and with your spirit. This is why mothering can be the most satisfying and the most challenging job in the world.

Love is not a decked out baby room. Love is not designer baby clothes. Love is not a possession or an acquisition. We all want to provide the best possible life for our children, but a lack of possessions does not mean a lack of love. You don't need things to meet the needs of your baby. You need love—God's love shining through you as you choose to meet your baby's needs with your presence and His grace.

You may not always feel love for your baby. Sometimes you will feel frustrated, tired, and angry. When you choose to put your feelings aside and meet your baby's needs instead, you are showing love. When you choose to feed your baby again, even though you really want to start dinner, clear the table, talk on the phone, or take a shower, you are showing love. You can be confident that *this sacrifice pleases God*.

In my distress I called upon the LORD, and cried unto my God: he heard my voice out of his temple, and my cry came before him, even into his ears.

Psalm 18:6

Chapter Eleven

Coping with Crying and Other Concerns

Miriam: I thought that after having five children and being a labor and delivery nurse and lactation consultant that I would know everything about newborns, but I was wrong. Caring for Shannon, my fifth baby, provided more opportunities to learn and grow as a mother. It is so satisfying to be able to soothe him when he is fussy, or decipher his cues when he is hungry or tired. I have enjoyed perfecting my mothering skills, and my husband, Shannon, takes great pride in his abilities as a father.

When Shannon and I were new parents we had so much to learn; there were many times when the baby would do something that perplexed us. Little did we know that the behaviors we saw were common to many newborns, and the solutions to many worrisome problems were usually simple.

This chapter covers many common concerns and questions that first time parents have. Some of the topics covered include crying, calming techniques, illnesses, finding safe health advice, and responding to problems with gentleness.

Crying

Babies cry! The sound of a baby crying is designed to be extremely distressing. You are hardwired to respond to your baby when he cries, but what does the baby's cry mean, and how can you decipher it?

Miriam: I remember shopping at the mall with a friend who had a new baby. He became hungry; so she stopped in a dressing room to nurse him. She came out after 10 minutes. The baby seemed content for two or three minutes then he began crying.

"I don't know what's wrong with him," she said, looking distressed.

"He's hungry."

"But he can't be. I just fed him."

"Well, he's hungry."

She looked at me skeptically, went back in the dressing room and fed him for 10 more minutes. After that, he slept for several hours. Later that day he was crying again.

"Why is he crying?" she asked.

"He's probably wet."

Guess what? He was wet. How did I know? I had two toddlers at the time, my problem solving skills had been thoroughly exercised, and I wasn't feeling overwhelmed with a new baby. Feeling overwhelmed has a negative effect on your critical thinking skills, which is why having helpers those first few weeks is important.

Responding to your baby's cry requires using both your emotions and critical thinking skills. If your emotions are working properly, you will experience a strong urge to quiet your baby's crying. God gave you emotions, so listen to them. God also gave you a mind to solve problems. The more time you spend with your baby, the better you will become at quickly and effectively meeting his needs. Instead of feeling overwhelmed, you will be able to respond intuitively.

The Cry Signals a True Need

The newborn's cry is a reflexive response to a need. Expecting the baby to resist the urge to cry would be like expecting you to avoid flinching if someone threw a dart at you. In fact, a baby who didn't exhibit the crying reflex would display a serious problem with brain function.

A newborn baby doesn't know what his cry means or have the ability to consider that "If I cry, she will feed me." It takes time for the baby to learn that specific intentional actions get specific results.

When your baby cries, he is simply communicating a need. The great news is you can meet it! If he's wet or dirty, change him. If he's hot or cold, subtract or add layers. If he's hungry, feed him. If he's lonely, comfort him. The need for your presence is legitimate, and can be easily met by cuddling him. All needs can generate a cry, because the baby is very limited in his ability to communicate.

Babies do begin with subtle, specific cues, but if subtle cues go unnoticed crying occurs. If the problem is not quickly addressed the crying will escalate, and is more difficult to quiet, because the baby is no longer giving all of the situation-specific cues. Now, the parent will need to find the cause of the crying, fix the problem, and calm the baby all while receiving a loud, distressing signal. No wonder listening to a baby cry is so upsetting!

Some babies give early cues more often and for longer periods, while others may skip most of the early cues and go straight for crying. As you observe your baby's cueing habits, you can find out a good deal about his personality. If your baby cues for a short time before crying, you will need to be more careful to respond to his early cues so that he will not be exasperated and will learn to trust you. Some babies are very laid back and will tolerate being ignored for long periods, but they still need their mothers to actively engage them throughout the day. Even in the newborn period you can influence your baby's personality! Through learning early cues and careful observation, you can become an expert about your baby!

Recognizing Cues and Responding to Needs

There are two amazing tools that will help you communicate with your baby and decrease crying. Identify his early, situation-specific cues, and then respond to his needs by using the simple strategies outlined in the following paragraphs. Choosing to engage in this delicate dance of communication takes some practice, but it is an incredibly rewarding experience!

Hunger: This involves sucking on hands, sucking movements with the tongue and mouth, turning the head and rooting, and licking the lips. Newborns will often give these cues for several minutes at a time and then fall back to sleep. Falling back to sleep doesn't mean the baby wasn't hungry, the rest period conserves his energy before beginning the next cueing sequence. If he could think in words, he would be saying, "No one fed me that time; I guess I'll try again later." As you begin to understand your baby's cues, you will be able to recognize and respond to the first cuing sequence. This will result in less crying, better breastfeeding, increased growth, and more contentment for mother and baby.

Burping: Babies who need to be burped will often cue their need by spitting up milk. Babies who spit up after nursing will often benefit from being burped before and after a feeding. You may not hear a burp, but this doesn't mean the extra air has not been expelled.

Gas or Bowel Movement: You may notice that your baby has a strained look on his face, draws up his legs, or is not taking a full feeding. The best way to avoid a gassy baby is to burp him often. If he doesn't have a lot of gas, he may not need to be burped as often. As one lactation consultant likes to say, "It's a lot easier to get rid of a gas bubble when it's in the tummy, than to wait till it passes all the way through the body." Laying the baby on his tummy or patting his back can help with gas discomfort. Babies who are straining to have a bowel movement or pass gas can be helped by allowing free movement of their legs. A baby will also have less straining in a sitting position with his back against your chest and knees flexed in front of the tummy (essentially a squatting position).

Discomfort: The baby may be uncomfortable and may cue for a position change by squirming or fussing. Always check him carefully if he continues to cry after other solutions have been tried. Check the toes and fingers for threads or hairs wrapped around them. Check zippers, snaps, and pins in the baby's clothing. Check for diaper discomfort from the diaper rubbing on baby's skin, diaper rash, or soiling.

Sleep: When babies are overtired they will no longer interact in a calm manner. They will cue for sleep by yawning, fussing, or looking away from your face or other stimuli. Tired babies may need help going to sleep. Rocking, singing, cuddling, and suckling can help an overtired baby drift off.

Although not scientifically verified, the work *Dunstan Baby Language* by Priscilla Dunstan regarding the cues babies give for specific problems may be helpful to some mothers. Her work discusses sounds newborns may make to indicate specific needs.

Anticipating Needs

A wonderful thing about being a mother is the intimate knowledge you will have of your baby. In time, you will come to understand him better than anyone else. Using a gentle routine (described in Chapter 8) can be a valuable tool as you learn to predict his wants. You will be able to meet some of his needs before they become a source of discomfort. *Anticipating your baby's needs is the best way to minimize crying.*

Just like the mother of a preschooler insists that he wear a sweater outside when it is cool or go to bed before he becomes exhausted in the evening, you will be able to predict your baby's needs. This doesn't mean that you are a bad mother if your baby cries, but you can strive to intervene before he experiences discomfort. Just as God knows what we require and provides for it, so we also anticipate needs and provide for our children.

> *Matthew 6:8 "Be not ye therefore like unto them: for your Father knoweth what things ye have need of, before ye ask him."*

Overstimulation

Sometimes babies cry for reasons that are not so obvious. Your baby may cry if he is over stimulated. The world has overwhelmed him. He's crying for his old home—the womb. If he was capable of expressing or understanding his need, he might say, "I am overwhelmed by all the new colors, noises, sounds, and space. I want back in my warm, cozy, predictable place."

Overstimulation is a bit more difficult to manage than say, feeding, diaper changing, or keeping him the right temperature. You cannot always prevent your baby from feeling overwhelmed or over stimulated, but you can work with him to help him feel at ease.

Recognizing that your baby has been over stimulated is challenging because your first thought is often about things like feeding and diapers. Also, your baby will be overstimulated long before you will feel the effects of too much activity. Put this possibility on your mental checklist and consider it the next time your baby is crying.

A Radically Different Environment

During his time in the womb, your baby never knew hunger or thirst. He never knew exhaustion, and there is a good chance he never experienced pain. Suddenly, after birth all of this changes. He experiences cold and hunger. For the first time, your baby knows loneliness. If your baby is separated from you, his cortisol (stress hormone) levels increase dramatically. He switches from a growing state to a survival state (Gunnar and White 2001). God made your baby's body to understand that he can't survive without your continued presence.

The act of crying is stressful for the baby. It causes a decrease in oxygen saturation, an increase in brain pressure, and a fast heart rate among other changes (Ahnert et al. 2004). A newborn cries to signal distress. Research shows that parents who swiftly respond to a newborn's cries will decrease the amount of crying that occurs (Bell and Ainsworth 1972).

You are primarily responsible to sustain the life of your baby. Consider this prayerfully before you decide to let your baby cry it out, as some would suggest. There will be a time for your baby to learn to soothe himself, but there is substantial research support to indicate this is not appropriate during the newborn phase (Thompson and Trevathan 2008).

Especially in the first few weeks, it is helpful to spend time skin-to-skin with your baby. This meets the baby's needs for security, warmth, and becoming bonded or attached to you. It is hard for us to comprehend how different the outside world is to your baby, but your nearness to him when he is out of sorts, over-stimulated, or even lonely can make a difference in how he responds and is able to learn and grow.

Calming Babies

What do you do if the baby is becoming overstimulated or is distraught? There are some great soothing techniques you can use to make his environment more quiet and comfortable.

1. Place him skin-to-skin by removing everything but his diaper and placing him on your bare chest. This is the best option.

2. Many people recommend swaddling your baby. This mimics the cocoon feeling of the womb. Swaddling is best used in the context of calming. It should not be used routinely; skin-to-skin is preferred. See Chapter 9 for more information on safe swaddling.

3. Use noise. Many babies are calmed by a loud, white noise sound. This sound may come from a vacuum cleaner or car motor. Some babies enjoy a loud floor fan or a "shhhhh" sound. Babies can also learn to be soothed by the sound of a special song or lullaby. When your baby was inside of you, he constantly heard the sound of your heart and the blood moving through the umbilical cord and large vessels. He also heard the noises of the digestive track and even heard the muted sound of your voice and other sounds around the home.

4. Turn down bright lights to mimic the womb.

5. Rock your baby. In the womb, he felt your movement; whenever you moved, the baby was rocked. Now your baby craves that same sensation. You can do this by rocking or holding him on your shoulder and "dancing" or jiggling him while patting his back or bottom.

    When patting your baby try different intensities. Some babies like gentle rubbing while others like firm patting. While patting your baby, *his head should always be supported.* You can also hold the baby on his side in your arms and jiggle him in small, fast movements. Never jiggle, pat, or shake the baby if you are angry.

6. Nonnutritive suckling at the breast or with a pacifier is very soothing to babies. Once your baby begins to calm, you can slow your movements and give him the opportunity to suckle.

7. Combining all these techniques can help when a baby is distraught. It may be helpful to use a clock to see how long you've been using the techniques, because a minute can seem like an hour when the baby doesn't settle quickly.

As you become more acquainted with your baby, you will be able to calm him more quickly. Some babies will need these soothing techniques very often in the first few months as they transition to the world outside the womb. We need to respond in love and concern to our babies, and the first few months require more hands on care. In fact, by four months, many babies will resist swaddling and other soothing techniques as they become more aware of the world around them and more independent from you. You are not spoiling your newborn when you respond to his needs for a period of adjustment after birth. In fact, you will be parenting like God does. God doesn't overwhelm us or give us more than we can handle. He shows compassion and mercy.

> Psalm 145:8 *"The LORD is gracious, and full of compassion; slow to anger, and of great mercy."*
>
> Psalm 86:15 *"But thou, O Lord, art a God full of compassion, and gracious, longsuffering, and plenteous in mercy and truth."*

Slings and Things

Using a sling or wrap is a great technique for calming a baby and is especially helpful with high need or difficult newborns. Wearing baby in a sling all day has been found to reduce crying (Hunziker and Barr 1986). Your baby was literally attached to you for nine months; it makes lots of sense that he will continue to need your physical presence. Wearing your baby often leads to frequent nursing and nursing for comfort. These behaviors, especially in the first few weeks, will increase the success of breastfeeding.

Baby-wearing is a great way to promote attachment for both breastfed and bottle-fed babies. It may be even more important for bottle-fed babies, because they may not experience as much skin-to-skin contact and handling as breastfed babies.

Perhaps you need to take a shower or check the oven. You can have another family member hold the baby when you're busy. If you don't have extra help available to you, you can get a newborn swing, which may help your baby be comfortable during those times when you cannot hold him. The kind that swings from side to side is very helpful. However, swings cannot substitute the interaction your baby needs with you.

Inconsolable Crying (a.k.a. Colic)

Although soothing techniques will very often be effective, no one technique or group of techniques will always work. Some babies do have periods of inconsolable crying. Culturally, we often refer to this as "colic," but that is not an accurate term as researchers have not found a clear link between gastric spasms and the crying that some babies do. Inconsolable crying is not solely a western culture phenomenon as it has been documented in many parts of the world.

Some babies will have a predictable time of crying every day. As researchers have studied crying, they have found that in some cases this inconsolable crying can be decreased (St. James-Roberts et al. 2006). Skin-to-skin contact, responding quickly to infant cues, and following a gentle routine can prevent crying jags for both of you!

There may be an identifiable cause for inconsolable crying. The baby may have reflux, a dairy allergy, or some other cause of discomfort. The baby's healthcare provider can identify a variety of problems the baby may be having. If the baby's cry is high-pitched and seems constant or difficult to settle, it is time to take him to his primary care provider for a check-up.

In rare instances, crying may be an indicator of injury during the birthing process. If your baby's primary care provider has already evaluated the baby and cannot determine a cause, you may consider complementary medicine. Many qualified chiropractors will see an infant for free to evaluate for a misalignment. It is very important that the chiropractor is experienced and gentle with infant adjustments and you are comfortable with this choice. A doctor of osteopathy (DO) or a doctor of physical therapy may also perform these types of adjustments and make helpful recommendations.

Miriam: I take each of my infants for a check-up with a chiropractor soon after birth. I began this practice when Beka had a torticollis of the neck.

If your baby's primary care provider says everything is fine, the baby is eating well, gaining weight, and you feel he is healthy, you may be dealing with inconsolable crying. This type of crying usually begins at two to four weeks, peaks at six to eight weeks, and then will begin to diminish at three to four months. Crying may occur at the same time every day and can last from 30 minutes to several hours.

These babies that cry inconsolably are sometimes termed high needs or difficult babies; they will cry at times when nothing seems to be wrong and nothing stops the crying. Having a baby with this temperament can be challenging and frustrating. However, it is comforting to know that they are within the range of normal newborn behavior. It is also encouraging to know that this type of crying will diminish and come to an end after a few months. Although it is distressing when you cannot console your baby, it does not mean that you are a bad mother.

Techniques for Coping with Inconsolable Crying

There are further techniques that you can try to decrease the length and intensity of the baby's cries. These interventions are proactive and will take some planning. Skin-to-skin contact and baby-wearing are the most effective techniques for calming inconsolable crying. See Chapter 10 for more information on skin-to-skin.

Perhaps a change of scenery will help. Take the baby for a walk outside or go for an outing to a park. Many infants calm when they are outside or in a different environment.

For other babies, increasing the predictability of his environment can help decrease crying. Whenever possible keep the baby in a quiet environment and follow the same general pattern on most days. Refer to Chapter 8 for help understanding appropriate patterns or schedules for newborns.

Coping Measures for Frustrated Mothers of Difficult Babies

You may be tired, cranky, and angry, because you have no explanation for the baby's crying. If this is the case, it is probably time to hand the baby off to someone else and take a short break.

Before you leave make sure that your baby does not need to cluster feed. Sometimes babies will need to nurse every hour to increase milk supply. This can be frustrating if you are not expecting it. If the baby stops crying while nursing, he may be cluster feeding. The best thing to do at this point is to put on a long movie and grab a snack. Refer to Chapter 6 for further information about cluster feeding.

If you have run through all the calming strategies and carefully evaluated that your baby isn't hungry, you don't have to be constantly present. There may be times when you feel overwhelmed. Seriously, leave the house for an hour or two. You may want to go to a friend's house to take a nap, do something with a girl friend, or just go for a walk. This gives you a chance to regain some perspective.

Allow another trusted caregiver to change, bathe, and comfort your baby for a short period. The caregiver who stays with a crying baby needs to be a mature person who is able to control his emotions and knows what to do in case of an emergency.

If you are all alone with a baby that is crying inconsolably, and you're feeling angry or unable to manage the situation, *put the baby down* in a safe place and step away. Peek in on the baby occasionally. Please be aware that most mothers occasionally feel helpless and angry, but this should not be a frequent, normal part of your postpartum experience. If you are often feeling angry and helpless, you may be having symptoms of postpartum depression. Please refer to the Appendix B on postpartum mood disorders.

Miriam: Once when my first baby was crying inconsolably, I had to call my husband at work and ask him to come home immediately. I felt pretty guilty. Maybe I wasn't a good mother if I couldn't handle her by myself. Happily, he didn't even question me. He was home within half an hour, and the three of us survived.

In Review: My Baby is Crying, What should I Do?

+ Are basic needs met? Think hunger, wet, dirty, cold, hot, lonely, or ready for a different environment.

+ Is the baby overstimulated? Skin-to-skin or swaddle; Jiggle/dance/pat; try different positions for baby like laying him on his side or tummy in your arms; white noise; dim the lights; allow baby to suckle at breast or on a pacifier; combine these techniques.

+ Is the baby sick? Does the baby have a fever? Has the baby been refusing to nurse or perhaps sleepy when he should be nursing? Has the baby been having four bowel movements a day after day four? Is the cry high pitched? Is the crying constant? Take the baby to his primary care provider if needed.

+ Is this a high needs baby? Consider skin-to-skin and baby-wearing.

+ Is the baby full but still crying? You may need to take a break and find another caregiver for an hour or two.

While crying is a primary concern for many parents, other issues can arise such as choosing a hospital, caring for baby illnesses, and dealing with relatives. These topics and more are covered in the rest of this chapter.

Choosing a Hospital

You may have received this book early in your pregnancy or even before you are expecting. If this is the case, you should think carefully about the choice of a hospital and healthcare provider. When thinking of where you will deliver, you should consider which facilities are available to you, as well as your goals for delivery and feeding.

If you plan to breastfeed your baby, you want to choose a hospital that is on board with your decision. Although, you will not find a hospital advertising that they don't promote breastfeeding, the level of support can be astonishingly varied.

The best way to facilitate early breastfeeding is to choose a facility that encourages mothers and babies to stay together after delivery. Hospitals that are designated as Baby Friendly will be the best choice for lactating mothers. In order for a facility to be designated Baby Friendly, everything about the mother and baby care areas must be examined to assure the best breastfeeding experience is possible. This requires policy changes, education for all levels of health care providers, and a clear commitment to facilitate the breastfeeding experience.

If a Baby Friendly facility is not available, be sure to take a look at the other facilities and evaluate them, looking for any areas of concern. You may ask for a tour of the birthing center before your baby arrives. Here are some questions to ask:

+ Are babies routinely taken from their mothers after delivery?

+ Will my baby be expected to go to the newborn nursery for admission?

+ Do you have a board certified lactation consultant on staff?

+ When is the lactation consultant available?

+ Is the lactation consultant available after discharge for phone calls and/or outpatient visits?

+ If my baby is healthy, will I be able to place him skin-to-skin immediately after delivery?

+ Is your facility willing to accommodate requests I have that differ from your normal way of doing things?

+ Do you encourage rooming in? (Rooming in means that the baby will share your room and will only be taken to the nursery on your request.)

Your tour guide's responses will give you a good idea of what to expect should you choose that facility. Choosing the obstetrician may determine the hospital or birthing center if the doctor only delivers at one facility.

It would also be a good idea to ask your health care provider what type of expectations they have immediately after delivery. Medical professionals have a duty to provide safe care. Parents should realize that some of their requests may not be able to be honored because of serious health or safety concerns; a great deal of care depends on the events of labor and delivery. However, you should feel confident that your wishes will be followed when possible by the hospital staff.

When choosing a healthcare provider you will want to explore their preferences and beliefs about labor, delivery, and infant care. You may have to ask direct questions to get this information. For instance if a vaginal delivery is important to you, you could ask, "What is your c-section rate?" or "Do you feel comfortable with a doula in the room?" or you might ask "Were your children breastfed?" Other questions could be asked in a similar manner.

Although your provider may not agree with you on every issue, he should be willing to educate you on his views or agree to disagree to some extent. If you are careful to have some flexibility about your goals while carefully communicating them, many providers will work hard to keep your business. It is wonderful to find a provider who shares your values and can support your goals.

Baby Illness

Babies do not have a strong immunity to fight off colds and other viruses. Fortunately, providing your baby with breast milk can protect him from the viruses you are exposed to. The antibodies you build against the virus in your body pass to your baby through breast milk. Your milk not only provides antibodies that actively attack germs, but it also creates a barrier in your baby's gut that prevents many viruses and bacteria from reaching his blood. His immune system has a limited opportunity to interact with these germs, which allows the strengthening of his immune system. This is why common germs rarely cause severe illness in a breastfed baby.

Daycare can lead to exposure to many more germs than if your children stay home. That isn't necessarily a bad thing, as exposure allows your child to build immunity to those germs. Breastfeeding mothers can help their babies gain immunity to the germs at daycare by periodically going to the facility and handling the items that the baby touches. This will expose her to the same organisms that her baby is exposed to, thereby causing the mother to develop antibodies to those organisms and pass them in her breast milk. This will protect the baby from becoming ill.

Some concerning signs displayed by your baby include fever, loss of appetite, true vomiting, and cough. If your baby is not keeping feedings down and appears dehydrated (the fontanel is sunken or mouth and other mucous membranes are dry) it is an indication that the baby is not getting enough fluids. If your baby has these symptoms, call his healthcare provider. If your baby skips two or more feedings or is difficult to waken, these are indications the baby needs to be evaluated by a medical professional immediately.

Colds and Viruses

Nasal congestion can be a sign of an allergic response to something in the baby's environment. It may also be a sign of exposure to the common cold virus (rhinovirus) or a respiratory virus. Some viruses, particularly RSV, can be dangerous to newborns.

Some infants will need to be hospitalized if they have difficulty breathing or an inability to eat due to an increased respiratory rate. RSV does cause fever and produce large amounts of mucus and a bad cough. You can help protect your newborn from colds, RSV, and flu by staying away from large crowds or people who show symptoms of illness, especially during flu season and the winter months.

To keep your baby's nose clear so he can breathe, you need to suction it with a bulb syringe. This is not an enjoyable task for the mother or baby, but it is very effective and is about the only way to clear out a baby's nasal passages. It is not safe for babies to take cold and congestion preparations from the store. That is why the bulb syringe is important.

In the first six weeks of life, check with your healthcare provider before giving the baby any over the counter (OTC) medication for fever or fussiness. When the baby is fussy, you don't want to mask a fever that may indicate a more serious problem.

Many pediatricians do not recommend any anti-fever medications unless a fever is over 101° and the baby is clearly uncomfortable. Fever is part of the body's natural defense mechanism to kill bacteria, virus, or other organisms. By giving acetaminophen (Tylenol®) or ibuprofen (Motrin® or Advil®) you may actually be lengthening the course of symptoms. Babies should not be given ibuprofen before six months of age.

When a baby begins having a fever over 99° with an ear or forehead thermometer, then the pediatrician or nurse practitioner should be called. A baby less than three months old needs to be seen by his primary care provider for any temperature over 100.4°. Sometimes babies will have a drop in temperature along with other symptoms of illness. This can be an indication of infection as well. A typical viral fever lasts three days, but no more than five days.

Germs: The Good, the Bad, and the Ugly

Germs cover every millimeter of our environment. There are an abundance of antibacterial products advertised, especially soaps and cleaning products. It may seem like a good idea to kill the bacteria on a surface; however, the cleaning products do not discriminate between the good and bad bacteria. All of the germs are killed. It is not necessarily a good thing to use a substance that kills all the bacteria because it eliminates the good, protective bacteria. When dangerous bacteria are introduced to the surface, there are no beneficial bacteria to stop the dangerous germs from growing and forming a massive colony.

It is best to only use disinfectant products in your kitchen and bathroom when you will be dealing with bacteria like E. Coli from feces or various germs from poultry. During and after an illness it can help to vigilantly wipe down all surfaces to prevent the spread of the virus or bacterial illness. Using a sanitizer cycle on a dishwasher can be helpful if it is available. Use disinfectant products with discernment. Regular soap and warm water should be used routinely for the house, children, and pets.

Another strategy some mothers use to protect their children from germs is to isolate them from other children and give very frequent baths. Research has shown that a baby in an ultraclean environment is more prone to allergies and illnesses, because the baby's immune system is never challenged and therefore, it never develops.

Babies need good bacteria. In fact, at birth the baby is sterile and the trip through the birth canal, plus skin-to-skin contact helps colonize the baby's body with friendly bacteria. This is why it is important not to pass around your baby to everyone right after delivery. He needs his exposure limited to the bacteria living in and on his mother.

The nurses and doctors should wear gloves and gowns during the birth and should not cuddle the baby against their uniforms. Stethoscopes should be wiped down before placed on your baby's skin. The baby needs to touch his parents first. Other contact should be limited until baby has had extended skin-to-skin exposure with his mother and father.

You can influence your baby's health profoundly by taking measures to ensure your body has high levels of beneficial bacteria. Kefir, yogurt, homemade sauerkraut, homemade pickles, nattō, and sourdough bread are all loaded with healthy bacteria that can positively impact your health. A body full of friendly bacteria can prevent leaky gut syndrome, an overgrowth of bad yeast, and many other illnesses.

Baby's Output

Many moms express concern that their babies are not getting enough to eat. The baby's weight is the best indicator of adequate breastfeeding, but the baby's output should also be considered. These are normal elimination patterns for newborns.

The baby's elimination patterns will change rapidly in the first week.

+ Day One – one wet diaper, one stool (black)

+ Day Two – two wet diapers, two stools (black)

+ Day Three – three wet diapers, three stools (black or green)

+ Day Four – four wet diapers, three or four stools (black or green)

+ Day Five – five or six wet diapers, three or four stools (green or yellow)

+ Day Six – six to eight wet diapers, three or four stools (yellow)

Counting wet diapers can be difficult, because disposable diapers are super absorbent. If you notice that some of your baby's diapers are soaked, you can focus on counting stools. Stooling is a great indicator of how well breastfeeding is going. The more times you feed your baby, the more stools he will have. Your baby should have three to four yellow stools that are quarter-sized or bigger per day.

Green, frothy stool after the fourth day can indicate that your baby is not getting enough of the fatty component of the milk (hind milk). To remedy this, he needs to nurse longer on the first breast during a feeding, until he comes off on his own. The fat component gradually increases during the nursing session on one breast, so the longer a baby stays on one breast, the more fat content he receives. This fatty milk stays longer with the baby and tends to decrease gas and hunger, while at the same time helping the baby grow. Assuring your baby gets plenty of fatty milk is a good preventive strategy against colic and gassiness.

Coping with Family

How can you deal with intrusive family members? It is vital to lay down clear boundaries. For example, if you don't want other family members besides your husband in your delivery room, let people know.

Be kind yet firm about the big things, such as, "No, the three-month-old cannot spend the night with grandma and grandpa," or "No, the baby can't ride with his aunt and the boyfriend we've just met." In many situations you will be able to quietly take your baby into a different room, or leave the gathering.

Try to be laid back about the little things. Don't push the grandparents to accept all of your choices. Unless they are living with you or care for your child several times a week, these things shouldn't be an issue.

Family is very important. They are the only ones who will love your child like you do. If you are expecting a baby and there is a family reunion an hour away, go to it, unless you are truly ill. Take the opportunities you can to strengthen those relationships.

While you are pregnant or just after you've had the baby, everything that happens may feel overwhelming, and it can be easy to hurt someone's feelings. Be kinder to your family than you think they deserve. Nurture that support system, unless they are a danger to you and your child.

You may feel like your family is not involved enough. Sometimes all it takes is asking for more involvement. It is very possible that your parents or your husband's parents had intrusive family members, and they are trying to give you privacy and space. It is always better to be honest in your communication in order to help your family understand your desires better.

Chaotic Afternoons

The late afternoons can be a time of chaos in the home; perhaps you are preparing dinner, the baby wants to be fed, and your spouse is arriving home after being away all day. The key to bring order to your home is careful planning. You may be able to prepare a meal in the morning while the baby is napping, something that can easily be popped in the oven an hour before dinner. A time-saving idea is to make a double recipe of a casserole, and freeze half of the uncooked entree for a meal in a week or so.

Pick a weekly menu and repeat it during the newborn period. Simple main dishes with a complement of fresh fruits and vegetables are always an easy fix. Healthy snacks like raw nuts can be helpful. With dinner out of the way you can focus on the people in your life.

You may need to nurse more often in the evening because your supply is lowest then. Curl up in your nest while you feed your newborn and read a book to your toddler. Have your older child sit beside you while you help him with homework. Light a candle and put on some calming music.

Sometimes the best planning does not keep all of the crazy out of your day. At these times, take a moment to call out to God for help. Imagine dealing with the situation with grace, in a way that will make Jesus happy. Then carry out those actions. Remember to be kinder than you normally would to your spouse, others, and yourself.

If you have several small children at home, consider getting a Mommy's Helper. A Mommy's Helper is a child, usually 9 to14 years old, that you can train to help you several afternoons per week. A Mommy's Helper may be a homeschooler in your neighborhood or a child in your church who can help during a busy afternoon.

These Mommy's Helpers can play with the toddler or other young children in the back yard, or rock the baby while you take care of dinner. Usually a Mommy's Helper will work for the training and attention you provide. Cookies and small gifts are appreciated. If this Helper is satisfactory, then a small hourly fee can be arranged.

Safe Health Advice

You should be cautious about where you seek advice on health care matters. The Internet is full of sites with information that has little scientific merit. There are women who have very minimal training in research interpretation or clinical practice who will advocate a variety of treatments and practices. Please use discernment when someone tells you to ignore the advice of your healthcare professional because something else worked for her.

Forums can be very helpful when moderated by a very experienced mother, or even one who is also an infant care professional. A forum populated by many inexperienced mothers may recommend a solution that hasn't had the consequences adequately evaluated.

Healthcare professionals monitor and treat many specific conditions. Some conditions, if left untreated, will have minimal consequences for some mothers and babies while others will experience severe effects if medical advice is ignored. For example, Group Beta Strep (GBS) infection may not kill every infant, but untreated GBS will kill some infants. They die quickly and miserably. Healthcare professionals have degrees and experience. They may treat hundreds or even thousands of mother and baby pairs per year. Their advice is worth listening to carefully.

Common Concerns

This section covers common concerns that first time mothers may not recognize. Many times these concerns can be easily addressed.

"My baby won't take a pacifier." Babies can learn to use pacifiers. It isn't hard, but it's a training process for most babies. You just have to hold the pacifier for him while he practices.

"My baby sleeps a lot during the day." You should offer feedings at regular intervals during the day. This will help your baby develop good sleep habits. Sleeping a lot may also mean that the baby has jaundice and needs to be seen by his healthcare provider. Newborns do sleep often during the day, but they should be awake enough to nurse appropriately. If they are too sleepy to nurse or even take a bottle, call your healthcare provider.

"My baby doesn't sleep at night." This behavior indicates that the mother may be holding her baby all day but is expecting the baby to sleep on a separate sleep surface at night. It could also indicate that the baby is not nursing enough or

sleeping too much during the day. Sometimes mothers will allow their baby to nap in a swing during the day and then expect them to lay flat for nighttime sleep. An approved sleeping device that allows the baby to maintain a slight angle will help a newborn sleep better at night.

"My baby is only two weeks old and she sleeps eight hours at night." A two-week-old baby sleeping this long at night is going too long without feeds. The baby will probably exhibit poor growth, and this behavior will affect the breastfeeding mother's milk supply. Breastfed babies should not sleep eight hours at night until at least the eighth week. Some mothers with small capacity breasts should never go more than four to five hours at night without feeding. Even bottle-fed babies shouldn't be sleeping eight hours a night at two weeks. They need to be awakened and fed.

"My eight-week-old is sleeping 12 hours at night, and it's great." This is too early for such a long period of sleep, especially for a breastfed baby. The mother's milk supply may not be affected immediately, but even a mother with average capacity breasts will eventually be affected. Older babies who have mothers with large capacity breasts should not go longer than 10 hours without a feed.

"I just dried up at four months" Milk supply and demand changes at four months. If you have allowed your baby to sleep for long periods of time and have only emptied your breasts four or five times per day you will very likely "dry up" after the fourth month. The solution is to add a feed. An early morning feed can be very helpful for increasing milk supply.

The solutions to these common problems are simple. However, they do take some thought. Don't hesitate to look for answers from good resources when you recognize a problem.

Responding to Problems with Gentleness

Sometimes mothers are made to feel badly for responding to their child's cries and other needs. A mother may be told "You are not a slave to that baby. You are in charge. Don't let that baby rule your life." While there is a nugget of truth in these statements (mothers should be guiding the day and making sure their own needs are met) it is important to remember that nowhere in the Bible does God tell a mother to delay responding to her baby or that her desires and needs are more important. In fact, the Bible teaches that we are to put others before ourselves. Our children will learn to do the same as they follow our example in the home.

We also do not find commands to respond harshly to infants. There are usually several ways to accomplish any task, but we need to think beyond the situation at hand. The way we complete a task or deal with a problem is very important. Responding harshly may work more quickly in the short term, but there are negative long-term consequences. Acting with gentleness towards our newborns will cause both mother and baby to reap many rewards. Scripture promotes responsive, loving, and gentle mothers.

> *1 Thessalonians 2:7-8 [7] "But we were gentle among you, even as a nurse cherisheth her children: [8] So being affectionately desirous of you, we were willing to have imparted unto you, not the gospel of God only, but also our own souls, because ye were dear unto us."*

In this passage, Paul is comparing his loving care of the new Christians to the loving care a nursing mother gives her baby. The word "gentle" is the Greek word *epios*. This word was used in other Greek literature to describe the forbearance and care that a nursing woman would give a difficult child or the patience she would exhibit when caring for a sick or needy child. The word "nurse" means nursing mother. The nursing mother sustains the life of the child with her own life.

The word "cherisheth" is the word *thalpo*. This word has the idea of imparting heat. The nursing mother gives the heat of her body to warm her child. The child is held in such close proximity as to be literally warmed by her body.

The next idea, "affectionately desirous" is the word *homeiromai*, which means passionate, longing, ongoing love. This love is compelling and unsurpassed. It is not enough for the mother to meet the physical needs of the child. She is compelled to ensure that all of the child's needs are met.

The warmth of her body, the sweetness of her milk, her gentle caresses all work to calm her child. This pattern of responsiveness and self-giving is the expected action of mothers towards their babies. Paul assumes that all the people reading his letter will know how babies should be cared for. As Christians we may often pray, "Christ use me. I want to please You." As a mother, you have the opportunity to be used in Christ's service to your baby. In a very real sense, responding to your baby's needs is a form of worship.

> *Matthew 10:42 "And whosoever shall give to drink unto one of these little ones a cup of cold water only in the name of a disciple, verily I say unto you, he shall in no wise lose his reward."*

He Giveth More Grace

He giveth more grace as our burdens grow greater,
He sendeth more strength as our labors increase;
To added afflictions He addeth His mercy,
To multiplied trials He multiplies peace.

When we have exhausted our store of endurance,
When our strength has failed ere the day is half done,
When we reach the end of our hoarded resources
Our Father's full giving is only begun.

Fear not that thy need shall exceed His provision,
Our God ever yearns His resources to share;
Lean hard on the arm everlasting, availing;
The Father both thee and thy load will upbear.

His love has no limits, His grace has no measure,
His power no boundary known unto men;
For out of His infinite riches in Jesus
He giveth, and giveth, and giveth again.

(Flint ND)

Section Four

Putting It All Together

Grace be to you, and peace, from God our
Father, and from the Lord Jesus Christ.

Ephesians 1:2

Faithful is he that calleth you,
who also will do it.

1 *Thessalonians* 5:24

Chapter Twelve

Grace from God to You

*T*his book has covered much information on mothering and infant care. Now it is time for you to put this information into practice. Adjusting your expectations while having an attitude of humility will put you in a position to experience God's grace and help as you parent (James 5:5).

As you share your life with your children, they will see your example, and you will have the opportunity to plant good seeds that can produce godly fruit in their lives. You will find joy in meeting your family's needs through everyday tasks, when you focus on praising God and offering your work as worship to Him.

God's Grace for Parenting Mistakes

As much as you desire to be a godly parent, you will make mistakes. Thankfully, God is merciful. God doesn't change our actions or always prevent their consequences, but He is able to send others to meet a need that we have caused by our ignorance or self-will. Or, He may provide His grace to the one we have wronged to help them accept and love us anyway. Those are just two of the ways God can overcome our errors. Despite our failures He loves us.

Here are some encouraging thoughts and verses to help you understand and overcome difficulties. If you have accepted Christ as your Savior, you are at peace with God because of Christ's work on the cross. He is not out to get you when you fall. Instead, He is there to help you learn to live in ways that bring Him glory and bring you joy. Isn't that a wonderful thought?

> Romans 5:1 "Therefore being justified by faith, we have peace with God through our Lord Jesus Christ:"

We have learned to trust God as He uses the circumstances in our lives for our good. Even when challenging times come, we can trust that God is at work; He doesn't forget us.

> Romans 8:28 *"And we know that all things work together for good to them that love God, to them who are the called according to his purpose."*

God is so gracious and so wise that He can use the difficult times in our lives to make us more like Him. He does not give up on us, but continually draws us into fellowship with Him.

> James 1:2-4 ² *"My brethren, count it all joy when ye fall into divers temptations;* ³ *Knowing this, that the trying of your faith worketh patience.* ⁴ *But let patience have her perfect work, that ye may be perfect and entire, wanting nothing."*

God's Grace for Evaluating and Adjusting Expectations

Miriam: My parenting style has become more relaxed, because my expectations about infants and being a mother have changed. I had many unrealistic expectations regarding the way things were "supposed to be." For instance, before my milk transitioned to mature milk, Rebekah wanted to nurse for 45 minutes out of every 90 minutes, and I wasn't expecting that. It was exhausting!

As Rebekah grew, I expected her to sleep through the night. Even when I ignored her crying until she fell asleep, she would wake again in an hour or so hungry! It was frustrating. What was I doing wrong? It took a lot of courage to ignore the advice I had received to use a strict schedule, and instead rely on her cues and my Mommy Sense.

There was so much I had to learn, and so many changes I had to make as a new mom, but it was wonderfully satisfying when I could meet Rebekah's needs. Those early weeks with my first child were filled with great challenges and great joy! I'm so glad that God gave me grace and patience as I was learning to be a mother.

Women struggle when they feel they have to mother in a certain way and have very specific ideas about the way things should work in their families. There are books and groups that stereotype what a good Christian mother should be. One person may have an image of a good Christian mother as someone who has many children, home schools, doesn't work outside of the home, breastfeeds, uses cloth diapers, and maybe has an herb garden. Another person may have the image of a mother who attends every one of their children's sporting and musical events, sends them to Christian school, and provides for every conceivable material and financial need. With God's grace any type of woman can be a successful, happy mother.

It is important that you consider the expectations you have for your family. Have you considered how your culture will influence your parenting? What images of family life come from your culture? What are the choices that you feel are nonnegotiable for your children in areas like nutrition or education? While we all want to fit into our community of friends, it is important that you and your spouse decide what will work for your family. There may be many good parenting practices that are a part of your culture, but these practices may not be required to be a good or godly parent.

Sometimes there is a big difference between your family or cultural expectations and God's expectations. There can be differences between the Bible's teachings on family life and a group's interpretation of the Bible's teachings.

> Acts 17:11 *"These were more noble than those in Thessalonica, in that they received the word with all readiness of mind, and searched the scriptures daily, whether those things were so."* God will bless you for following His Word and the leading of the Holy Spirit.

The specific choices made in each home are up to that particular family. Sometimes this may mean that you and your family do not choose to do something that others around you and perhaps even you would value very highly. Although that choice may sadden your heart, you would need to accept that situation and trust that God has your family's best interest at heart.

> Ronda: My daughter takes violin lessons, and she is doing well. If we increased her lessons to three times a week, she could excel even more. However, I have four children and limited resources to pay for music lessons. What is best for Sarah's musical ability is not always what is best for our family. Instead of three lessons a week, we make the decision to only have one and spend the rest of the money on other necessities. Another family may choose to pay for the three violin lessons a week, because they want to make that sacrifice. I can live with the fact that Sarah will not get a full scholarship to Julliard School of Music, because we didn't sacrifice in that way for her. Bob and I made the choice, and we are comfortable living with it. That is what we each must do.

God knows and understands your situation in life. There is not one path for all of us to take, each is unique. He will give us the grace to go down that path, even when it isn't the one that we would prefer. You may not be able to provide all of the things you would like for your family. However, we can trust God to meet our needs. Sometimes it is difficult to recognize God's best for our family when it looks different than what we would have chosen.

> *Matthew 6:33 "But seek ye first the kingdom of God, and his righteousness; and all these things shall be added unto you."*

God's Grace to Serve Faithfully

As you are evaluating choices, it is easy to become overwhelmed. Focus on the important question, "God, what do You require from me as a woman, a wife, and a mother?" Answering this question often brings peace as we discover pleasing God is less complicated than we often think.

> *Micah 6:8 "He hath shewed thee, O man, what is good; and what doth the Lord require of thee, but to do justly, and to love mercy, and to walk humbly with thy God?"*

God wants mothers with humble hearts who seek fellowship with Him. That requires time spent alone with God on a daily basis. For the new mother who is overwhelmed with the activities of her life, that may seem impossible. God is gracious to us. He doesn't expect you to spend hours of time with Him alone while your baby cries in the other room or dinner burns in the oven. He wants to meet with you where you are, while you are nursing, cleaning, or rocking your baby.

God wants women to guide and guard their homes through wisdom, discernment, and prayer. Women have a responsibility to guard their homes from external distractions, time wasters (read television and Internet here), and even visitors who might have a destructive influence on their families.

God wants women to love their husbands and children. Sometimes this can be difficult. If we aren't careful about guarding our time with the Lord, we will not be spiritually refreshed and able to take the daily emotional and physical stress. When our resources are gone, we tend to take it out on those around us. What an effect that can have on our husbands and children! We must ask God to give us the grace to love at those difficult times.

Christian author and speaker, Nancy Leigh DeMoss, describes God's ambulances of grace that are ready for any emergency. They are loaded with just the right resources that we need and are waiting for our call. If we can avail ourselves of that grace each time we are struggling, what a difference it would make (2007).

Follow God's leading in your life and make your decisions based on what He shows you through His Word, the Holy Spirit, science, and your own Mommy Sense. Learn how to evaluate infant care practices using the different ways of knowing discussed in Chapter 1. God will help you provide for the needs of your baby as you trust Him and rely on His grace.

When you seek to glorify God in your choices, you will find joy in mothering and the freedom to fulfill your role in a way that is your own. After all, you are the image bearer of God, a joint heir with Christ, and a vessel of the living God.

> *Ephesians 2:1-10* [1] *"And you hath he quickened, who were dead in trespasses and sins;* [2] *Wherein in time past ye walked according to the course of this world, according to the prince of the power of the air, the spirit that now worketh in the children of disobedience:* [3] *Among whom also we all had our conversation in times past in the lusts of our flesh, fulfilling the desires of the flesh and of the mind; and were by nature the children of wrath, even as others.* [4] *But God, who is rich in mercy, for his great love wherewith he loved us,*
>
> [5] *Even when we were dead in sins, hath quickened us together with Christ, (by grace ye are saved;)* [6] *And hath raised us up together, and made us sit together in heavenly places in Christ Jesus:* [7] *That in the ages to come he might shew the exceeding riches of his grace in his kindness toward us through Christ Jesus.* [8] *For by grace are ye saved through faith; and that not of yourselves: it is the gift of God:* [9] *Not of works, lest any man should boast.* [10] *For we are his workmanship, created in Christ Jesus unto good works, which God hath before ordained that we should walk in them."*

Appendices

My people are destroyed for

lack of knowledge:

Hosea 4:6a

Appendix A
Reading Research Articles: What You should Know

When reading information about a medical subject, we are presented with information that is stated as fact with a reference cited that may or may not be meaningful to us. We usually depend on the author's integrity and the journal editor's evaluation to assure the accurate reporting of findings. It is helpful to have some personal understanding of how research is conducted. There are many examples of articles and stories that report opinion as fact or misinterpret research findings to make their own point. You can understand the findings much better if you look at the actual study. Of course, there are times you may find that the author does not cite a source or he reports his own research. In scientific writing today, researchers are expected to publish their findings in peer-reviewed journals as a means of establishing the research's integrity. If you are reading a book where an author is reporting his own research, he should cite a journal article where he has previously published a report of the study. If this is not done, it should raise a red flag as to why the research was not submitted for peer-review.

It is relatively easy to get access to many studies today through the Internet. Sometimes researchers publish in an online journal that should have the same peer-reviewed process of evaluation, but the journal doesn't actually have a print version of its editions. Other times, authors will report information online in a blog or information web page that does not have the oversight of a journal. Although there can be some very accurate reporting in these sites, there can also be a great deal of inaccuracy presented. This type of source should cause you to consider carefully the author's background and purpose in sharing this content.

Reading a Research Report

When you first get a research study or journal article to examine, you should look at the title, authors, and introduction. The first page often gives information about the authors' affiliations and any conflict of interest, like being paid by a company who makes the product they are evaluating for this study. Review the abstract, which is a two to three paragraph summary at the beginning of the article. This can give a brief overview of the study's relevance to your area of interest. The references used in the article should be fairly recent unless they are foundational studies; less than five years is the standard for recent articles. Foundational studies, on the other hand, are studies that may be a number of years old but provide ground-breaking information in a subject area. The method of conducting the research as explained should make relative sense to you. Sometimes reading a research report can be rather dry, due to the jargon and passive voice. Just keep drinking lots of water, and you can make it through.

Introduction

In this section of the report, the authors will review what is already known and established about the subject based on previous research. Look to see that the author cites studies that are both supportive of as well as contradictory to the premise he is planning to study, at least as much as is available. You also want to see that the studies are linked to each other and properly explain why the research is being done.

Method

The researchers will explain how the study was conducted. It is important to look at the type of study. Rarely in human and social science literature do we find experiments, because we don't desire or can't ethically force people to engage in specific behaviors for the purpose of a study. For example, you won't find a study that has mothers required to use a specific, exclusive option, either artificial milk or breast milk, for two years of a baby's life, just to find the outcomes in the baby's and mother's health. The type of study usually done is called *ex post facto*, or done after the fact. This type looks at the mothers and babies and what they are already going to do (breastfeed or formula feed), then sees which outcomes are related to the two types of feeding. Although this is the only way to study this type of information, the fact that other variables can influence the results, causes this to be a weaker method of study than experiments. Usually to compensate for this, researchers will try to get the largest sample size possible.

Even small method details can make a big difference in the findings of a study. For example, if a study is testing a drug that needs to be refrigerated but does not provide adequate refrigeration, the results will be invalid, but you only notice this if you know about the drug and the procedure that was used. Yes, this really happens! Also, if results of an intervention are recorded at different times for different studies, such as the amount of drug in the blood after an oral dose measured at one hour in one study and at two hours in another, the results cannot be compared accurately. Study procedures can influence findings in significant ways.

Sample size

The studied sample size is a very important detail. In a general sense, the larger the group the more likely the results can be accepted. That does not eliminate the possibility of using the results of studies with small samples; but understand that the small sample is less likely to represent all the possible subjects that weren't in the study. So, the findings of a study that examines 1000 babies are more likely to occur again in another sample, than the findings of a study that uses 5 babies in their sample.

Interpretation

The researcher will then report the statistics used to calculate the results and will report his result analysis. This is called the interpretation and can be the most difficult written part of the study to understand. Sometimes studies don't have the expected results, so the researcher has to try to understand why that occurred. This is one of the places that peer-review really helps, because having other people check a researcher's work and interpretation will make him more careful about making bold statements of the findings not based on the results. It should be cause for concern if the results that are reported don't match up with the conclusions made by the researcher.

Researchers have to be aware of competing explanations for why something occurred in their results. Consider if a researcher studied the effect of Vitamin D supplements on rickets symptoms and included only children in southern states and during summer months. In this example, exposure to sunlight might have a greater influence on rickets symptoms than the actual supplementation. Exposure to sunlight would be a competing explanation for the results, since it may have a greater effect on rickets symptoms than Vitamin D supplements. The researcher would need to talk about that possibility and account for it in the way the study was interpreted. If you find yourself asking questions like, "Well, yes, but did they take *this* into consideration when they made that conclusion?" you may have found a limitation or weakness in the study. There are always competing explanations for research results, but the researcher needs to recognize and write about them.

Review studies with a critical attention to how the research was compiled and how the findings are explained. This will give you confidence in the reported results and conclusions.

It is helpful when studying a particular subject to get an overall idea of previous studies. Literature reviews are compilations of multiple research studies on a specific topic. Cochrane reviews are a highly valued type of review, but some subjects have not been researched sufficiently to require a review or the studies may not meet the rules for inclusion in a Cochrane review. If a review is not available, one can read through several studies on a specific topic including studies with conflicting results. Always look at conflicting studies with the same attention to method, sample size, results, and conclusions. You may also be able to find written critiques or study evaluations on the Internet. Some of these critiques may be well written and complete, while others may be less so. Critiques are a person's opinion of a research study, so you need to watch carefully for bias in the content (Rankin and Esteves 1996).

The researcher and the reviewers need to work with honesty and fair handedness to establish accurate results and reporting. It is important that researchers complete their research and report their findings in a manner which honors God.

Be strong and of a good courage, fear not, nor be afraid of them: for the LORD thy God, he it is that doth go with thee; he will not fail thee, nor forsake thee.

Deuteronomy 31:6

Appendix B
Postpartum Mood Disorders

Psalm 40:1-3 [1] *"I waited patiently for the LORD; and he inclined unto me, and heard my cry.* [2] *He brought me up also out of an horrible pit, out of the miry clay, and set my feet upon a rock, and established my goings.* [3] *And he hath put a new song in my mouth, even praise unto our God: many shall see it, and fear, and shall trust in the LORD."*

Becoming a mother is a time of significant physical and emotional change. The new mother may have exerted herself during labor more than at any other time in her life. She needs to process her birth experience, and adjust to taking care of a new, vulnerable person at a time when she is also very vulnerable. All postpartum women need help during this time, even if everything appears to be going well.

There are more changes occurring now than any other time in the normal course of life. A mother is expected to handle these changes with dignity, self-discipline, grace, and joy! What a tall order! Occasionally, the challenges of new motherhood will overwhelm her physical and mental coping mechanisms. It is important to understand the prevention, common causes, and treatments of postpartum mood disorders.

Understanding Postpartum Mood Disorders

There are several types of postpartum mood disorders. The most common mood disturbance is commonly referred to as "the baby blues." About 85 percent of women experience the baby blues, a time lasting no more than two weeks where women experience mood swings, crying jags, fatigue, and feelings of being overwhelmed by the demands of motherhood. This can happen to mothers who are prone to being melancholy, but also to those who are normally very happy, dynamic women. Some women will experience symptoms lasting longer than two weeks. This is called postpartum depression.

All too often feelings of sadness are ignored. You may hear comments like, "Well, she's hormonal," "It's just the baby blues," or "It's normal after having a baby." Unless these occasions are the rare exception, they are not normal. *The baby blues should last no more than two weeks. Any symptoms lasting longer than two weeks need to be taken seriously.*

There are two other postpartum mood disorders—post traumatic stress disorder (PTSD) and postpartum psychosis (PPP) . Many mothers are traumatized by the birth and need help processing their experiences. If symptoms caused by the trauma are severe enough, the woman may be diagnosed with post traumatic stress disorder. About 1 in 1,000 women may experience postpartum psychosis, a disorder that is characterized by a break with reality.

Dealing with postpartum mood disorders proactively can decrease the severity and length of symptoms. It is important to seek treatment as soon as possible, because lengthy untreated postpartum depression can be more difficult to treat successfully (Kornstein and Schneider 2001).

Symptoms of Postpartum Depression

+   Inability to experience joy in life
+   Feelings of shame or guilt
+   Feeling overwhelmed by life and the demands of motherhood
+   Severe mood swings
+   Difficulty bonding with the baby; mother may feel the baby does not belong to her
+   Inability to find joy in the companionship of others, especially family and friends
+   Thoughts of harming the baby, yourself, or other children. These thoughts are intrusive; people experience them even if they want or attempt to avoid them.*
+   Obsessive-compulsive behaviors
+   Feelings of abandonment by God and others

+ More than usual loss of interest in sex (after the initial six to eight week postpartum period)

+ Loss of appetite

+ Anger

+ Feeling tired all the time

+ Inability to sleep

*Often women with postpartum depression (PPD) experience intrusive thoughts, or thoughts they can't control. These thoughts can include hurting the baby or imagining how the baby may be injured. They are very upsetting, although the woman can recognize that the thoughts are abnormal or wrong. Mothers will go to great lengths to avoid the thoughts or avoid the possibility of injuring the baby (Kendall-Tackett et al. 2009).

Preventing Postpartum Mood Disorder

There are some very helpful, natural things that all women can do to improve health, prevent disease, and prevent postpartum mood disorders. These specific measures have a basis in current research and are part of healthy living. Although some of these seem basic and common sense, they can have a profound effect on your health. Please consider implementing them in your life.

1. Add fish oil to your diet. This adds the essential fatty acids that cannot be found in plant based supplements. Begin supplementing at a dose of 200-400mg of DHA per day. The fish oil will contain both EPA and DHA. It is important the source is not contaminated and not rancid. Because pregnant women should not consume a lot of seafood (due to high levels mercury), they will not be able to consume enough DHA from food sources, so a supplemental source is very helpful (Kendall-Tackett et al. 2009).

2. Moderate exercise for 20-30 minutes should be done a minimum of 2-3 times per week. An early morning walk in the sunshine is one way this could be accomplished.

3. Optimization of the body's vitamin B-12 level above 400 and the vitamin D level above 30 should be maintained. These blood level tests can be ordered by your primary care provider.

4. Four to five hours of continuous sleep at night. Even if you cannot achieve this every night after the baby is born, even three nights a week will make

a significant difference. Four hours of continuous sleep may be unrealistic during the first two weeks, but hopefully after that time, the baby will have moved the long nap of the day to nighttime.

5.   Bright light therapy or daily time out of doors in the sunshine

Getting Help

If you have been having symptoms of depression for more than two weeks, it is time to seek help. How can you get help? Who should you approach? Because depression is often caused by a combination of factors, you may need more than one type of help. Discussing these issues can be very difficult. It can also be difficult to admit to yourself or your family that you have a problem, but if you do not acknowledge it, you may not get better. It is really important that you make the effort to get help for yourself and your family.

Help from Your Healthcare Provider

There are common physical problems that can cause depression. Because some of these causes can be treated or ruled out quickly, see your health care provider right away. The doctor will usually recommend the mother follow-up with another appointment in a month, or earlier when there is cause for concern. He will often recommend the mother gets counseling as well.

Some healthcare providers are not reliable at treating and properly diagnosing depression. Make sure you ask specifically for help. You may need to make suggestions regarding treatment. If you believe that your healthcare provider is not offering an effective treatment plan ask for a referral. Getting a second opinion is often helpful.

Help from a Counselor

Some women have relationship problems that contribute to postpartum depression. This does not mean that every case of postpartum depression has a relational component or that mothers should be blamed for their depression. Research suggests that counseling is an effective treatment for depression. When choosing a counselor use one that approaches counseling from a Biblical worldview and is trained to help depressed people. Since all truth is God's truth, counselors can be very effective by providing you with truthful insight into your problem.

What the counselor tells you should line up with God's Word. Carefully evaluate what you are told.

The Bible has much to say about relationships, and we can turn to this advice first! A Christian counselor who relies on God's Word as a therapy basis can be very helpful. Neuthetic counseling, often available as a church resource, applies Biblical principles to an identified problem.

Interpersonal therapy has been shown in some studies to be as effective as medications in working through the problems of relationships. This therapy can also give the mother hope for the future.

Another type of therapy mentioned in Chapter 2 is cognitive behavioral therapy (CBT). This therapy changes the way you think about a problem area, and helps you to change your behavior based on that new way of thinking. The Bible speaks directly about this concept in Ephesians 4:22-24 and Colossians 3:9-10, where it commands "Put off... put on." We are told to replace wrong thinking or behaviors with new behaviors that honor God.

Feeling Good: The New Mood Therapy by David Burns provides a do-it-yourself approach to cognitive therapy. This book may be helpful as Burns does offer effective techniques for recognizing and rejecting the lies and negative self-talk that depressed people commonly experience.

It is helpful for the counselor to allow the mother to talk through the problems she is having, and to be able to identify the ways she is thinking about a situation. Oftentimes counselors will give homework. They will expect the client to make effort to change behaviors and thought patterns that contribute to depression. This is a valuable aspect of having ongoing success in managing and preventing depression recurrence.

Counseling is a critical component on the journey to wellness for the woman with postpartum mood disorders. If you are counseled by someone who discourages you from seeking further help (especially professional or medical help), states that your depression is a result of unknown sin, ignores physical causes of depression, or has a narrow approach to discussing your problems, you might need to find another counselor.

Other Places to Get Help

There are many other places to get help. Your pastor or a mature woman in your church may be able to help you. Many churches now have counselors available.

They may not have training in specific therapies, but many of them will be helpful and able to refer you to a counselor who has this advanced training.

Many websites offer resources and information about postpartum depression. One group, Postpartum Support International (www.postpartum.net) has a website where you can find resources in your area (Get Help – Support Groups and Area Coordinators 2011). Books are also additional resources. Several books and websites are included in the Resource chapter at the end of the book.

Treatments

Medications

Your healthcare provider may prescribe a medication to help with postpartum mood disorders. You should carefully consider this recommendation. Medications may be necessary to treat postpartum mood disorders, especially major depression, and medications are required for postpartum psychosis. If you are having trouble with your daily activities and personal hygiene or are having serious sleep disturbances, you may need medication.

The class of antidepressants known as SSRIs are considered the safest for pregnant and breastfeeding mothers. Other medications may be prescribed if the mother has been on them before. If your primary caregiver wants to prescribe an anti-depressant, you should check with another source about the safety of the medication with breastfeeding.

Dr. Thomas Hale, the foremost authority on medications during pregnancy and breastfeeding has sponsored an online source at www.infantrisk.com/content/webforum that gives direction for safe medication during pregnancy and breastfeeding (Hale 2011). This is one of the best places to get valid information. Information provided by the pharmaceutical maker of the medication will always be overly cautious to protect them against lawsuits. Following pharmaceutical company recommendations would leave you with very few medications to take for any problems.

There are other treatments that can help with postpartum mood disorders. Some of these treatments we will discuss can be done while you are taking medication or as a stand alone treatment.

Supplements

Some research suggests that antidepressants do not help everyone (Gartlehner et al. 2007). There is no explanation for why they seem to work for some people but not others. The good news is that there are other therapies that have been shown to be as effective as antidepressants.

There are complementary supplements, such as 1,000 mg of EPA, usually in combination with DHA (these are Omega-3 fatty acids), St. John's Wort, SAMe, and 5-HTP that have been effective as well. These are recommended to be used alone or in combination with prescription medication for mild or moderate depression.

It is important that your primary healthcare provider knows the names and dosages of any complementary therapies you are using, especially St. John's Wort, as there are drugs with which it is incompatible. Please use herbal supplements under the direction of a healthcare provider.

If you choose to use SAMe, it is important that your vitamin B levels are normal or taking it will be counterproductive (Kendall-Tackett et al. 2009). Some primary healthcare providers will be happy to work with these complementary supplements. Although these therapies are labeled as supplements it is worth noting that research shows they can be very effective. You should seriously consider these options with your healthcare provider.

Complementary Therapies

Complementary therapies such as acupressure, acupuncture, and chiropractic may be helpful, but they should be considered as complements to traditional medicine, especially in urgent, serious situations like major depression and postpartum psychosis. Sometimes complementary medicine can provide a solution when traditional medicine cannot, and sometimes traditional medicine works beautifully with complementary medicine.

Vitamins

All mothers should have their vitamin levels (B-12 and D particularly) checked. Taking a vitamin supplement can be a simple way to resolve low vitamin levels. The B vitamins have many functions and play a role in mood regulation. It is helpful to take a B complex vitamin, but if your B-12 level is low, you may be encouraged to also take a dissolvable B-12 supplement.

Vitamin D3 also plays a role in mood regulation. Most of the population has low vitamin D levels. It is very easy to supplement with vitamin D3 as these supplements are readily available. If you live in a sunny part of the country, spending 20 minutes a day in the sunlight may raise your vitamin D3 levels, although it may not increase the level enough to make an appreciable difference.

Exercise

Exercise has been shown to make a significant positive difference for depression sufferers. It can even help with severe depression. The best type of exercise is aerobic. 2-4 times a week for 20 minutes for mild depression has been shown to be effective. 3-5 times a week for 40-60 minutes is needed for severe depression. Exercise has been shown to be as effective as medication. As long as you are otherwise healthy, vigorous exercise can be done by breastfeeding mothers. Because exercise is such an effective treatment, it should not be ignored.

Nutrition

Nutrition is another area that should not be ignored. A diet full of fresh fruit and vegetables with whole grains, eggs, and meats is perfect for most postpartum women. Healthy fats are especially important, like those found in avocados and coconuts. Grass fed meat is preferable.

Thyroid

Problems with the thyroid gland can cause depression. It is always a good idea to have this ruled out. Your healthcare provider can order some blood work to test the following hormones.

+ Thyroid stimulating hormone (TSH)

+ Triiodothyronine (T3)

+ Thyroxine (T4)

Your provider should check all of these levels, because a complete profile of your thyroid will give more information than checking just the TSH level. Some women do have symptoms even when their levels are at the low end of normal.

Summary

Even the best cared for mothers may experience postpartum mood disorders. The baby blues, postpartum depression, and postpartum psychosis can provide challenges for women, but with God's grace they can come through these times with a closer relationship to God.

Depression, unfortunately, is a part of the human condition, but we have an amazing God who is good. He is able to redeem all the aspects of our lives as we turn them over to Him. We praise Him for His goodness, and proclaim His love.

Ronda: One of my favorite passages these days is Psalm 34. We've shared the first ten verses here. What promises we have when we trust in the Lord!

Psalm 34:1-10 [1] *"I will bless the LORD at all times: his praise shall continually be in my mouth.* [2] *My soul shall make her boast in the LORD: the humble shall hear thereof, and be glad.* [3] *O magnify the LORD with me, and let us exalt his name together.* [4] *I sought the LORD, and he heard me, and delivered me from all my fears.* [5] *They looked unto him, and were lightened: and their faces were not ashamed.* [6] *This poor man cried, and the LORD heard him, and saved him out of all his troubles.* [7] *The angel of the LORD encampeth round about them that fear him, and delivereth them.* [8] *O taste and see that the LORD is good: blessed is the man that trusteth in him.* [9] *O fear the LORD, ye his saints: for there is no want to them that fear him.* [10] *The young lions do lack, and suffer hunger: but they that seek the LORD shall not want any good thing."*

I waited patiently for the LORD; and he inclined unto me, and heard my cry. ²He brought me up also out of an horrible pit, out of the miry clay, and set my feet upon a rock, and established my goings. ³And he hath put a new song in my mouth, even praise unto our God: many shall see it, and fear, and shall trust in the LORD.

Psalm 40:1-3

Appendix C

When Mourning Comes: Responding to Miscarriage

A Look at Loss

For some women, a miscarriage may be the first significant loss they have experienced. Many other women have dealt with loss or trauma perhaps early in their lives. No matter when it occurs, loss is a painful part of life. God says, *John 16:33 "These things I have spoken unto you, that in me ye might have peace. In the world ye shall have tribulation: but be of good cheer; I have overcome the world."*

Tribulation or trouble is a normal part of life in this fallen world. We should expect it and prepare for it when we can. The best way to prepare for trouble is to maintain closeness with God, so that we are willing and quick to call out to Him.

Genesis 3:16a "Unto the woman he said, I will greatly multiply thy sorrow and thy conception; in sorrow thou shalt bring forth children." Many Bible commentators believe this does not refer to just the pain of labor but also to family problems causing emotional pain. Anyone who has experienced problems in marriage, with children, or the loss of a child can attest to the fact that the pain of these experiences can be overwhelming.

For anyone experiencing pregnancy loss or a struggle with infertility, it is important to have the intellectual and spiritual knowledge to deal with this most intimate source of grief in a healthy way. A person's first encounter with significant loss is very important. It lays the groundwork for how that person is likely to continue responding to life's challenges. This appendix will address dealing with miscarriage from a physical, emotional, and spiritual standpoint.

Physical

Many pregnancies end in loss, often before a woman is aware she is even pregnant. Women who use early pregnancy tests or chart their ovulation and cycles may be more aware of a pregnancy. Many miscarriages occur due to an early problem in replication of cells, where chromosomes may be missing. The vast majority of these have nothing to do with heredity. 10 to 15% of known pregnancies in the first 12 weeks end in loss. Up to half of these losses are related to a blighted ovum—a fertilized egg that never develops a baby. Other types of losses may occur when a tiny baby in the embryonic stage or the placenta does not grow properly.

Maternal factors that can cause or contribute to pregnancy loss include problems with the cervix, uterus, or ovaries, genetic problems, hormone imbalances, and vitamin deficiencies. Some problems can be resolved with a minor surgical procedure, taking hormones, or increasing the intake of certain vitamins. Many times the cause of infertility is never identified. Sometimes otherwise perfectly healthy women are unable to conceive.

Miriam: My sister experienced five consecutive miscarriages over a two and a half year period before she had a healthy baby. The doctor never identified a specific cause of pregnancy loss. Her hormone levels were normal, and she was able to have extensive blood work and ultrasounds performed. In her case, she began a baby aspirin and L-methylfolate daily. Her blood work showed a MTHFR gene mutation. The very first pregnancy after beginning these two treatments was a healthy one. She is now the mother of a healthy baby boy and is expecting a second child.

When a woman is having a miscarriage, her physician may offer to perform a Dilation and Curettage (D&C). During this procedure, the doctor will dilate the cervix and gently scrape out the uterus. A D&C is necessary when a miscarriage doesn't complete on its own; that is when the baby has died or, in the case of a blighted ovum, when the pregnancy has failed to progress, but the woman's body does not recognize the loss and doesn't expel the tissues. Infection can occur if this happens.

A D&C can also be done when a woman has had multiple miscarriages, if she and the physician decide to perform diagnostic tests on the products of conception (such as the placenta or embryo). The doctor may offer a D&C to hurry the process. Otherwise it may take several weeks before the miscarriage is completed naturally.

Research suggests that women respond very differently to miscarriage and there is no best way to manage it (Smith et al. 2006). Some women feel they need time to grieve and a surgical procedure would be more difficult than a miscarriage at home. Others feel the need to end the process in order to move on. The procedure is not without risk. There is a small chance of rupturing the uterus or leaving scar tissue.

It is important that the doctor you choose does these procedures on a regular basis. Some doctors may use other procedures to assist with the miscarriage.

Allowing the body to naturally expel the pregnancy can be done at home. Some women prefer this, as it allows them time to deal with the loss. Miscarriages done at home are difficult and painful. This depends on the age of the baby. Many women are told to expect bleeding and cramping like a heavy period. This is only an accurate description if the pregnancy loss occurs before six to eight weeks. Even then, large blood clots may be passed.

Pregnancies that are further along than six or eight weeks are more painful with severe contractions or cramping and bleeding over a number of days, especially when the baby is expelled. During this time, a woman should not be left alone. She will need to be watched carefully for excessive bleeding. Excessive bleeding is completely filling one sanitary pad per hour for two consecutive hours.

After the products of conception have been passed, the bleeding should lessen. Continued heavy bleeding could signal a problem. After a time of initial heavy bleeding, the vaginal discharge should lessen and darken. The blood may look brown, but any vaginal discharge should not smell foul. Foul smelling discharge or a fever are signs of infection. If a fever or continued heavy bleeding is experienced, contact your healthcare provider.

Burial Information

Women who have a miscarriage when the baby is recognizable may desire to conduct a burial. If the miscarriage occurs in the hospital with a D&C, the parents may request the remains to be buried or cremated. Miscarriages that occur at home under the care of a physician do not require the baby be buried in a cemetery.

A cemetery burial is only required when a baby has reached a viable age, usually 20 weeks, depending on your state. If a baby is big enough for an official burial, it is considered a stillbirth instead of a miscarriage. This delivery will need to be done at a birth center, hospital, or at home with the attendance of a certified nurse midwife.

Physical Recovery

Many doctors recommend waiting two to three cycles before attempting another pregnancy. This is good advice. It will allow time for hormone levels to normalize and the mother to heal physically. A woman may experience memory loss, hair loss, and irregular cycles. It is important to consult with a healthcare provider if cycles do not return to normal.

Fertility Issues

Since most early pregnancy losses occur because of replication problems with the fertilized eggs, many doctors will not begin an infertility work-up unless a woman has a second trimester loss or stillbirth. Doctors will also do infertility work-ups after two or more consecutive miscarriages. You may be referred to an endocrinologist or fertility specialist.

Some of the blood work and other testing are very complicated. A specialist handles these specific tests and treatments on a daily basis. Seeing a specialist may be better than a regular obstetrician, but it depends on access and the individual doctor's experience.

Emotional

Immediately during or after a pregnancy loss, particularly if the baby is recognizable, a woman will often need to experience closure by holding, seeing the baby, or having a memorial service and burial. This opportunity should be offered to the parents at the hospital. If some time has passed without a memorial service and either parent is still struggling with the loss, a ceremony can still be arranged.

A woman may be devastated by a pregnancy loss. She may feel confused, afraid, and a failure. Women undergo many physical changes in early pregnancy, which affect their emotions. A pregnancy that results in a stillbirth will cause significant hormonal changes in the mother that will continue for some time after delivery.

A woman begins the emotional work of becoming a mother as soon as she finds out she is pregnant. Becoming a mother and readying herself for care of a tiny baby are significant jobs. During pregnancy, it is normal to have feelings of ambivalence. Women recognize that a new baby will drastically change their lives. Even women who look forward to a baby may not look forward to all of the changes needed to accommodate this new person. These feelings of ambivalence coupled with an unsuccessful pregnancy outcome can result in guilt. Many women immediately ask "What did I do wrong?" and "What could I have done differently?" Often the answer is "Nothing."

Pregnancy loss is an assault on a woman's identity. Women are biologically meant to reproduce. When a loss occurs, it is a direct emotional attack and can be more difficult to handle than a serious physical illness.

Husband's Response

No two people deal with grief the same way. Men and women tend to have divergent responses to grief. A young father may not know how to deal with the loss of a pregnancy or stillbirth, and he is unlikely to know how to help his wife. A very early pregnancy loss before the father sees an ultrasound picture or feels the baby move may seem unreal.

Sometimes men try to deal with loss by becoming busy. They do not undergo the dramatic hormonal changes that accompany a baby's loss. They may have a stress response, but a man's hormones are not undergoing significant changes. The father may feel helpless knowing he had no control over the pregnancy and no control over the way his wife responds. Sometimes when men experience a lack of control, they quickly move to an environment where they can exert control, causing them to spend more time engaging in hobbies or work.

The woman may feel that this shows insensitivity to her feelings or even a lack of concern for the baby. Women appreciate emotional strength in their men. That emotional stability can also help a woman overcome her own grief. Men are better at compartmentalizing their emotions. It is very important to accept the way that your spouse grieves. Many good marriages have been destroyed after a loss. Generally, one or both partners are unable to deal with their own grief or to accept the way their partner grieves.

As much as we love and need our husbands, we must not expect them to respond like we do or to be perfect in understanding our needs. Inexperienced or young men are often not up to the task of responding to a woman's grief. Learning to meet the needs of a woman takes a willingness to learn, maturity, and trial and error. Men need space and acceptance. We must recognize that men are different than women and respect these differences in times of grief.

Spiritual

Pain and suffering are part of this world. Human beings will suffer, and we should understand that this does not contradict God's love or compassion for us. It also does not indicate that God isn't at work in the world. When we consider the depravity of man and the holiness of God, our perspective changes and we begin to understand God's mercy and graciousness.

We live in a depraved world, and each of us is deserving of God's holy wrath. God in His great mercy provided Jesus to take away the sins of the world and allowed us fellowship with Him. As believers, we can be thankful for the blessings, grace, and mercy God has bestowed in our lives.

> *John 16:33 "These things I have spoken unto you, that in me ye might have peace. In the world ye shall have tribulation: but be of good cheer; I have overcome the world."*

Obtaining a right perspective on one's purpose in life can help change the perception of life events. When we consider that *God's chief desire* for each of us is *to become like Christ*, we can get a glimpse of how He views the trials He knows will come. It is difficult to grasp that thought when we find ourselves in the midst of a difficult, heart-breaking situation. God's love is with us even then, and He wants to come and give us the grace we need to face the next minute, hour, day, or week.

Peace is found in a reliance on Christ. We have to come to the point where we realize that trouble is part of this world. Sometimes sorrow is so overwhelming that it seems like the only reality, but this is a lie (Romans 8:18). We have victory over the trials of life through Jesus. Even when bad things happen we know that ultimately all will be made right.

When you are hurting, Jesus hurts with you. He is there even when you feel alone. He is so kind and so wise that He can redeem even the saddest parts of our lives. He promises to always be there (Hebrews 13:5) and to help you through the problems that come your way (1 Corinthians 10:13).

Summary

Miscarriage as well as other types of loss may come in our lives. There are physical causes and effects of miscarriage. The emotional response can be very different for the husband and wife, and it is important for both spouses to be responsive to the other, yet allow for those differences. The grieving parents can be comforted spiritually by recognizing God's heart towards His children, His purpose for their lives, and understanding His promise to be with them through suffering.

for your heavenly Father knoweth that ye
have need of **all** these **things**.

Matthew 6:23

Recommended Resources

Books:

Collins, Nelia. 1999. *To Glorify God*, 2nd ed. Indianapolis, IN: Colonial Hills Press.

Cross, John and Ian Mastin. 2004. *The Lamb*. Olds, Alberta, Canada: GoodSeed International.

Hale, Thomas. 2012. *Medication and Mothers Milk*, 15th ed. Amarillo: Hale Publishing.

Karp, Harvey. 2003. *The Happiest Baby on the Block: The New Way to Calm Crying and Help Your Baby Sleep Longer*. New York: Bantam Books.

Klaus, Marshall and Phyllis Klaus. 1998. *Your Amazing Newborn*. Reading, MS: Perseus Books.

Mohrbacher, Nancy and Kathleen Kendall-Tackett. 2010. *Breastfeeding Made Simple*, 2nd ed. Oakland, CA: New Harbinger Publications.

Murkoff, Heidi, Sandee Hathaway, and Arlene Eisenberg. 2008. *What to Expect the First Year*, 2nd ed. New York: Workman Pub.

Pantley, Elizabeth. 2002. *The No-Cry Sleep Solution*. Chicago: Contemporary Books.

West, Diana and Lisa Marasco. 2009. *The Breastfeeding Mother's Guide to Making More Milk*. New York: McGraw-Hill.

Wheat, Ed and Gaye Wheat. 1981. *Intended for Pleasure*. Old Tappan, NJ: F.H. Revell Co.

Wiessinger, Diane, Diana West, and Teresa Pitman. 2010. *The Womanly Art of Breastfeeding*, 8th ed. New York: Ballantine Books.

Videos:

Bergman, Jill and Nils Bergman. 2011. *Grow Your Baby's Brain*. Kangaroo Mother Care. www.kangaroomother.care.com

Stark, David. 2011. *BabyBabyOhBaby:Incomparable Parenting Series*. Stark Productions. www.babybabyohbaby.com Two DVDs present current evidence-based information on breastfeeding and infant massage best practices in a warm and relaxing way, with real mothers and babies.

Smilie, Christine. *Baby-Led Breastfeeding...The Mother-Baby Dance*. Los Angeles: Geddes Productions.

Websites:

Baby Sleep Site – babysleepsite.com – This site provides information about sleep problems that go beyond the advice in this book and may require a sleep consultation.

Breast Crawl References – breastcrawl.org/science.shtml – A site that provides references to studies and details of a baby's physiology. This concerns early initiation of breastfeeding by the infant navigating unaided from the mother's midchest to a position compatible with breastfeeding.

Breastfeeding Law –www.breastfeedinglaw.com – Lawyer and breastfeeding advocate, Jake Aryeh Marcus J.D, has a website information regarding breastfeeding laws with interpretations specific to the individual state laws.

Breastfeeding Made Simple – www.breastfeedingmadesimple.com/animatedlatch.html – This site has good information about breastfeeding. The link provided is to an animation graphic of a good latch.

Consumer Product Safety Commission – www.cpsc.gov/ – The site that lets parents know which products are unsafe.

Dr. Jack Newman's website – www.breastfeedinginc.ca – Dr. Newman's site is a great resource related to getting babies to latch and breastfeed despite difficult circumstances. Click on Online resources, then Videos to view several different clips about latching.

Dunstan Baby Language – www.dunstanbaby.com - The site discusses the different sounds a baby makes that can be linked to specific problems or needs, using a language for baby.

Focus on the Family – www.focusonthefamily.com – This site provides great resources on depression and postpartum depression, as well general family content.

Home for the Hearts of Women – www.incourage.me – There are many blog posts that discuss various aspects of spirituality and encourage women towards Christ-likeness.

Infant Risk Center – www.infantrisk.org – This website is sponsored by Dr. Thomas Hale and Texas Tech University Health Science Center. They have an online search engine and a call center for questions about various drugs, pregnancy, or breastfeeding. There is also info about nausea and vomiting during pregnancy, depression, alcohol and substance abuse, herbal medications, and chemicals. You can also call the center at 806-352-2519.

Kegel Exercises – www.sgsonline.org/sgsinc/patiented/educate_articles/ edpi002.htm – Although the instructions include a number of typographical errors, this website has the clearest explanation of how to do Kegel exercises and how to increase the frequency of exercises over time.

KellyMom – www.kellymom.com – This site is a great online resource for information about infants and breastfeeding. It is managed by Kelly Bonyata, a lactation consultant in South Florida.

Making More Milk – www.makingmoremilk.com – This site addresses concerns about low supply and teaches mothers how to have healthy babies who are gaining weight appropriately without jeopardizing breastfeeding.

Mayo Clinic website – www.mayoclinic.com – This site is a solid source for information regarding any concerns you have about your baby.

Mother-Baby Sleep Lab at Notre Dame – cosleeping.nd.edu/safe-co-sleeping-guidelines/ – This is the home of Dr. James McKenna and his many studies and articles relating to co-sleeping as well as his safe sleep guidelines.

National Conference of State Legislatures – www.ncsl.org – This site provides up-to-date information about state breastfeeding laws.

New Hampshire Breastfeeding Task Force – www.nhbreastfeedingtaskforce. org – This site provides an outstanding curriculum for healthcare providers about postpartum depression.

Oral Health - My Water's Fluoride – apps.nccd.cdc.gov/MWF/Index. asp – This webpage provides info about each community's level of water fluoridation. Here you can look up the amount of fluoride in your water supply.

Period of Purple Crying – www.purplecrying.info – This is an informative site that can help parents cope with inconsolable crying and high needs babies.

Physician Quality websites – These are sites to help you compare physician evaluations:
Health Grades – www.healthgrades.com
Vitals – www.vitals.com
U Compare Health – www.ucomparehealth.com
Everyday Health – www.everydayhealth.com

Revive our Hearts – www.reviveourhearts.com – This is an excellent source for encouragement to lead a godly life.

Uppity Science Chick – www.uppitysciencechick.com – This site provides information about breastfeeding and depression related research.

Support Groups:

La Leche League – www.llli.org – These groups meet locally for mothers to come, learn more, and share with each other about breastfeeding. Essentially, it is a support group for breastfeeding mothers, but it is so much more. Often new mothers find others who they can connect with and build lasting connections.

Moms in Prayer International – www.momsintouch.org – This is a ministry to mothers that encourages "moms to get together and pray for their children and schools, believing that through prayer God releases His power."

Mothers of Preschoolers (MOPS) – www.mops.org – These groups usually meet in a local church and are another resource for mothers who have small children and are looking for an adult connection. Through friendship, creative outlets, and instruction, women are encouraged that "mothering matters."

Postpartum Support International – www.postpartum.net – This is an excellent resource for women experiencing anxiety or depression during or after pregnancy. Here you can find support groups in your state.

Mobile Resources:

Text4baby – Texting BABY to 511411(or BEBE for Spanish) will allow you to receive free text messages each week, timed to your due date or baby's date of birth. The messages focus on a variety of topics critical to maternal and child health, including birth defects prevention, immunization, nutrition, seasonal flu, mental health, oral health and safe sleep. Text4baby messages also connect women to prenatal and infant care services and other resources.

Phone Apps – There are a number of free mobile phone apps available to help with managing information about a new baby. Be wary of any that are sponsored by a formula company as they tend to have negative messages about breastfeeding success in their content.
One positive app (available only for iPhone at this time):
iLetDown – allows mom to record baby's sounds and picture to use when pumping at work to help encourage a let down response.

References

Ablett, Anne-Marie. 2011. "Foremilk and Hindmilk: In Quest of an Elusive Arbitrary Switch." The Funny Shaped Woman. Accessed October 30. http://thefunnyshapedwoman.blogspot.com/2011/05/foremilk-and-hindmilk-in-quest-of.html. (Chapter 6)

ABM (Academy of Breastfeeding Medicine) Protocol Committee. 2010. "ABM Clinical Protocol #22: Guidelines for Management of Jaundice in the Breastfeeding Infant Equal to or Greater Than 35 Weeks' Gestation." *Breastfeeding Medicine* 5 (2): 87-93. doi:10.1089/bfm.2010.9994. (Chapter 3)

Adolph, Karen. 2000. "Specificity of Learning: Why Infants Fall Over a Veritable Cliff." *Psychological Science* 11(4): 290-295. (Chapter 3)

Ahnert, Lieselotte, Megan Gunnar, Michael Lamb, and Martina Barthel. 2004. "Transition to Child Care: Associations with Infant-Mother Attachment, Infant Negative Emotion, and Cortisol Elevations." *Child Development* 75 (3): 639-650. doi:10.1111/j.1467-8624.2004.00698.x. (Chapter 11)

AAP (American Academy of Pediatrics), Section on Breastfeeding. 2005. "Breastfeeding and the Use of Human Milk." *Pediatrics* 115 (2): 496-506. doi:10.1542/peds.2004-2491. (Chapter 6, 9)

AAP (American Academy of Pediatrics), Section on Breastfeeding. 2012. "Breastfeeding and the Use of Human Milk." *Pediatrics* 129 (3): e827-e841. doi:10.1542/peds.2011-3552. (Chapter 6, 9)

AAP (American Academy of Pediatrics), Subcommittee on Hyperbilirubinemia. 2004. "Management of Hyperbilirubinemia in the Newborn Infant 35 or more Weeks of Gestation." *Pediatrics* 114 (1): 297–316. doi:10.1542/peds.114.1.297. (Chapter 3)

AAP (American Academy of Pediatrics), Task Force on Sudden Infant Death Syndrome. 2011. "SIDS and Other Sleep-Related Infant Deaths: Expansion of Recommendations for a Safe Infant Sleeping Environment." *Pediatrics* 128 (5): e1130-e1139. doi:10.1542/peds.2011-2284. (Chapter 7)

Baddock, Sally, Barbara Galland, Barry Taylor, and David Bolton. 2007. "Sleep Arrangements and Behavior of Bed-Sharing Families in the Home Setting." *Pediatrics* 119 (1): e200-e207. doi:10.1542/peds.2006-0744. (Chapter 7)

Ball, Helen. 2009. "Bed-Sharing and Co-Sleeping." *New Digest* 48:22-27. (Chapter 7)

Barrett, Julia. 2006. "Children's Health: Breastfeeding: Nature's MRE." *Environmental Health Perspectives* 114:A25-A25. doi:10.1289/ehp.114-a25a. (Chapter 6)

Bell, Silvia and Mary D. Salter Ainsworth. 1972. "Infant Crying and Maternal Responsiveness." *Child Development* 43 (4): 1171-1190. (Chapter 11)

Bergman, Nils and L.A. Jürisoo. 1994. "The 'Kangaroo-Method' for Treating Low-Birth-Weight Babies in a Developing Country." *Tropical Doctor* 24 (2): 57-60. (Chapter 10)

Blass, Elliott and Lisa Watt. 1999. "Suckling- and Sucrose-Induced Analgesia in Human Newborns." *Pain* 83 (3): 611-623. doi:10.1016/S0304-3959(99)00166-9. (Chapter 5)

"Breastfeeding State Laws." 2011. National Conference of State Legislatures. Accessed Oct 26. http://www.ncsl.org/default.aspx?tabid=14389. (Chapter 6)

Brown, Matthew. 2005. "Delivered from Storm, Mother Gives Birth in Attic." *The Times-Picayune*, September 1. http://www.nola.com/katrina/pages/090105/a2.pdf. (Chapter 6)

Browne, Joy. 2008. "Chemosensory Development in the Fetus and Newborn." *Newborn & Infant Nursing Reviews* 8 (4): 180-186. doi:10.1053/j.nainr.2008.10.009. (Chapter 3)

CDC (Centers for Disease Control and Prevention). 2011a. "Overview: Infant Formula and Fluorosis." Centers for Disease Control and Prevention. Accessed October 29. http://www.cdc.gov/fluoridation/safety/infant_formula.htm. (Chapter 9)

CDC (Centers for Disease Control and Prevention). 2011b. "Sudden Unexpected Infant Death (SUID)." Centers for Disease Control and Prevention. Accessed October 29. http://www.cdc.gov/sids/. (Chapter 7)

Colson, Suzanne. 2010. "What Happens to Breastfeeding When Mothers Lie Back? Clinical Applications of Biological Nurturing." *Clinical Lactation* 1 (1): 11-14. (Chapter 5, 6)

Colson, Suzanne, Judith Meek, and Jane Hawdon. 2008. "Optimal Positions for the Release of Primitive Neonatal Reflexes Stimulating Breastfeeding." *Early Human Development* 84 (7): 441-9. doi:10.1016/j.earlhumdev.2007.12.003. (Chapter 6)

Cross, John and Ian Mastin. 2004. *The Lamb.* Olds, Alberta, Canada: GoodSeed International. (Chapter 10)

Cubero, J., V. Valero, J. Sánchez, M. Rivero, H. Parvez, A. B. Rodríguez, and C. Barriga. 2005. "The Circadian Rhythm of Tryptophan in Breast Milk Affects the Rhythms of 6-Sulfatoxymelatonin and Sleep in Newborn." *Neuroendocrinology Letters* 26 (6): 657-661. (Chapter 7)

DeMoss, Nancy. 2007. "Good News for Imperfect People." Revive Our Hearts. Accessed November 6, 2011. http://www.reviveourhearts.com/radio/revive-our-hearts/good-news-for-imperfect-people-1/. (Chapter 12)

Eidelman, Arthur. 2006. "The Talmud and Human Lactation: The Cultural Basis for Increased Frequency and Duration of Breastfeeding Among Orthodox Jewish Women." *Breastfeeding Medicine* 1 (1): 36-40. doi:10.1089/bfm.2006.1.36. (Chapter 6)

Fact Sheet #73: Break Time for Nursing Mothers Under the FLSA. 2010. Washington, D.C.: U. S. Department of Labor. Accessed October 26, 2011. http://www.dol.gov/whd/regs/compliance/whdfs73.htm. (Chapter 6)

Field, Eugene. 1891. A Dutch Lullaby. In *A Little Book of Western Verse.* New York: Charles Scribner's Sons. p. 128-130. Accessed December 15, 2012. http://archive.org/stream/alittlebookwest02fielgoog#page/n6/mode/2up. (Chapter 3)

Flint, Annie. 1928. He Giveth More Grace (No. 3). In *The Christ We Forget and Twenty-One Other New Songs.* Philadelphia: Rodeheaver Co. (Chapter 11)

Gartlehner Gerald, Richard Hansen, Patricia Thieda, Angela DeVeaugh-Geiss, Bradley Gaynes, Erin Krebs, Linda Lux et al. 2007. "Comparative

Effectiveness of Second-Generation Antidepressants in the Pharmacologic Treatment of Adult Depression." *Comparative Effectiveness Review No. 7.* Rockville, MD: Agency for Healthcare Research and Quality. Accessed August 24, 2012. http://www.effectivehealthcare.ahrq.gov/repFiles/Antidepressants_Final_Report.pdf. (Appendix B)

Genna, Catherine W. and Diklah Barak. 2010. "Facilitating Autonomous Infant Hand Use During Breastfeeding." *Clinical Lactation* 1 (1): 15-20. (Chapter 6)

"Get Help – Support Groups and Area Coordinators" 2011. Postpartum Support International. http://www.postpartum.net/Get-Help/Support-Resources-Map-Area-Coordinators.aspx (Appendix B)

Gettler, Lee and James McKenna. 2010. "Never Sleep with Baby? Or Keep Me Close but Keep Me Safe: Eliminating Inappropriate Safe Infant Sleep Rhetoric in the United States." *Current Pediatric Reviews* 6 (1): 71-77. doi:10.2174/157339610791317250. (Chapter 7)

Gilmore, Rick and Mark Johnson. 1995. "Working Memory in Infancy: Six-month-olds' Performance on Two Versions of the Oculomotor Delayed Response Task." *Journal of Experimental Child Psychology* 59: 397–418. (Chapter 3)

Grandjean, Phillipe and Phillip Landrigan. 2006. "Developmental Neurotoxicity of Industrial Chemicals." *The Lancet* 368 (9553): 2167-2178. doi:10.1016/S0140- 6736. (Chapter 9)

Gunnar, Megan and Barbara White. 2001. "Salivary Cortisol Measures in Infant and Child Assessment." In *Biobehavioral Assessment of the Infant*, edited by Lynn Singer and Philip Zeskind, 167-189. New York: Guilford. (Chapter 11)

Hale, Thomas. 2011. "Webforum" InfantRisk Center at Texas Tech University Health Science Center. Accessed September 28. http://www.infantrisk.com/content/webforum (Appendix B)

Hawks, Annie and Robert Lowry. 1872. *I Need Thee Every Hour.* Cincinnati, OH: National Baptist Sunday School Convention. (Chapter 9)

Hixson, J. B. 2008. *Getting the Gospel Wrong: the Evangelical Crisis No One is Talking About.* N.p: Xulon Press. (Chapter 10)

Howard, Cynthia, Fred Howard, Bruce Lanphear, Elisabeth deBlieck, Shirley Eberly, and Ruth A. Lawrence. 1999. "The Effects of Early Pacifier Use on Breastfeeding Duration." *Pediatrics* 103 (3): e33. doi:10.1542/peds.103.3.e33. (Chapter 5)

Hunziker, Urs and Ronald Barr. 1986. "Increased Carrying Reduces Infant Crying: A Randomized Controlled Trial." *Pediatrics* 77 (5): 641-648. (Chapter 11)

Ip, Stanley, Mei Chung, Gowri Raman, Priscilla Chew, Nombulelo Magula, Deirdre DeVine, Thomas Trikalinos, and Joseph Lau. 2007. "Breastfeeding and Maternal and Infant Health Outcomes in Developed Countries." *Evidence Report/Technology Assessment No. 153*. Rockville, MD: Agency for Healthcare Research and Quality. Accessed February 24, 2012. http://www.ahrq.gov/clinic/tp/brfouttp.htm. (Chapter 6)

Jelovsek, Frank. 2011. "How to Do Pelvic Floor Muscle Exercises (Kegel's)." Society of Gynecologic Surgeons. Accessed October 26. http://www.sgsonline.org/sgsinc/patiented/educate_articles/edpi002.htm. (Chapter 4)

Jenik, Alejandro, Nestor Vain, Adriana Gorestein, and Noemí Jacobi for the Pacifier and Breastfeeding Trial Group. 2009. "Does the Recommendation to Use a Pacifier Influence the Prevalence of Breastfeeding?" *The Journal of Pediatrics* 155 (3): 350-354. doi:10.1016/j.jpeds.2009.03.038. (Chapter 5)

Ken, Thomas. 1755. A Morning Hymn. In *Manual of Prayers for the Use of the Scholars of Winchester College*. 28th ed. London. Accessed December 15, 2012. http://archive.org/stream/amanualprayersf02kengoog#page/n132/mode/2up/search/awake. (Chapter 8)

Kendall-Tackett, Kathleen, Zhen Cong, and Thomas Hale. 2011. "The Effect of Feeding Method on Sleep Duration, Maternal Well-being, and Postpartum Depression." *Clinical Lactation* 2 (2): 22-26. (Chapter 6, 7)

Kendall-Tackett, Kathleen, Lynn Duffy, Linda Zollo, Laurie Geck, Alison Holmes, Judy Dodge, and Jolenne Porter. 2009. "A Breastfeeding-Friendly Approach to Depression in New Mothers." New Hampshire Breastfeeding Task Force. Accessed October 26, 2011. http://www.nhbreastfeedingtaskforce.org/pdf/breastfeeding_depression.pdf. (Appendix B)

Kirsten, Gert, Nils Bergman, and F. Mary Hann. 2001. "Kangaroo Mother Care in the Nursery." *Pediatric Clinics of North America* 48 (2): 443-454. (Chapter 1,6)

Klaus, Marshall and John Kennel 2001. "Care of the Parent." In *Care of the High-Risk Neonate*. 5th ed., edited by Marshall Klaus and Avroy Fanaroff, 195-222. Philadelphia: W. B. Saunders Company. (Chapter 3)

Kornstein, Susan and Robert Schneider. 2001. "Clinical Features of Treatment-Resistant Depression." *Journal of Clinical Psychiatry* 62 (Supplement 6): 18-25. (Appendix B)

LLLI (La Leche League International). 2008. "I Have Just Learned I am Pregnant with Twins. What Do I Need to Know to Breastfeed under these Circumstances?" La Leche League International. Accessed October 29, 2011. http://www.llli.org/faq/twins.html. (Chapter 6)

Marcus, Jake Aryeh. 2011. Breastfeeding Law: Know Your Legal Rights. Accessed Oct 26. http://breastfeedinglaw.com/state-laws/. (Chapter 6)

Marlier, Luc, Benoist Schaal, and Robert Soussignan. 1998. "Neonatal Responsiveness to the Odor of Amniotic and Lacteal Fluids: A Test of Perinatal Chemosensory Continuity." *Child Development* 69 (3): 611-623. (Chapter 11)

Marston, Cecily, Agustín Conde-Agudelo, Julie DaVanzo, Katherine Dewey, Shea Rutstein, and Bao-Ping Zhu. 2007. "*Report of a WHO Technical Consultation on Birth Spacing*." World Health Organization. Accessed February 29, 2011. http://www.who.int/making_pregnancy_safer/documents/birth_spacing.pdf. (Chapter 4)

Mayo Clinic Staff. 2011. "Infant Jaundice: Lifestyle and Home Remedies - Mayoclinic.Com." Mayo Clinic. Accessed October 26. http://www.mayoclinic.com/health/infant-jaundice/DS00107/DSECTION=lifestyle-and-home-remedies. (Appendix B)

McClintock, John and James Strong. 1894. *Cyclopaedia of Biblical, Theological, and Ecclesiastical Literature*. New York, NY: Harper & Brothers, Publishers. p. 892. http://archive.org/stream/cyclopaediabibl00mcclgoog#page/n8/mode/2up. (Chapter 6)

McKenna, James and Thomas McDade. 2005. "Why Babies Should Never Sleep Alone: A Review of the Co-Sleeping Controversy in Relation to SIDS,

Bedsharing and Breast Feeding." *Paediatric Respiratory Reviews* 6 (2): 134-52. doi:10.1016/j.prrv.2005.03.006. (Chapter 7)

McKenna, James. 1996. "Babies Need their Mothers Beside Them!" The Natural Child Project. Accessed September 8, 2012. http://www.naturalchild.org/james_mckenna/babies_need.html. (Chapter 7)

McKenna, James. 2011. "Safe Cosleeping Guidelines." Mother-Baby Behavioral Sleep Laboratory. Accessed October 26. http://cosleeping.nd.edu/safe-co-sleeping-guidelines/. (Chapter 7)

Mirmiran, Majid, Yolanda Maas, and Ronald Ariagno. 2003. "Development of Fetal and Neonatal Sleep and Circadian Rhythms." *Sleep Medicine Reviews* 7 (4): 321-334. (Chapter 7)

Mohrbacher, Nancy. 2010. "Rethinking Swaddling." *International Journal of Childbirth Education* 25 (3): 7-10. http://www.icea.org/sites/default/files/09-10 (Reduced).pdf. (Chapter 9)

Mohrbacher, Nancy and Kathleen Kendall-Tackett. 2010. *Breastfeeding Made Simple.* 2nd ed. Oakland, CA: New Harbinger Publications. (Chapter 1,5,7)

Mohrbacher, Peter 2011. "Animated Version of the Latch." Breastfeeding Made Simple. Accessed August 25. http://www.breastfeedingmadesimple.com/animatedlatch.html. (Chapter 5)

Moore, E. R., G. C. Anderson, and N. Bergman. 2007. "Early Skin-to-Skin Contact for Mothers and Their Healthy Newborn Infants." *Cochrane Database of Systematic Reviews* Issue 3. CD003519. doi:10.1002/14651858. CD003519.pub2. (Chapter 10)

Newman, Jack 2011. "Breastfeeding Videos." Breastfeeding, Inc. Accessed August 25. http://www.breastfeedinginc.ca. (Chapter 5)

Newman, Jack and Edith Kernerman. 2009. "Breast Compression." Breastfeeding, Inc. Accessed September 8, 2012. http://www.breastfeedinginc.ca. (Chapter 5)

Olds, Sally, Marcia London, and Patricia Ladewig. 2000. *Maternal-Newborn Nursing: A Family and Community-Based Approach.* 6th ed. Menlo Park, CA: Addison Wesley. (Chapter 3)

Pantley, Elizabeth. 2002. *The No-Cry Sleep Solution.* Chicago: Contemporary Books, p. 43. (Chapter 7)

Pearl, Debi. 1999. "My Two Cents." No Greater Joy Ministries. Accessed October 26, 2011. http://www.nogreaterjoy.org/articles/general-view/archive/1999/july/01/my-two-cents/. (Chapter 3)

Peterson, Eugene. 2002. *The Message: The Bible in Contemporary Language.* Colorado Springs: NavPress. (Preface)

Quillin, Stephanie and L. Lee Glenn. 2004. "Interaction Between Feeding Method and Co-Sleeping on Maternal-Newborn Sleep." *Journal of Obstetric, Gynecologic, and Neonatal Nursing: JOGNN* 33 (5): 580-588. doi:10.1177/0884217504269013. (Chapter 7)

Rachlis, Val and Patricia Petryshen. 1992. "Investigation of Newborn Hyperbilirubinemia: Helping Family Physicians Identify Newborns at Risk." Canadian Family Physician 38: 73-6. (Chapter 3)

Rankin, Marlene and Maureen Esteves. 1996. "How to Assess a Research Study." *AJN: American Journal of Nursing* 96 (12): 32-37. (Appendix A)

Riordan, Jan and Karen Wambach. 2009. *Breastfeeding and Human Lactation.* 4th ed. Sudbury, MA: Jones and Bartlett Publishers. (Chapter 1)

Roberts, Debbie. 2011. "Preventing Musculoskeletal Pain in Mothers: Ergonomic Tips for Lactation Consultants." *Clinical Lactation* 2 (4): 13-20. (Chapter 4)

Scragg, R. K., E. A. Mitchell, A. W. Stewart, R. P. Ford, B. J. Taylor, I. B. Hassall, S. M. Williams, and J. M. Thompson. 1996. "Infant Room-Sharing and Prone Sleep Position in Sudden Infant Death Syndrome." *Lancet* 347 (8993): 7-12. (Chapter 7)

Siegel, Jerome. 2005. "Functional Implications of Sleep Development." *PLoS Biology* 3 (5): e178. doi:10.1371/journal.pbio.0030178. (Chapter 7)

Smith, Lindsey, Julia Frost, Ruth Levitas, Harriet Bradley, and Jo Garcia. 2006. "Women's Experiences of Three Early Miscarriage Management Options: A Qualitative Study." *The British Journal of General Practice: The Journal of the Royal College of General Practitioners* 56 (524): 198-205. (Appendix C)

St James-Roberts, Ian, Marissa Alvarez, Emese Csipke, Tanya Abramsky, Jennifer Goodwin, and Esther Sorgenfrei. 2006. "Infant Crying and Sleeping in London, Copenhagen and When Parents Adopt a 'Proximal' Form of Care." *Pediatrics* 117:e1146-e1155. doi:10.1542/peds.2005-2387. (Chapter 11)

Stuebe, Alison, Walter Willett, Fei Xue, and Karin Michels. 2009. "Lactation and Incidence of Premenopausal Breast Cancer: A Longitudinal Study." *Archives of Internal Medicine* 169 (15): 1364-1371. doi:10.1001/archinternmed.2009.231. (Chapter 6)

Terman, Michael and Jiuan Su Terman. 2005. "Light Therapy for Seasonal and Nonseasonal Depression: Efficacy, Protocol, Safety, and Side Effects." *CNS Spectrums* 10 (8): 647-63. (Chapter 4)

Thompson, Laura and Wenda Trevathan. 2008. "Cortisol Reactivity, Maternal Sensitivity, and Learning in 3-Month-Old Infants." *Infant Behavior & Development* 31 (1): 92-106. doi:10.1016/j.infbeh.2007.07.007. (Chapter 11)

UNICEF Maharashtra. "Initiation of Breastfeeding by Breast Crawl." YouTube video, 6:08. Posted by LactationSensation, June 27, 2007. http://www.youtube.com/watch?v=zrwfIcPB1u4. (Chapter 6)

Uvnäs-Moberg, Kerstin, Gianfranco Marchini, and Jan Winberg. 1993. "Plasma Cholecystokinin Concentrations after Breastfeeding in Healthy 4 Day Old Infants." *Archives of Disease in Childhood* 68:46-48. (Chapter 5)

Vennemann, M. M., T. Bajanowski, B. Brinkmann, G. Jorch, K. Yücesan, C. Sauerland, E. A. Mitchell, and GeSID Study Group. 2009. "Does Breastfeeding Reduce the Risk of Sudden Infant Death Syndrome?" *Pediatrics* 123 (3): e406-410. doi:10.1542/peds.2008-2145. (Chapter 7)

West, Diana and Lisa Marasco. 2009. *The Breastfeeding Mother's Guide to Making More Milk*. New York: McGraw-Hill. (Chapter 5)

WHO (World Health Organization). 2007. "Guidelines for the Safe Preparation, Storage and Handling of Powdered Infant Formula." World Health Organization. Accessed October 29, 2011. http://www.who.int/foodsafety/publications/micro/pif2007/en/. (Chapter 9)

Wiessinger, Diane, Diana West, and Teresa Pitman. 2010. *The Womanly Art of Breastfeeding*. 8th ed. New York: Ballantine Books. (Chapter 5, 6)

Wolf, Jacqueline. 2008. "Got Milk? Not in Public!" *International Breastfeeding Journal* 3:11. doi:10.1186/1746-4358-3-11. (Chapter 6)

Index

The index is primarily organized topically, so you may need to look for the broader topic area to find the content you desire.

Made in the USA
Lexington, KY
20 April 2013